ECONOMICS OF PEASANT FARMING

T0299864

ECONOMICS OF PEASANT FARMING

Doreen Warriner

Reader in Social and Economic Studies of Eastern Europe,
School of Slavonic and East European Studies, University of London

Routledge
Taylor & Francis Group

LONDON AND NEW YORK

First published 1939 by Frank Cass & Co. Ltd.
Second Edition 1964

This edition published 2013 by Routledge
2 Park Square, Milton Park, Abingdon, Oxon OX14 4RN
711 Third Avenue, New York, NY 10017

*Routledge is an imprint of the Taylor & Francis Group,
an informa business*

First issued in paperback 2016

© 1964 Taylor & Francis

ISBN13: 978-0-7146-1257-7 (hbk)
ISBN13: 978-1-138-99329-7 (pbk)

CONTENTS

LIST OF ILLUSTRATIONS

LIST OF ILLUSTRATIONS

FOREWORD TO FIRST EDITION

IN all the East European countries which I visited in 1935, 1936, and 1937, I received much help from peasants and large landowners, as well as from economists and administrative officials. In Poland I received much hospitality and help from Professor Heydel, M. Poniatowski, and Dr. Styś, who introduced me to peasant villages in Central, Eastern, and Southern Poland, and from Miss Ewa Estreicher of the State Statistical Office. In Czechoslovakia my thanks are chiefly due to Dr. Milan Hodža, who first drew my attention to the economic problems of this part of Europe. In Rumania my thanks are due to Dr. Manuila, of the State Demographic Institute, who enabled me to visit the villages where his teams of trained investigators were working; in Yugoslavia to Dr. Marković of the Export Institute; in Hungary to Dr. Varga and Dr. Matolcsy; and in Bulgaria to Dr. Koestner of the National Bank, and Dr. Zagaroff of the State Statistical Office.

Mr. H. D. Henderson and Mr. P. Lamartine Yates read the typescript of the book, and I am very grateful to them for many suggestions.

I am indebted to the Ethnographical Museum in Cluj for permission to reproduce three photographs of Transylvania taken by Mr. Denis Galloway.

With the partition of Czechoslovakia the European agrarian problem enters on a new phase. The basis of agricultural prosperity, the connexion with industry, has been destroyed by the division of the industrial and agricultural regions of Bohemia, and it is impossible for the state as it now exists to maintain the same standard of living. German economic policy is designed to keep the remainder of the country as a source of food-supply for the Reich, and as such it cannot employ its present population in the land. The need for emigration is now almost as acute in Czechoslovakia as it is in the other countries of Eastern Europe.

DOREEN WARRINER

PRAGUE,
November 1938

INTRODUCTION TO THE SECOND EDITION

THIS book, first published in 1939, was originally conceived as an investigation of peasant farming in Europe—a horizon which then seemed wide enough. At the time that it was written, in the years of the agricultural depression of the nineteen-thirties, the habit of generalizing about 'the peasant' was prevalent, even in serious academic discussion. He was doomed, or he was eternal, according to the underlying outlook. I wanted to find out the facts, and found that in the singular he did not exist.

What I found was an immense contrast between the well-capitalized commercial peasant farming of Western Europe and the poor subsistence farming of the remotest parts of Eastern Europe; and between these two extremes a wide range of variation in standards of living and farming efficiency. This observation is now a commonplace, and the student will find fuller and more exact comparisons in specialized studies of European agriculture. But at the time that I wrote the range was not charted, nor had it been related to differences in the course of economic and social development during the nineteenth century.[1]

Within Eastern Europe, there proved to be sufficient contrast in economic and social conditions to make a book about peasant farming in that region only. As I studied the agrarian countries, I found that they suffered from over-population, resulting from a low rate of capital investment and a high rate of population growth; so the book became a study in what is now called under-development. As such it was in advance of its time.

In considering the remedies for farm poverty, as I called it then, I was concerned with various practical possibilities rather than with ideal solutions or models of development.

[1] For the nineteenth-century background, see *Contrasts in Emerging Societies: Readings in the Social and Economic History of South-Eastern Europe in the Nineteenth Century*, by G. F. Cushing, E. D. Tappe, V. de S. Pinto, and P. Auty, ed. Warriner, University of London, Athlone Press, 1964.

It was logical to begin with unbalanced trade, caused by the shrinkage of the market for the grain and meat surpluses of the agricultural exporters, since in the nineteen-thirties this was the immediate problem, and the only one which engaged the attention of economists. 'The German solution', then imminent, did offer a market for these surpluses, but would not touch the deeper underlying imbalance of the economic structure, due to the preponderance of agriculture over-supplied with manpower.

As to the prospects of raising rural living standards by improving farming efficiency, there was what would now be called a distortion in the pattern of land use, correlated with maldistribution of rural population. The naturally fertile Danubian plains, which could have been Europe's Corn-Hog Belt, were cultivated too extensively, in large estates or in peasant farms alike, and their great potential neglected, while the poor mountain soils were over-cultivated, because they were too densely settled. The plain regions could have been developed by means of public investment in irrigation and more intensive farming generally, and this development was needed, to raise the rural living standard—which in Rumania it could certainly have transformed. But it was not likely to increase employment in agriculture sufficiently to absorb labour from the poor regions.

As to land reform, the measures carried through after the First World War had been a remedy for one generation only. There was not, at that time, a broad general prospect for relieving farm poverty by further redistribution of land, because, excepting in Hungary, most of the land was already peasant owned. 'The Russian solution', in the sense of collectivization, was no solution for countries which had no great expanses of uncultivated land; there were some prospects for industrialization through planning on the Russian model.

The conclusion was that either the agrarian countries must industrialize, or their populations must migrate. This conclusion still seems a sound diagnosis of the situation as it was before the war, though it was much attacked at the time for its pessimism.

I

By way of introduction to this second edition (which is a re-issue of the first, except for corrections to mistakes in the original text), it seems necessary to give the reader some idea of how the agrarian situation in Eastern Europe has changed since the book was written.

This is difficult, for two reasons. Twenty-five years is a long time. The region experienced 'the German solution' in its terrible totality. To Poland and Jugoslavia, the war brought death and destruction on a scale inconceivable in any period of European history. After the war, Poland was shifted westwards into new frontiers. The expulsion of eleven million Germans meant a migration out of the region on an unprecedented scale. These vast changes cannot be described here; and yet they are what my generation most remembers.

The other reason is that the results of 'the Russian solution' cannot be assessed in relation to the main theme of the book, the desirability of raising the peasants' standard of living, for that is not its aim. In the years immediately after the war, it did indeed seem as if communist policy were doing the things that needed to be done. Industrialization was the chief aim, and it was certainly needed; for agriculture, the target was quick recovery to the pre-war level of production, which would have meant a considerable increase in food consumption in the countries with smaller populations; and for the poorest peasants there were radical land reforms. There was then much greater scope than before the war for redistribution of land, because the German exodus left large areas available for resettlement. In the post-war chaos, it was good to meet again peasants from the over-crowded villages of Southern Poland on their large new farms near Wroclaw, and to find that the destitute farm labourers of Northern Hungary had become owners of sizable farms.[1]

Since that hopeful interim, the full solution has been applied: the expansion of heavy industry and collectivization.

[1] For the results of these reforms, see Warriner, *Revolution in Eastern Europe*, London, 1950, Chapter VII.

For communists these policies are ends in themselves, because they signify power. In so far as higher wages in industry are needed to secure increased production, the achievement of these ends implies a rise in urban living standards. So far as the peasants are concerned, the aim is to lower their living standards, even at the cost of food production, unless supplies are reduced to a level which threatens the towns with starvation.

If this is not understood, and it is believed that the object of planning is to raise living standards in general, then the policy appears an unintelligible failure, and there is no solution to the problem of why economies that have been investing at high rates for a long period should show such poor results. In Poland, for example, where the much needed increase in food production on the poor sandy soils depends mainly on fertilizers, one might easily conclude that the planners are insane when one finds that even by 1958 fertilizer production had not recovered to the pre-war level (within the present frontiers, where consumption was much higher than in the old Poland), and learns that fertilizers have been exported to China. Refrigerators, expensive and unsaleable in the shops, are hollow symbols when meat and milk are luxuries; and one might argue that investment has been misdirected, if one assumes that necessities should come first. But from the communist standpoint, such things are not mistakes: industry comes first, and agriculture is the buffer sector.

So all that can be done is to take the situation as described in the book point by point, and note the main changes in outline, with more detailed observations on Jugoslavia and Poland, where the peasants have to some extent come back into their own, within the limits uneasily set by dogma.

In the first place, the pre-war trade balance is now reversed. Eastern Europe is now a grain deficit region. Net grain imports in 1958–60 averaged 3·5 million tons per annum, of which Poland and Czechoslovakia each imported 1·6 million tons, Jugoslavia 200,000 tons (with an export surplus in 1960 for the first time since the war), Hungary 188,000 tons and

Bulgaria 70,000 tons; Rumania's net exports averaged only 180,000 tons. The explanation of these large and generally increasing imports is presumably higher consumption, since grain output per head of population is now at the same level as before the war (see Table I). Higher consumption in the countryside may account for the need to import food for the towns, which suffer chronic shortage of meat and milk and occasional shortages of bread.

So the priorities of 1939 are now reversed. Then industrial development was the first; now it is increased food production. The movement of population into industry creates a demand for food which agriculture cannot supply, partly for lack of capital, and partly for lack of incentive.

Next, agricultural over-population. This was shown to exist in two forms: (i) a failure of agricultural production to keep pace with the growth of agricultural and total population —a rather muted Malthusian devil, because there were then the export surpluses to fall back on; (ii) labour redundancy on the land, since hypostasied by others into the monster of 'the surplus'. How have these conditions changed?

(i) As regards the first condition, the following table shows changes in grain production between the pre-war average and the average of 1958–60, in relation to total populations, for the countries for which agricultural production statistics are available. Since the war Rumania and Bulgaria have not published agricultural production statistics on a basis comparable with pre-war, but following the Russian practice quote figures of 'biological yields', instead of the normal barn yields; this inflates the figures to an unknown extent.

Table I shows that grain production did not recover to the pre-war level by 1948 or 1949, the targets set in the short-term recovery plans, except in Hungary, where agriculture had suffered comparatively little from war devastation. In Poland and Jugoslavia the pre-war level was not reached until 1957, and in Czechoslovakia not until 1960. During the early fifties, when the process of collectivization reduced production, grain output per capita fell, but by 1958–60 it was up to

TABLE I

Changes in Grain Production and Population in East European Countries

	POLAND	HUNGARY	JUGOSLAVIA	CZECHO-SLOVAKIA
Grain Production (million metric tons) 1934–8 Average Present Frontiers	13·3	6·1	8·1	5·6
1948	11·3	6·3	7·6	4·9
1949	11·9	5·2	7·3	··
1950	11·6	5·4	4·6	4·9*
1951	11·0	6·2	7·2	··
1952	11·7	4·0	3·8	··
1953	10·0	6·2	7·5	n.a.
1954	11·0	5·4	5·1	n.a.
1955	12·7	6·6	7·4	5·1
1956	12·1	5·3	5·9	5·4
1957	13·5	7·0	10·2	5·2
1958	13·5	5·7	7·5	4·8
1959	14·1	7·3	12·1	5·5
1960	14·3	6·9	11·0	5·8
Average 1948–50	11·6	5·6	6·5	4·9
1958–60	14·0	6·6	10·2	5·4
Populations (Present Frontiers) (millions)				
1937	34·5	9·1	16·3	14·4
1949	24·6	9·2	16·1	12·3
1959	29·3	9·9	18·4	13·6
Increase or Decrease per cent. in Grain Production				
Pre-war to 1958–60	+ 5·3	+ 8·2	+25·9	− 3·6
1948–50 to 1958–60	+20·0	+17·9	+56·9	+10·2
Increase or Decrease per cent. in Population				
Pre-war to 1959	−15·0	+9·3	+12·9	−5·6
1949 to 1959	+19·1	+7·6	+14·3	+9·9
Per Capita Grain (metric tons)				
Pre-war	0·39	0·67	0·50	0·39
1959	0·48	0·66	0·55	0·40

* The only available figures relate to 1948 and to the average of 1948–52.

Sources: For Poland, *Statistical Yearbooks*; for the others, FAO, *Yearbooks of Food and Agricultural Statistics*.

or slightly above the pre-war level. Hungary still shows a much higher per capita level than the other countries, and throughout the post-war period food has been much more plentiful than in Poland and Czechoslovakia, as might be expected, now that Hungary's formerly large export surplus has turned into a small import surplus.

Thus the grain supply position is not worse than before the war, and there has certainly been an increase in consumption. None the less, for Poland, with an adverse trade balance, the outlook is graver than it was, because population is now increasing at a higher rate than before, and higher yields cannot be attained without much more investment in agriculture. If the agricultural potential of the Danubian plain were to be developed, production could of course be increased at much lower costs, and Hungary and Rumania could export to the rest of the communist bloc, thus reducing its dependence on grain imports from Russia. But in agriculture each country is autarchic, and no attempt has been made to utilise the most fertile land more productively, except in Jugoslavia, which therefore shows a much higher rate of increase in grain production than the other three countries.

Although it is in grain cultivation that large-scale operation might be expected to show better results than peasant farming, grain production in the later nineteen-fifties increased faster in Poland and Jugoslavia, where collectivization had been abandoned, than in Hungary and in Czechoslovakia, where it was still proceeding. Czechoslovakia shows the poorest results, partly because the once well-farmed German lands went out of cultivation after the war (according to recent reports about half a million hectares are still uncultivated). Official indices of total agricultural production show the same broad contrast between the countries, but show Poland in a more favourable position; owing to its more rapid increase in livestock production, which is encouraged in order to squeeze out an export surplus of pigs and bacon.

(ii) As to the existence of labour redundancy on the land, agricultural populations are now smaller, both relatively and absolutely (with the possible exception of Rumania, where the only figures available show an absolute increase). Changes in the size of the agricultural populations up to 1950 were mainly due to changes in frontiers and total populations. From 1950 to 1960 the decreases were due to the growth of industrial employment, which has been large enough to absorb the increase of the working population and also to draw labour off the land. The following table shows these changes.

TABLE II

Total and Agricultural Population in East European Countries

(Present Frontiers, except where otherwise stated)

Column 1   Total population at census date, millions.
Column 2   Agricultural population at census date, millions.
Column 3   Agricultural as per cent. of total population.

| | Pre-War | | | Post-War | | | | | |
| | | | | 1950–59 | | | 1960 (1961) | | |
	1	2	3	1	2	3	1	2	3
Poland	(1931)*32·0	19·1	60	(1950) 25·0	11·6	47	29·7	11·2	38
Czechoslovakia	(1930) 14·0	4·6	33	(1950) 12·4	3·1	25	(61) 13·7	2·7	19
Hungary	(1941) 9·3	4·5	49	..	..	..	10·0	3·6	36
Jugoslavia	(1931) 14·5	11·1	79	(1953) 16·9	10·3	61	(61) 18·5	9·3	51
Bulgaria	(1934) 6·1	4·4	73	(1956) 7·6	4·2	55	..	..	..

* Pre-war frontiers
Sources: Official Statistical Yearbooks, FAO Production Yearbooks.

In spite of these large shifts in the balance of occupations, the proportion of the total population in agriculture is still high by comparison with Western Europe, except in Czechoslovakia, where it is similar. Although labour productivity by comparison with Western Europe is still low, it must have risen considerably, since a larger volume of output is now produced by a smaller labour force. Unfortunately recent labour force figures are scanty, and their comparability with pre-war uncertain; moreover the growing practice of combining agriculture with industrial employment renders comparison difficult. However, such figures as are available may be quoted to show the large absolute reductions in the agricultural labour force in Poland and Czechoslovakia, and the much smaller reductions in Hungary, Jugoslavia and Bulgaria. The Rumanian figure quoted shows that the proportion of the labour force in agriculture was still high in 1956.

TABLE III

Total and Agricultural Labour Force in East European Countries

(Present Frontiers, except where otherwise stated)

Column 1   Total active population at census date, millions.
Column 2   Active agricultural population (both sexes) at census date, millions.
Column 3   Column 2 as per cent. of Column 1.

	Pre-War			Post-War					
				1950–59			1960 (1961)		
	1	2	3	1	2	3	1	2	3
Poland	(1931)*15·0	9·6	64	(1950) 13·2	7·0	53	..	..	..
Czechoslovakia	(1930) 6·7	2·5	37	(1950) 5·8	2·2	38	(61) 6·1	1·5	25
Hungary	(1930) 3·8	2·0	53	..	..	..	4·9	1·8	38
Jugoslavia	(1931)* 6·5	5·1	78	(1953) 8·4	5·4	64	(61) 9·0	4·8	52
Bulgaria	(1934) 3·4	2·7	80	(1956) 4·1	2·6	64	..	..	..
Rumania	(1941) ..	6·5	..	(1956) 10·4	7·3	70	..	..	..

* Pre-war frontiers
Sources: Official Statistical Yearbooks, FAO Production Yearbooks.

Has industrialization absorbed the surplus of labour on the land? Put in this way, the question cannot be answered. Any estimates of excessive manpower based on pre-war conditions are out of date in the countries where there have been large changes in populations. Moreover, for reasons explained below, the surplus was not precisely measurable in numbers. The degree of mechanization in agriculture is still low, except in Czechoslovakia, but it must have affected labour requirements to some extent. There is certainly a shortage of farm labour in Czechoslovakia now, which is not surprising, since excess of manpower was formerly localized in Eastern Slovakia, and also in Ruthenia, which is now in Russia. In Hungary also a shortage is reported, which is surprising, since the reduction in the farm labour force between 1930 and 1960 amounted to only 200,000 workers. As to Poland, the man: land ratio is now more favourable, and on this overall basis there should now be no surplus labour; but there is still an excess of farm population in Southern Poland, though there is a shortage in the north-west. As to Jugoslavia, there is certainly some surplus labour still in the poorest regions, though in other regions there are shortages. So although no reassurance can be found in figures, it can be concluded that in these four countries there is less surplus labour in agriculture than there was.

Another aspect of occupational imbalance is now much more striking: the maldistribution of labour between industry and services. In industry there is much obvious underemployment, while too little labour is employed in transport and distribution. The transport bottleneck is one of the main causes of urban food shortage. In agriculture itself, whatever the labour supply situation, more capital and labour should now be employed in improving the infrastructure, through land reclamation, farm roads, transport and marketing facilities. So today the problem of occupational imbalance is too complex to be stated in terms of the simple old antithesis between agriculture and industry.

From the standpoint of this book, the important question is whether the movement of labour into industry can be shown to have relieved the extremes of farm poverty. As the map on p. 71 shows, Southern Poland and Jugoslavia south of the Sava were the regions most densely populated in relation to farm land, and as Chapter VII shows, they were among the poorest, with no prospect of agricultural development, and therefore greatly in need of alternative employment. How has industrial development affected them?

The Polish government has followed a policy of industrial dispersion, in consequence of which peasants in the southeastern region (formerly Southern Poland) have benefited by the expansion of the new industrial centre of Krakow, round

the new steel works in the suburb of Nowa Huta, which
houses some of the recruits to industry; they also find work
in the old industrial centre of Katowice, also expanding,
though not so fast as Kraków. Movement into industry
largely takes the form of daily migration from the countryside
by small farmers or members of their families. In the mid-
fifties 'peasant-industrial workers' were estimated to number
between 900,000 and 1,200,000 in Poland as a whole. In
1960 there were estimated to be 400,000 such workers in
Kraków voivodship alone, in a total population of 2·3 million.
They are the best off among the industrial workers, since the
farm, even if small, provides a secure food supply; the wages
earned by the commuting members of the family provide cash
for consumption goods, and also for new farm equipment and
building. According to a sample survey covering 80 villages
in Poland in 1947–57, nearly half the peasant families in the
south-eastern region derived some income from industrial
employment, and one quarter of them derived over 60 per cent
of their income from off-farm earnings.[1]

Official opinion holds that this is a temporary situation,
since for orthodox doctrine these commuting peasants are
two-timers in the class war. None the less, it is cheaper to
provide double-decker railway carriages for them than to build
more new urban housing. So commuting makes the best of
two bad jobs, because industrial wages are low, food dear and
urban housing hard to get. It is the peasants' answer to
planning, just as it is the peasants' answer to the economic
miracle in Western Germany.

The Jugoslav government has also followed a policy of
industrial dispersion, for strategic, political and social reasons.
This has resulted in a relatively larger increase in industrial
employment in the regions south of the Sava, although the
absolute increases are much greater in the old industrial
centres.[2] Power stations and new plants have been located
in the agriculturally over-populated republics, in Bosnia and

[1] *Spoleczno-ekonomiczna struktura wsi w Polsce ludowej,* B. Gałęski, Instytut
Ekonomiki Rolnej, Warsaw, 1960.

[2] F. E. I. Hamilton, *Recent Changes in Industrial Location in Jugoslavia,*
London University Ph.D. thesis, 1962.

South Serbia for economic as well as social reasons, and for social reasons in Macedonia, Montenegro and Kosmet-Metohija, the regions officially described as backward.

In old and new centres alike, the to-and-fro movement is very evident. Huddled forms with swaddled feet on the stations are the daily commuters, who travel up to 2 hours daily each way, to work in the factory from 6 a.m. to 2 p.m., and then return to work on the farm. When the journey home is too long, the bread-winning wife or child will carry food to the station where the commuter sleeps. A floating mass of temporary migrants from still remoter districts comes to work for two or three months in the towns, and then returns to the farms for the harvest, tired of factory discipline and having earned enough cash for the moment. About half the industrial labour force are estimated to be peasant-industrial workers of one kind or another.

So in these regions industrialization does to some extent absorb the surplus, including the part-time workers and the seasonal slack. Manpower is more fully employed and earnings have increased. Probably the poorer peasants are better off than they were, even though their conditions of work are exhausting.

Peasants in general would also have benefited from industrialization if the increase in the urban demand for food had raised prices and stimulated production. But communist policy has kept farm incomes down, by fixing low prices for compulsory delivery quotas, thus eliminating the price inducement to higher productivity. Some improvement in village living standards has come through industrialization, as for example rural electrification. But when a Polish planner explains that the peasants are now allowed to build again, as if this were an immense concession, one realises that even in Poland the peasants are still an oppressed class.

So far as collectivization is concerned, the arguments of the book have stood the test of time. Nothing was learnt from the Russian experience, except a more sophisticated strategy; the results were far less disastrous, because the process was far less brutal. When the process started in 1948–49 (in Bulgaria in 1945), laws were passed to the effect that membership of the various forms of co-operative, set up to provide a framework for the transition to collective farming, should be voluntary; in practice, coercion was used.

Economic incentives were also used. Co-operative farmers were given higher prices, cheap or free credit, all supplies of new farm equipment, and were lightly taxed. At the same time, 'private' farmers were subjected to various penalties, such as lower prices, higher delivery quotas, higher taxes, while their savings were wiped out by currency conversions. These punitive measures reduced production, as shown in Table I above. By 1953 the whole region faced a food crisis, which forced a revision of the policy: prices were raised and quotas reduced; the pressures were relaxed and the process slowed down.

Jugoslavia tore into collectivization with characteristic élan and snapped out of it with equally characteristic decision after the catastrophic harvest of 1952, the lowest within living memory. Poland never went far, and tacitly gave it up after the October Revolution of 1956. In Hungary, after the rising in the same October, most of the co-operatives broke up; after the rising was crushed, the process was resumed. Collectivization is now complete in Bulgaria and all but complete in Hungary, Czechoslovakia and Rumania. The co-operative façade has now been abandoned; the statutes of the collective farms in Czechoslovakia and Bulgaria are now identical with those of the Russian kolkchoz.

Peasant attitudes are as hostile as they were in Russia, but more sophisticated. Czech farmers continue to cultivate well, as they always did, but express their hostility in the traditional Czech manner through a Schwejk conspiracy to keep targets low. Hungarian farmers also cultivate well, but the bulk of the meat and poultry supplies now comes from the tiny fraction of the land held in private plots—the same ridiculous misuse of land as in Russia. In Poland, according to an eminent economist, 'pressure on the peasants was sufficient to induce them to join the co-operatives, but not sufficient to induce them to increase production'. In practice, this meant

that the co-operative farmers earned higher incomes by re-
selling their cheap fertilizers to the individual farmers at
black market prices. Still, the peasants have suffered, as
they were meant to do, since for them socialism is intended
to be a punishment.

However, the industrial workers, for whom it is intended to
be a reward, have suffered also. If farmers have had to pay
the price of industrialization in shortage of consumer goods,
townspeople have had to pay the price of collectivization in
food shortage as well. Much capital has been invested in
farm buildings and machinery which brings in no return
in increased food supplies. Even in communist terms, the
policy has been self-defeating, because scanty foreign exchange
must be used to buy grain instead of capital equipment. No
doubt when Russia abandons collective farming the satellites
will thankfully follow suit.

In the meantime, the interesting question is how to organise
agriculture after collectivization has failed. In Poland and
Jugoslavia, the conflict between dogma and common sense
presented a real dilemma, dragged out for years in dreary
debate about 'the peasant', while production slowly recovered.
In Jugoslavia the communist party at length found a com-
promise solution in 'the break-through on a narrow front',
i.e. concentrating state investment in the fertile lands of the
Voivodina, through state farms and a new type of co-operative,
which provides farm equipment for its members and also
tractor service, against payment. This is the policy adum-
brated on pp. 137–8 of this book; as Table I above shows, it
has been successful, though unfortunately the rapid rate of
increase in 1957–60 has not been sustained.

In Poland, the problem has been tackled less vigorously.
The Agricultural Circles grow slowly, owing to mistrust of
their ultimate objective; they are a loose form of co-operative
organization, financed from the proceeds of the difference
between the prices paid to farmers and the market prices of
farm produce; with these funds the circles buy tractors and
other equipment for the use of their members. The old and
genuine dairy co-operative societies have been revived. Compulsory delivery quotas are now fixed at only 30 per cent of

production; under a system of contracts, at favourable prices, produce is sold to state bacon, sugar-beet and oil seeds factories. The government is wisely undertaking land reclamation on a large scale. Poland has in fact, though not in theory, more or less reverted to a West European pattern of farm organization.

To-day the disparity in farm income levels between Eastern and Western Europe is greater than ever. For in Western Europe agricultural production has increased much faster, while the farm labour force has continued to decrease. Peasant farming, with no change in the structure of farm ownership, is now highly mechanized.[1] Now it is the Western European farm surpluses which cannot find markets. So superficially at least the conditions of 'Europe's farm problem' appear to have been reversed; but Europe as a whole is better fed by fewer people than it was in 1939, so that in reality there has been progress.

II

Since the book has acquired broader connotations than it was originally intended to have, it seems necessary to use the opportunity of this introduction to explain how far I have found its arguments applicable in other contexts, and why they can be misinterpreted, as in one important respect they have been, if they are applied to under-developed countries in general.

The chief source of misinterpretation has been the idea of surplus population in agriculture, about which so much nonsense has since been written. This condition, though it was

---

[1] See UN/FAO: *European Agriculture, A Statement of Problems, Geneva,* 1954; Warriner, 'Changes in European Peasant Farming', *International Labour Review,* Geneva, 1957, and *Why Labour Leaves the Land,* I.L.O., Geneva, 1960.

real enough, can be seriously misleading if it is used as a key
to the problems of under-development. Excessive manpower
in agriculture is not a condition specific to under-developed
countries. On the contrary, even in countries which are
developing fast, with rapid movement of labour from agriculture into industry, pockets of surplus farm labour may
persist, because the least efficient farmers are often the least
mobile, for various reasons, such as age, poverty, small scale
or remote situation, which prevent a change of occupation.
But where such groups form only a small fraction of a relatively small agricultural population, as in the United States
and in several West European countries, such differential
mobility is not an obstacle to development, but a consequence
of it: labour is redundant only in relation to a rising general
standard of living and a rising level of productivity in agriculture, which these farmers cannot attain.

In the agrarian countries of Eastern Europe, by contrast,
the existence of surplus labour on the land *was* a serious condition, because the level of productivity in agriculture was not
rising, but tending to fall. The real problem, of which excessive manpower was only one aspect, was that agricultural
production did not keep pace with the growth of agricultural
(and total) population. Over-population meant that there
were too many mouths, not merely too many hands; and the
primary need was to make the hands more productive, in
order to feed the mouths. Because this was the primary need,
I estimated the numbers who did not have enough to eat
(p. 88), before I guessed at the numbers who could not be
employed by the development of agriculture (pp. 138–9). I
attempted to gauge the scope for increasing agricultural production and employment, which was large, but not large
enough to absorb all the surplus labour from the poorest
regions. Thus the employment of the surplus was a residual
problem, and not the starting point.

Unfortunately, economists and demographers have since
made it their starting point, by concentrating on the labour
aspect of over-population to the exclusion of the food aspect,
and have busied themselves with elaborate calculations of the
number of redundant bodies in agriculture, disregarding the

question of how these bodies were to be fed. One estimate calculated the size of the surplus in Eastern Europe in the existing pre-war conditions.[1] Another authority worked out the hypothetical surplus, on two different standards of labour requirements,[2] an exercise which certainly demonstrated under-employment among statisticians. Observation made me wary of such precise estimates; and reflection has reinforced this scepticism.

One of the difficulties in such calculations is that in any system of farming subject to much seasonal variation in labour requirements, it is difficult to isolate all-the-year-round redundancy from seasonal unemployment. It was particularly difficult to do so in the agrarian countries of Eastern Europe, where the seasonal variation was much greater than in Central and Western Europe, because livestock husbandry was backward and arable cultivation was extensive and one-sided. Any estimate of the size of the labour surplus which is made by relating manpower actually available to labour requirements in man-days (whether these are calculated for the country concerned, or on a standard derived from other countries) will inevitably exaggerate the size of the surplus, because such estimates take only total man-days into account, and not their timing, so that the seasonal variation is ignored. If, that is to say, the annual labour requirements of a farm are 270 man-days throughout the year, then one man can do the work, but if the man-days must be worked during three months of the year, then three men will be needed. Or to put it another way round, if all the workers are unemployed for half the year, it does not follow that half the workers are surplus, though some of them may be. The real surplus consists of those workers who are employed only for a short period in the peak season, and who could work throughout it, if they had larger farms, or could find work on other farms. Where the amount of land per worker in agriculture is very small, in such extensive systems, then there is a true surplus

---

[1] P. N. Rosenstein Rodan, in an unpublished memorandum for the Royal Institute of International Affairs.

[2] Professor Wilbert E. Moore, *Economic Demography of Eastern and South-Eastern Europe*, League of Nations, Geneva, 1945.

of workers who could leave agriculture without reducing production. It is for this reason that I used density of farm population as my main criterion, and referred to overpopulated *regions*. However, for practical purposes it is impossible to distinguish, in precise numbers, between the true surplus and the seasonal slack, because the length of the peak season is imprecise. My guesses at the proportion of the actual surplus (p. 68) and the numbers of the residual surplus (pp. 138–9) were deliberately rough, and were possibly too high, because I did not take the seasonal variation sufficiently into account.

Another difficulty in estimating the size of the surplus is that the labour force in agriculture is usually heterogeneous, and in this region was particularly so. Farmers differ in ability; workers differ in skill and strength, and in their part-time contributions to the work of the farm. If a large number of good farmers are expelled, as in the case of the Germans from the Czech borderlands, or from the Voivodina, agricultural production will fall, because good farmers are not easily replaced. If the same number of young men move to the towns from small farms in poor regions, it is probable that the older men and women can work harder, and maintain the low level of production, so that in this case the surplus is reduced. In family farming (which in this region offered fuller employment than large estates, cf. pp. 148–50) it is always difficult to assess the contribution made by part-time women workers, and the extent to which they could take on fuller employment. Though women worked hard on the land in the agrarian countries, as several of the illustrations show, they could not, as a rule, take over the whole of the work of the farm, as the effects of wartime mobilization proved. From the concrete examples in the text, the reader will note that it was easy to observe *symptoms* of labour redundancy, such as waste of labour on poor land (pp. 136–7) or an inordinately large number of workers on a group of small farms (pp. 130–1), and yet difficult to *identify* the surplus workers. But the fact that the surplus was not precisely measurable does not mean that it did not exist, only that rough guesses are more honest than precise figures.

The post-war experience in Eastern Europe has shown that the surplus was certainly large. How otherwise account for the fact that in Poland in 1957 the pre-war grain output was produced by an agricultural population of 11 million, instead of the pre-war 19 million? Apart from a low degree of mechanization, there have been no changes in methods of farming or capital inputs which would explain such a great increase in output per head of agricultural population (there are unfortunately no comparable figures for active agricultural population). As to Jugoslavia, the change is less striking, but there too production recovered by 1957 to the pre-war level with a smaller labour force and very little capital input (though the recent rapid increase in production is due to new capital investment). Why then labour the point that precise calculations of the size of the surplus are not possible? They drew attention to a serious condition, a type of disequilibrium which economists had hitherto ignored.

The real objection to calculations of this kind is not merely that they cannot be precise; it is that they tend, by their apparent precision, to convey the impression that the surplus of labour is an absolute magnitude, i.e. a definite number of workers who cannot be employed in agriculture in any conditions. But all estimates of agricultural surplus population are of course relative to given conditions; the type of farming, technical methods and agrarian structure must be assumed to be fixed. In a short period this assumption is legitimate, but in a longer period it is unrealistic, because agricultural policy can quickly induce changes which increase employment (such as the encouragement of intensive crops and livestock production, or the development of irrigation), as well as changes which decrease it. Yet in discussion, as so often happens, the basis of the estimate tends to be forgotten, and the assumption of 'given conditions' tacitly translates itself into a belief that agricultural employment cannot be increased. From the apparently hard fact that there are, say, one million surplus workers on the land, it may then be inferred that there are one million workers who can be employed *only* in industry. Economists then proceed to draw up development plans based on the rate of industrialization needed to absorb this number.

By a process of cumulative error, they may even go so far as to argue that it is advantageous for a country to have a surplus of this kind. One look at Southern Poland would have dispelled that idea.

So the ultimate effect of all this paper work was to give a wrong twist to the discussion of development policy, because it concentrated attention on one aspect of agricultural over-population, labour redundancy, to the exclusion of the other, the long-term decline in output per head. Consequently the emphasis was placed on industrialization as the sole remedy, while the equally great need for increasing agricultural production was ignored—with what effects in practice can be seen in Communist Eastern Europe today. If the expertise deployed in calculating the elusive surplus had been devoted instead to a review of the figures showing the long term decline in output per head, or to a survey of land use and agricultural potential, it might have offered a better guide to the formulation of development plans.

In those under-developed countries where the race between population and agricultural production today is a far grimmer reality than it was in the old Eastern Europe, the use of the concept of surplus labour as a starting point for development plans is definitely dangerous, since it may bias policy off the right approach, the need for increasing food output. Consider Egypt, for instance, where a tiny cultivated area, one-tenth the size of that of Bulgaria, has to support a population four times as large as the Bulgarian. Would it be helpful to calculate the size of the labour surplus, on the basis of the Bulgarian or any other European standard of labour requirements? Clearly it would be absurd, because Egyptian farming is the most intensive in the world. There is a surplus of labour, no doubt; but its extent does not measure the true gravity of the situation, the tendency for output per head to fall as a result of growing pressure on the land. No practicable rate of industrialization can counteract this, or change the course of the race. Fortunately for Egypt, the planners have not thought in terms of 'absorbing the surplus'. Although industries are being developed, the main point of the Five Year Plan is to make more land, through increasing the supply of water from the

High Dam, and economizing the precious water on the land already cultivated. Perhaps under-developed countries need a new economics, treating water as an independent factor of production.

Nor are estimates of the extent of surplus manpower relevant when over-population appears in its most serious form, the destruction of the fertility of the soil through over-cropping, as is happening now in parts of tropical Africa. The primary need there is to evolve a more productive and stable agriculture, which may require a complete change in the type of farming. What is needed are not calculations of the amount of surplus labour under a given system, but estimates of the extent to which it would be possible to evolve a new system, in which a more productive type of agriculture would conserve soil fertility.

So the existence of surplus labour in agriculture, however it is estimated, does not in itself provide a basis for decisions as to the priorities of development. Calculations of labour requirements in agriculture can of course be useful for specific purposes, as for example in relation to policies of land reform or schemes for land settlement, when it is essential to calculate the minimum size of holding needed to support a family, so that the holdings granted to the new owners will give them the standard of living considered adequate. Where there is much variation in soil or rainfall, then such calculations must be based on soil surveys and rainfall averages in each area. In Egypt and Italy, the standard minimum holding is calculated with reference not to the existing system of farming, but to the more intensive system which it is intended to introduce. This is a different method of approach, since it is positive, and starts from the ground up.

So far as land reform is concerned, the more I have seen of countries still dominated by landlordism, the more convinced I am that peasant farming offers better conditions of employment than large estates (Chapter VIII). In the Middle East, during the war, I realized that I had scarcely seen real agrarian poverty before. Nor had I ever seen extortionate absentee landowners. When I first saw the share-rent levied—the fat smiling Lebanese landowner collecting his half of the heap of grain from the kneeling cultivator—I remembered that it was this very thing that the peasants of the Balkans had fought to abolish for over a century, from 1803 to 1918. In 1944, it seemed high time that this system should be abolished in the Middle East.

Yet if one looked at the situation historically, there was no reason for the anger which sprang from remembrance of another world. In the Balkans the struggle for national independence against alien rulers had gone hand in hand with the struggle for peasant ownership against alien land-lords. But in the Arab world the bad old Ottoman system had survived the disruption of the Ottoman Empire. The landowners were not alien; the cultivators were not cast in the heroic Balkan mould; and liberal ideas had not influenced the urban middle class to the extent of arousing their interest in the countryside. Seen against this background, the peasant life of Eastern Europe, though technically backward, appeared to be a highly evolved society which had matured through a long series of revolutions and reforms, and satisfied social aspirations still. The old Peasant Parties, once weighed and found wanting in economic foresight, had, after all, given many people more of what they wanted, a criterion of good government which should not be out-of-date even today.

The second argument of Chapter VIII, that peasant society will not, of itself, invest in long term large scale improve-ments in agriculture, is surely true in other parts of the world? In writing reports for the United Nations, I have carried this argument further, and, in the language of the international forum, have urged that governments undertaking land reforms should do so as part of 'an integrated comprehensive program' to link reform with better farming, by measures to help new farmers through easier credit, co-operative marketing, agri-cultural education and so on. This simple lesson from the past seems obvious common sense, but has proved rather a counsel of perfection. Apart from a few countries, there has been little real progress in land reform in under-developed countries in the last decade. It is the first step, the redistribution of ownership, that proves the stumbling block, not the supplementary measures.

In these international discussions, it sometimes seems as if governments in under-developed countries were quite genuinely puzzled about the objectives of agrarian reform. Thoroughly sophisticated as they are about economic growth, they would like to be sure that they get the latest land reform model, in the choice of which they may be bemused by experts prating of the Kolkchoz, the Kibbutz, and the Gezira Scheme, as if these were new makes of car. The Ground-Nuts Scheme is conveniently forgotten. As to collectivization, it has now been enforced, in the rigid old-fashioned style, in a variety of conditions and in different types of farming; and its results have been bad: the countries which have abandoned it have increased production much faster. No under-developed country which is concerned to increase food production— and which is not?—can afford to risk it. Planned investment in agriculture is obviously necessary, but the recent East European experience demonstrates that the kolkchoz is a wasteful way of undertaking it. If schemes of group farming are to be tried, then it would be wiser to look at the new types of co-operative organisation which have been introduced in Poland and Jugoslavia since the failure of collectivization.

The moral of the East European experience, today and yesterday, is that governments undertaking land reform should consider, first and foremost, what their people want; no change in the agrarian structure can really be called a social reform unless it does that. To take social aspirations into account is also economically sound, since ownership can be a powerful incentive if it is encouraged by an active government policy. Though I would not go quite so far as Colin Clark, who says that 'the peasant works, and nothing else does', I believe that peasant farming is a good foundation. Nothing in agriculture works wonders. What works best, judging from the experience of Western Europe, is co-operation between the state, the co-operative movement and the peasant farmers. To work on these lines is likely to give better results than the import of foreign models: a pragmatic approach can adapt and evolve.

So I hope that in under-developed countries young people will not waste time discussing 'the peasant', or sit in offices computing the size of their surplus populations, but will *walk* through the villages and see farms and talk to farmers, to learn what can be done about farm poverty.

April 1963   DOREEN WARRINER

CHAPTER I

EUROPE'S FARM PROBLEM

1. AGRICULTURE AND ECONOMIC DEVELOPMENT

IN the present economic situation in Europe two factors of outstanding importance influence the standard of living: the low level of earnings in agriculture as compared with earnings in industry, and the policy of agricultural protection. The difference between earnings in agriculture and industry is, of course, not a feature peculiar to Europe: farm workers are generally underpaid by comparison with industrial workers, and farm capital in general earns a lower rate of return than capital invested in industry. Everywhere farmers see that economic progress does not bring them the same gains as other producers receive, and under the pressure of falling prices and rising costs they conclude that there is a conflict of interests between town and country, and that the whole trend of modern civilization is against them.

In Europe, however, the low level of earnings in agriculture has a special cause, apart from the universal disability which affects food producers in general. European farmers have to compete with overseas producers who work with more land per head and more capital, and can therefore sell food products cheaper, while maintaining a good standard of living. To stave off the effects of this competition from their home producers, the countries of Western Europe, which were formerly large food importers, have raised tariff barriers and cut food imports to nothing. But protection, though it increases the farmers' share in the national income at the expense of the industrial population, does not equalize earnings on the land with earnings in industry, and in spite of high tariffs the level of incomes per head in agriculture remains lower than in industry, because labour is less productive, working with less capital.

So important is the policy of agricultural protection likely to remain in the future development of world trade that it is hardly necessary to stress the importance of examining the system of food production in Europe as a whole. It is the difficulty of adjustment to the increase in productivity in agriculture which lies at the root of Europe's economic problem, and it is obvious that very far-reaching changes in methods of production may be necessary for Europe if this adjustment is to be made.

To understand the real nature of the present farm problem in Europe we must examine the economic basis of the peasant farming system, and ask how far it determines the policy of high protection to agriculture, and how far it is responsible for the low level of earnings on the land. The most striking feature of agricultural organization in Europe is, of course, the small size of the food-producing enterprise, and the almost universal prevalence of family farming. It is natural to conclude that this indicates a weak and inefficient form of organization, since economic progress usually seems to go hand in hand with an increase in the size of the producing unit. In the development of modern industry the advance of large-scale production through the concentration of capital in large firms has been the chief means through which the productivity of labour has increased; but in agriculture there is no parallel movement of concentration.

Before we turn to examine the farm problem in Europe itself, therefore, it is necessary to look at the relation of farm organization to economic progress in a wider perspective, to see why in general the scale of operations remains smaller than in industry.

It is not only in Europe that the scale of farming operations is small. Even the large family farms of the United States and Canada, with 200–500 acres, are small businesses compared with the average industrial undertaking, and even in England, when farms over 50 acres take up about 80 per cent. of the farm area, farm businesses are small, reckoned in turnover, as compared with industrial firms. England is usually regarded as a country of large farms, yet one out of three workers on the land is a farmer. In Europe, however, the scale of farming operations is smaller still. Measured in acres, the typical peasant farm is very small, about 8 hectares (20 acres) in Western Europe, about 3 (7 acres) in the East, excluding the Baltic.

The following table shows the range within which average farm sizes vary in Europe. The average, of course, is a misleading figure for countries like Hungary, where great numbers of dwarf holdings exist beside the large estates and bring the average down. But in general the dispersion round the average is close enough to allow comparison between countries, although the contrast between *typical* peasant farms in Eastern and Western Europe is not sufficiently clear, owing to lack of statistics for the Balkans.

Farm Workers and Farm Sizes

(1935 or nearest census date)

	Occupied in agric., millions	Farm land, million hectares	Number of farms, millions	Average size of farm, hectares	Average number of workers per farm
Germany . .	9:4	28·7	3·0	9·6	3·1
Belgium . .	0·6	1·7	1·1	1·5	0·5
Denmark . .	0·6	3·1	0·2	15·5	3·0
France . . .	7·7	34·9	4·0	8·7	1·9
Great Britain and N. Ireland . .	1·6	19·6	0·6	32·7	2·7
Eire . . .	0·7	4·7	0·4	11·7	1·7
Italy . . .	8·0	21·5	4·2	5·1	1·9
Holland . .	0·7	2·3	0·2	11·5	3·5
Norway . . .	0·4	1·0	0·3	3·0	1·0
Austria . . .	1·0	4·3	0·4	10·7	2·5
Sweden . . .	1·0	4·9	0·6	8·2	1·7
Switzerland .	0·4	2·2	0·2	11·0	2·0
Portugal . .	1·9	..	..	..	..
Spain . . .	4·5	39·0	..	..	..
Total and average for Western Europe (excluding Spain and Portugal) . .	32·1	128·9	15·2	8·48	2·11
Poland . . .	10·3	25·6	3·3	7·8	3·1
Czechoslovakia .	2·7	8·4	1·6	5·25	1·7
Hungary . .	2·0	7·5	1·3	5·8	1·5
Rumania . .	6·5	18·3	3·2	5·7	2·0
Bulgaria . .	2·5	4·1	0·7	5·9	3·6
Jugoslavia . .	4·9	14·2	..	..	..
Greece . . .	1·5	2·2	..	..	..
Turkey . . .	4·4	..	..	..	..
Eastern Europe (excluding Jugoslavia, Greece, and Turkey)	24·0	63·9	10·1	6·33	2·28
Baltic States . .	3·5	13·9	0·85	16·35	4·12
Europe . . .	59·6	206·7	26·15	7·90	2·28

(Table based on *Statistisches Jahrbuch für das Deutsche Reich*, 1937.)

With the exception of certain regions in Eastern Germany, Hungary, and Poland, small farms are everywhere the rule and if they continue to exist, it is a proof that they can offer the worker an income at least as high as big farms. We ought not to conclude that large farms are more efficient, unless there is a marked tendency for farms to increase their size as businesses; and this tendency is not apparent, either in Great Britain or in Europe.

There is, of course, a long-period tendency for farms to increase their size as businesses, by increasing their farming equipment, in the form of live stock, machinery, and feeding-stuffs. But to a large extent this capital investment is a substitute for labour, and is not accompanied by an increase in the numbers of men employed per farm. As we shall see, it is the countries which have the larger capital investment per unit of labour, not those which have the largest farm units, which have the highest rural standards of living. (Similarly, farm-accountancy results suggest that the largest profits are earned by the farms with the largest capital equipment in relation to labour, not by the large farm units as such.) In farming, therefore, the increase in the productivity of labour appears to occur without a fundamental change in the size of farming enterprises.

The reasons why this should be so are not difficult to find. On the technical side, there is no need for the development of large-scale capitalistic enterprise, because there is no need for large indivisible units of capital equipment, above all, no need for power-supply; on the economic side, the prospects of profits are so low that the risk of large-scale investment is too heavy. Capital can usually find a better return elsewhere, and in consequence the bulk of capital invested in agriculture is supplied by the farmer himself, since he is the best judge of the risk of investment in his own enterprise. Consequently, the farmer remains to a large extent capitalist, entrepreneur, and labourer at the same time.

Further, of course, the long periods of falling prices necessarily means that the cost of capital investment in new processes is too high. In any industry, at any time, there are always available better technical methods, or methods of increasing the physical productivity of labour: but whether these methods are used or not depends on whether they will save on total costs. An instance of this is the grass-drying process in England, which, though it saves labour, and produces a better product than hay, is at the moment too costly; another instance is that of the tractors and reaping machines in Hungary, which stand idle because labour is cheaper. It is quite possible that the big farms can use better technical methods, but these methods need not necessarily be more economic. In a branch of production like agriculture, which has to meet long periods of falling prices, there will necessarily be many processes which are too dear to use.

If, therefore, we view the question of agricultural organization in relation to the movement towards combination in industry, it appears that the connexion between low returns and small farms should really be reversed: farm incomes are not low because farms are too small; farms remain small because the scope for making profits in agriculture in general is low, and in consequence the investment of capital in large units is never likely to be highly profitable, apart from exceptional circumstances. The explanation of the low rate of profit is, of course, a very simple one: agriculture can never be expected to earn the same rates of return as industry does, because of the fundamental conditions of supply and demand. The demand for the chief foodstuffs remains stable, or expands only in proportion to the growth of population, while in the past fifty years the rate of increase in the supply of foodstuffs has been very rapid. It is simply *because* farmers have shown remarkable efficiency in using new methods to increase output that returns are low: even when food prices fall, output tends to increase. The relatively low rate of return is a sign that the community wants other goods more than it needs food; wages and profits will rise in the industries producing those 'other goods' and labour will tend to move out of agriculture into better-paid occupations. In a progressive economy, resources must continually tend to move out of farming.

Farmers naturally resent this process, which appears to them to mean an unjust distribution of rewards for labour and enterprise; yet, as the following chapters will show, where industry does not develop, and there is no rural exodus, the condition of the farm population is far worse than it is in an industrial economy. As industry expands and the farm population moves into industry, the amount of land and capital per head of the rest of the farm population increases, and the productivity of labour rises. The movement out of agriculture is in fact a sign of increasing productivity and a high rate of capital accumulation. An economic system with a low level of productivity will necessarily be obliged to keep most of its labour on the land, to satisfy its demand for food; as productivity increases, less labour need be used in food production. The rise in income per head means a shift in demand and a shift in the distribution of resources between occupations. Consequently the tendency for the farm population to decline must be regarded as a necessary feature of advance to a higher level of productivity.

Thus the relatively low level of earnings in food production is a necessity of economic progress and lies outside the sphere of agricultural policy. Farmers' influence in politics is often exerted as a demand for equality of return to farming interests, yet in the nature of things this demand cannot be met. The only way in which farmers can raise their incomes is to reduce their numbers on the land, but complete equality can never be attained so long as demand expands so slowly.

Further, the lower level of earnings cannot be much affected by experiments in farm organization: the idea that some form of large-scale joint-stock farming can raise the earnings of capital and labour to the level of earnings in industry is an illusion.

Hence it is not wise to regard the prevalence of small-scale farming as the result of a choice of independence rather than efficiency. In any branch of economic life where returns are low as a general long-period tendency, there is little tendency to the concentration of firms, because little tendency to large-scale investment. For the type of farming practised in European conditions the family farm (and, as we shall see, the family farm may be, and in England usually is, a large land unit) has undoubted merits: it maintains capital equipment, promotes capital accumulation, and gives full employment to the family. For reasons which will be examined at length in Chapter V, it is perhaps only suitable in certain conditions; but for these conditions it is undoubtedly an efficient type of *economic* organization.

It is, of course, true that the intangible advantages of peasant life loom very large to Europe's rural population. The security attached to land ownership, greater equality, the scope for earning as a family—all these allow the peasantry to satisfy their social aspirations. But these considerations would be of little importance, if labour on the peasant farm did not offer at least as good an income as labour on large farms, as a general rule.

Of course, if we say that, comparing their lot in similar economic conditions, the peasant farmer is better off than the farm labourer, it does not follow that the peasant farm can offer an adequate standard of living in an over-populated agrarian economy. The economic level of the farm population is dependent on the economic level of the country as a whole, that is, on the productivity of labour in general, and this is determined by the supply of capital and land in relation to the supply of labour. If general economic conditions, in the sense of capital and land shortage, keep output low, the peasant farm will not be able to raise it.

In the historical development of the system of peasant proprietorship the economic and political influences are closely interwoven, and to see their significance we must examine the origin of peasant society in some detail. But at the outset it must be emphasized that the peasant system is not, as it is so often thought to be, a political asset and an economic liability. In general, in European conditions, there is good reason to think that peasant farming is efficient in the sense that the productivity of labour is as high as on large farms, and that peasant farming as such offers no hindrance to technical progress.[1]

2. THE ORIGIN OF PEASANT SOCIETY

Against this view it might be argued that the coming of technical changes in British agriculture swept away the peasantry. In England the Agricultural Revolution—in the sense of the introduction of live-stock farming and better methods of cultivation—was accompanied by far-reaching changes in the farming system; inclosure means a transition to large capitalistic farms, employing labour, and the disappearance of numbers of small owners or small tenants. If peasant farms have survived in

[1] For the facts on which this view is based, see Chapter V and Chapter VIII.

Europe, it may naturally be concluded that it can only be because the peasantry has resisted technical progress and not adapted farming to new methods. In many English minds the idea lingers that the peasants of Europe are living in the same economic conditions, and using the same technical methods, as the eighteenth-century English peasant under the open-field system.

Yet a very little study of the European peasant system will show how far from reality such a conception is. For Western Europe the history of the past century has been one of steady and continuous technical progress in farming; corn yields have risen, live stock increased in numbers and improved in quality; the art of making pastures has made great progress. Because the conditions of Western Europe do not favour extensive corn production there has been little large-scale mechanization; but for the kind of farming practised machinery is not necessary, and in fact, of course, at the time of the inclosures machinery had very little importance. The earliest machine of any importance was the threshing engine, discovered in 1784, and even this did not come into general use in big farms until the twenties and thirties, when inclosure was all but complete.[1] The Agricultural Revolution was simply the use of root crops and clover —unlike so many technical improvements, it really merits the name of revolution, because it at one blow doubled the productivity of land and provided food for live-stock fattening. But this change has occurred universally in Western Europe, within a system of small ownership. To understand the scope of these changes we must look at the old field system.

This system was ancient and universal over Northern and Central Europe, from England to the Polish plains. There are many futile disputes about its origin; many German historians claim that it is Germanic, and there has been deep feeling about this in the learned world.[2] In fact it was a form of production well adjusted to the technical conditions of the Middle Ages, and it is simply necessary to look at each of its features from the

[1] Cf. Ernle, *English Farming Past and Present*. In 1837 'little or no machinery was employed in any operation of tillage—hand labour alone gathered the crops'.

[2] Fustel de Coulanges told the English historian Seebohm that it never had existed in France for this reason.

standpoint of the practical farmer to see why it had to exist as it did.

First, the strip layout. The land of the village had to be used mainly to grow bread crops for the consumption of all the families in the village. Each family had to have enough land to feed itself, and as in a primitive state the quality of land varies much more than when it can be improved by drainage and manuring, each family had to share in the good land and the bad. As more land was taken into cultivation it was divided up among all owners.

Second, the compulsory rotation. Almost all the cultivated land was under corn crops, except for a few meadows near the stream and the houses. Continuous cropping under corn exhausted the soil, and to avoid this it had to be left fallow every third year. Of course this was an immense waste; one-third of the land produced nothing; but with no alternative crops and very little manure it could not be avoided. The rotation followed was the so-called three-field—winter corn (rye or wheat), spring corn (wheat or barley), and fallow. This course had to be enforced on all owners, otherwise the crops of one would have spread into the fallows of the others. (This system can be seen in some very remote villages of Eastern Europe: the land divided into three areas, which appear like enormous fields of a big estate under the same crop, but in reality are composed of the strips of two or three hundred owners.) It was also necessary that all the crops should be the same in each area, because after harvest the cattle of the village grazed in herds on the fields and had to be let in on the same date. Thus the feature which later became an obstacle to progress was inevitable in medieval conditions; it was no hardship to be compelled to grow crops in a certain rotation when no others could be grown.

There was a more or less permanent shortage of food for 'the beasts', because no green crops or roots could be raised. The amount of live stock which each man could keep on the common grazing land and on the stubble fields had to be limited according to the amount of his arable land. In these conditions live stock had to be kept mainly for cultivation; fattening in the modern sense was a luxury. The rolls of the English manors record a constant struggle between the farmers to overstock the common by putting on more beasts than their 'stint'.

When root crops and clover were introduced the old system immediately lost the reason for its existence. The productivity of the land could be raised by sowing clover on the fallow; it increased the yields the following year, and provided winter food for the beasts. Not only that, but bad land could be brought into cultivation. The basis of agriculture was changed by the scientific rotation; live-stock fattening became as important as bread crops.

As soon as this discovery was made, two at least of the features of the old system had to disappear: the field rotation and the common grazing. The other feature, the strips layout of holdings, could remain, unless there was conversion to land for grazing.

In some parts of Europe where grazing is important the system as a whole has disappeared, and compact peasant farms are universal (Northern Germany, Denmark).

In Central Europe, however, the open-field layout remains: in South Germany, Switzerland, Bohemia, the landscape still looks like the old maps, strips of land under different crops side by side. But the old system in its essentials has disappeared; the commons have been taken into cultivation, and the compulsory rotation lapsed long ago.[1] The business of farming is intensive cultivation of the soil to produce hay, clover, and roots for fodder, as well as bread crops for sale. All that remains is a trace of the old economic structure, the field layout. (It goes without saying that this survival is irrational and wasteful: even in Canton Aargau, urbanized and advanced, it is not uncommon to find a holding of 7 hectares in 40 or 50 pieces.)

Thus in Europe the transition to modern methods of farming occurred without a change in the distribution of property, or in the scale of farming. Where big properties were extended (that is, in Prussia and in Hungary) at the same time, this was a result of the legal procedure of emancipation, and not a result

---

[1] Compulsory rotation with a six-year course *does* still exist in Württemberg. The complete system, with three-year course and bare fallow, exactly as in the Middle Ages, still exists in remote parts of Slovakia and Transylvania. See Chapter II.

THE FIELD SYSTEM
Jugoslavia. *Lika in the Karst region*
Czechoslovakia. *East Slovakia, typical 'American' village*

of technical changes. There was no general extension of large farms owing to the technical revolution as there was in England.

In England the extension of large farms was such a striking phenomenon that historians assume too readily that the end of the open fields necessarily meant the end of small farms also, as in reality it did not.

It was inevitable that the agricultural revolution should be introduced much more rapidly in England, because it originated in the experiments of English landlords on their estates: and it was their great service to economic progress that by investing capital on a large scale in drainage and land reclamation they brought new land under the plough very quickly and increased the food-supply to keep pace with the growth of population. Unlike the aristocracy in Europe, the landlords were commercially minded; they had incomes derived from investment in trading companies and were ruined at intervals by financial crises and bought up by financiers as they have been ever since. The growth of population made an expansion of wheat production urgently necessary and offered them the opportunity of making great profits by developing their estates.

But it was not inevitable that in the process of transforming the system of cultivation the small owners and tenants should be eliminated. The new technical processes had to be introduced by large farms with capitalistic resources, but once introduced there was no reason why small men should not use them. It is absurd to suppose that a small man could not grow clover on his arable land or cultivate root crops. If the revolution had meant machinery which could only operate on a big area, then the argument that only the big farm could succeed would no doubt hold good, but as we have said, at that time machines were not in use.[1]

The spread of large farms was in a large measure an attempt by the lords to extend their *properties*, and not the size of farming

---

[1] If Arthur Young's proposals for 50-acre holdings owned by the parish (in fact the small-holdings of the modern type) had been incorporated in the Inclosure Act of 1801, as they nearly were, there was no reason why the small farm should not have been established on a larger scale. Small-holdings legislation then was not a means of settling more people on the land, for the agricultural population increased, and continued to increase for half a century after, so long as corn prices remained high.

units. The new technique needed capital investment and improvement on the large farms, not an extension of ownership.

If the method of inclosure had been designed to meet the small man, or if he had had some political representation, the process could not have occurred. The small farms would have continued to play a larger part in the nineteenth century if the ruling class had not been landowners; if, that is, the whole political history of the seventeenth and eighteenth centuries had taken a different course, there was no reason why the transition to individualistic farming could not have occurred, without the violent social change involved in the extension of big farms.

This argument suggests that we cannot expect any development of capitalistic farming to occur in Europe, as it did in England. Under normal circumstances the prospects of profits in farming are too low, and land values too high, to make large-scale investment profitable. Unless there is an unusual combination of social and economic factors, a powerful landed oligarchy with commercial motives, and an urgent need for increased food output, the English development is not likely to occur. Except in East Prussia, the feudal landlord has never performed the function of entrepreneur: he may own a model farm, but the function of introducing new methods, mobilizing capital, and investing in industry lies outside the sphere of the aristocracy. Technical progress in farming had to be carried through by the peasantry, mainly through co-operative action.

Looking at the high degree of efficiency attained by peasant farms in such countries as Switzerland and Denmark, it can hardly be doubted that the liquidation of the peasantry in England was the result of political influence and not of technical necessity. Where political conditions were similar to the English, as in Hungary, the big estates survived the end of feudalism: where the peasantry or the monarchy could assert themselves, peasant proprietorship became established.

A short survey of European systems of land tenure will show that this is true. A broad division exists between the countries of small owner farms and the countries of big estates and landless labourers. In the first group come both the most advanced and the most backward—France, Switzerland, Holland and Belgium, Denmark, Western and Southern Germany, Czechoslovakia (in the main a country of medium-sized farms), and the purely peasant states of Jugoslavia, Rumania, Bulgaria, and Greece. In the second group come the big grain producers, Northern and Eastern Germany, Poland and Hungary. In these countries, of course, peasant farms also exist: the big estates cover about 40–50 per cent. of the total area. (In Poland conditions vary because after the eighteenth-century partition the three divisions developed on different lines.)

This contrast in distribution of property is mainly the result of political factors. The way in which the land is now owned was decided centuries ago, when the old agricultural structure began to break up. Since tenant farming is uncommon, both in peasant farms and in the big estates, the way the land is owned also determines the way the land is farmed. It is important to understand this point, for it might be concluded that economic and natural conditions determine the scale of farm operations, and it is certainly true that they do influence the size of the peasant farm within a certain range. But soil and technique are not responsible for the main line of division between the latifundia and the peasant farm. If larger farms really indicate a higher degree of efficiency, one would expect to find them in the countries which are economically most advanced, and where agricultural technique stands at the highest level. But in fact small family farms prevail in the most advanced countries as well as in the most backward, and large farms prevail when industry barely exists: they are feudal survivals, not modern capitalistic producers.

Therefore the reason for the contrast must be sought in political conditions. In the long and complicated process of dissolution of the old structure the eighteenth century is the decisive period, because it saw—in most of Europe—a great political change, the emancipation from serfdom, and a great economic change, the end of the open-field system. These two institutions dominated the rural world for centuries, from France to the Russian plain, giving economic and social life the same form over most of Europe; and as they declined, new ideas of government and new states arose, transforming the remains of the system in different directions, in some countries strengthening the peasant class, in others weakening it.

To understand why the dissolution of the legal framework of feudal society could stimulate development in two quite opposite directions, peasant farm or big estate, it is necessary to understand that feudalism was a system in which modern ideas of ownership did not apply. If introduced, they falsify the picture. The difficulty in understanding the system arises because the lord, in spite of his power over the serfs, did not own the village land or the forest in the modern sense of the term: he had rights as the serfs also had, but as there was no buying and selling of land there was no ownership. This point is very important, because when the system was transformed, according to modern ideas, into absolute ownership, one of two courses could be taken. The peasants, if strong enough, could refuse to go on giving labour service and rent, and claim that they owned the land. The lord, if strong enough, could claim that he owned the land and their services and would only release them from rent and services if they would surrender part of the land to him. As to the common, it belonged to neither. Of course the fact is, once the basis of military service was gone, that neither course was any more right than the other.

In the countries where the peasants are now a notably strong and vigorous stock they won their freedom very early. In South Germany, Tyrol, and Switzerland, in West Friesland and Holstein Dithmarschen, they threw out the overlords in peasant wars in the thirteenth and fourteenth centuries and emancipated themselves from serfdom centuries before the rest of Europe. In these countries the landed gentry have never been able to assert themselves again.[1] Why it happened in these districts precisely is difficult to say, but the most likely reason is that they were near the towns and trade routes which weakened the lord's power: early industrialization promoted the growth of a money economy.

In Western Europe, that is, France and England, emancipation also came early. The development in France and England followed roughly similar lines up to the sixteenth century. There it diverged, the English peasants getting freer and more prosperous, the French crushed beneath the feudal reaction. In France the lords had enormous judicial power, but little in-

[1] Cf. Laur, *Wirtschaftslehre des Landbaues*, p. 17.

fluence politically. They could impose on the peasants crushing
burdens of taxation and make their life unbearable by exercise
of privilege, but they could not dispossess the peasants (who
regarded themselves by this time as owners) by means of legislation. In England by contrast the lords had at this time little
judicial power, but in the eighteenth century the collapse of
the monarchy made them all-powerful politically. In consequence the English peasant was not subjected to heavy taxation
or oppressed by arbitrary decisions, but he had no remedy
against legislative action by the lord to divide up the commons.
Possibly if the French Revolution had not occurred the lords
might have forced the peasants so far into debt as to make them
give up their land. But before this could happen the revolution
broke out. It did not legally abolish big properties, but by
bringing estates into the market it gave the peasants the chance
to buy and strengthened the small proprietors. It is the revolution which gave the peasantry of France its strength.

The wave of the revolution spread over Europe and caused
the final emancipation of the serfs in monarchist Prussia and the
empires of Russia and Austria. But in none of these countries
did emancipation create a strong peasantry; the aristocracy
remained in power until our own time. In Prussia the emancipation happened in a peculiar way, exactly the contrary of that
in Western Europe, as a result of legislation and not of the
peasants' own rising. To gain their freedom the peasants had
to buy it with their land, surrendering one-third or a half of
their holding to the lord. In this way under the 'colonial law'
of the east, where big farms always predominated, the property
of the lord was enlarged and the smaller owners were forced
to become labourers. Unlike the aristocracy in France and
Austria, the Prussian landlords became commercial farmers,
managing their own estates on the most modern lines, erecting
factories for sugar and potatoes, living only for their farm. (Why
the name Junker should connote a dangerous and sinister and
brutal group of magnates is a mystery: nowhere is feudalism
less repugnant than in East Prussia, since the competence and
expert knowledge of the landowner makes him indispensable
to his estate.) In modern Germany the legislation which
expropriated the peasant is regarded as a crime and the

pre-war and post-war land settlement movement was in part
an attempt to make restitution.

In Austria and Hungary the situation was very different.
Emancipation came late, in 1848. In Austria the peasants'
position was not weakened, though the latifundia covered
a big area. In the Slavonic provinces national divisions
strengthened the social division: the estate owner and his
officials were German, his labourers and peasants Czechs,
Ruthenes, Slovenes, or Poles. But in spite of the social gulf and
the unhealthy political division it created, the peasants in Austria
were not oppressed, at least not in Bohemia, where a strong and
intelligent peasantry survived from the time of the defeat of the
Czechs in the seventeenth century, and kept language and
customs and traditions alive under foreign domination.

In Hungary, on the other hand, peasants lost ground in the
nineteenth century. At the time of the emancipation itself the
wave of liberalism prevented any injury to the peasants as a
class. But after the emancipation, in the second half of the
nineteenth century, the process known as *commassation* began
(i.e. the concentration of strips similar to inclosure), and in
this process, of course, the lords had opportunities for doing the
peasants down, by giving bad land in exchange for good; and
in this way the peasants have been reduced to 'dwarf holders'
of a few acres. 'Commassation was robbery,' says the Slovak
to-day. 'Our land reform only returned what was taken away.'
As in Austria, the big estates were owned by a race foreign to
the peasantry in the greater part of the country. But the social
and economic gulf was far deeper between Magyar nobles and
the Slovak, Rumanian, Croat, and Ruthene peasants than between Austrian and Czech, because the Hungarian Constitution
excluded the peasantry, whether Magyar or Slav, from political
rights. In the Old Monarchy the land question and the national
question were one.

Thus where a landless proletariat exists to-day it has originated in the fact that the big landowners possessed political
power at the critical period in agrarian history. Hence in the
progressive west the remains of feudalism have disappeared. To
illustrate the importance of this political factor many examples
might be given of the survival of peasant farms in regions of

large-scale farming, for instance, the bishopric Ermland in East Prussia. Here the land belonged to the Church, and its serfs were freed unconditionally; and it is still a land of medium-sized peasant farms, in the middle of a country of big estates.

As for the changes which have occurred since the War, weakening the big estates in the Succession States and creating peasant proprietors, the historical approach should show that it is wrong to regard these mainly as a reactionary movement against Communism; they are more obviously the completion of a much earlier revolution, and represent the end of feudalism rather than a new social change.

For these reasons, therefore, the evolution of peasant ownership in Europe should be regarded as a sign of positive political achievement, not as a survival of an outworn mode of life. But it does not follow, as we have said, that the independent status of the farm worker, valuable though it is, will guarantee a good standard of living: to determine the conditions in which peasant farming can give an adequate standard of living we must turn to the economic factors which influence the farm community.

3. DIFFERENCES IN STANDARDS OF LIVING IN EUROPE

We have seen that it is the difference in political development which accounts for the difference in social standing of the farm population. It is the political forces which determine the agrarian structure in its broad lines, the prevalence of peasant proprietorship, or large estates and proletariat. But it is only the *social* status which is so determined; the size of the peasant farm, the amount of land per head, and the amount of capital per farm—all these are determined by the general economic development of each region. The rate at which population has increased, and the progress of industrialization, are the main determinants of the economic level of the farm population, and these factors, of course, differ from one region to another: in the East of Europe, farm population has increased fast and industrialization has made little progress; in the West, trade has expanded, industry has advanced rapidly, and the rural population grown slowly.

This distinction between political and economic influences is extremely important. Whether the people on the land are family farmers or labourers working for an employer is mainly a question of political development; whether they are rich or poor is a question of the economic level of the community.

There is no necessary connexion between the two. It is possible to find in Europe communities of well-to-do peasants, somewhat better off than the English farm labourer; it is equally possible to find peasants in a state of destitution, as in Poland. Similarly, it is possible to find relatively well-paid labourers on the German estates and destitute labourers on the latifundia of Hungary.

It is important to emphasize the distinction between farming in family units and farming with intensive application of labour, because the two are so frequently confused in discussion of peasant farming.[1] A country with most of its land farmed in family units need not necessarily keep a dense population on the land, or a large proportion of its labour in agriculture. Nor need family farming be done on a small scale, with labour intensive methods. Indeed, in social structure there is no essential difference between typical farming 'sections' of the United States (and the British Dominions) and the peasant regions of Europe, though in Europe the density of farm population is five to ten times as high and the average size of farm tiny compared to the American farming unit.

What, then, are the factors which determine the economic welfare of the farm population? It is impossible to distinguish those factors which determine the standard of living of the farm community from the factors which influence the standard of

[1] The distinction is a very obvious one, but must be emphasized because the two things are frequently confused in the discussion of peasant farming. Cf. Ashby, 'The Family Farm,' in *Proceedings of the International Conference of Agricultural Economists*, 1934, where family farming is very clearly distinguished from small-scale intensive farming. In the small-holdings controversy, arguments for an extension of family farming are always mixed up with arguments for more men on the land. Perhaps the English small-holdings legislation is responsible for this confusion, since the legal maximum for a small-holding is 50 acres, and to put families on farms of this size would certainly mean to raise the density of the farm population above the average for Great Britain. The maximum, it is now agreed, should be much higher.

THE TWO EXTREMES
Commercial dairy farm, Canton Aargau
Subsistence farming, Transylvania

living of the country as a whole, and of these factors, of course, the supply of capital is most important. There is a broad general contrast between the conditions of the farm population in Western Europe, where the standard of living is reasonably good because farmers work with adequate capital equipment, and that of the East, where the peasantry is extremely poor.

This difference can be indicated by saying that, roughly speaking, the farms of Western Europe are twice as large, carry twice as much capital to the acre, produce twice as much corn to the acre, and employ only half as many people to the acre as the farms of Eastern Europe.

To bring out the contrast in the productivity of labour in agriculture, we can compare the corn output per head of farm population, as shown on the map on page 83. Corn output is only a rough guide to the extent of the difference in productivity between regions, because in the more advanced countries meat and milk production is more important than corn. But it serves to show the contrast in the supplies of the factors of production in the different regions: when output is high, capital and land are plentiful in relation to the supply of labour.

Another guide to the efficiency of the farming system (in the sense of labour productivity) is the proportion of the total population engaged in producing food. If a country itself produces the bulk of its food supplies, a low proportion of labour in agriculture shows that it can satisfy the demand for food with relatively less labour (and relatively more capital and land) than a country with a high proportion on the land. Thus, for instance, Germany has 29 per cent. of its labour in agriculture and imports only 5 per cent. of its food: each farm family must therefore supply about three families, including itself; in Poland, with 70 per cent. of its labour on the land, and exporting about 10 per cent. of its output, each family farm can only supply one and a half families, including itself. (Actually, of course, the difference in productivity is greater even than this comparison suggests, since in Western Europe both farm and town consumers eat more food.)

The following table shows the proportion of labour engaged in agriculture; with the exception of Great Britain, which imports about two-thirds of its food, and Denmark, which exports a large proportion, most European countries are largely self-supporting, and the proportion of labour on the land therefore indicates roughly their economic level.

Proportion of Population in Agriculture

Country	Census year	Percentage of working population in agriculture
United Kingdom . . .	1931	5·7
Switzerland	1930	20·1
Netherlands	1930	20·6
Germany	1933	28·9
Austria	1934	26·0
Denmark	1930	30·3
Norway	1930	31·0
Czechoslovakia . . .	1930	34·2
France	1931	34·5
Hungary	1930	50·8
Poland	1921	72·3
Bulgaria	1926	80·0
U.S.S.R.	1926	83·2

If we attempt to make a picture of Europe as a whole, combining both political and economic factors, we can distinguish three kinds of farm organization.

(1) First, the highly intensive farming of Western Europe, where live-stock production is the basis of the farming system, either specialized dairy production, as in Denmark or Switzerland, or meat production (usually of rather low quality), as in Germany and France. The arable is highly cultivated for corn and live-stock feeding-stuffs, with intensive application of both labour and capital. The density of the farm population is relatively low, because for the last two generations most of the increase of agricultural population has moved into the towns.

This system of cultivation is carried on in the main by family farms, of medium size, from 12 to 50 acres; in some regions of France and Germany much larger peasant farms are general. Within this region there are, of course, rather large differences in technical standards and economic levels. Denmark, Switzerland, and Holland, with their highly intensive and well-organized production, stand out as countries with well-to-do peasants mainly because they supply large urban markets with high standards of living, Great Britain, and in Switzerland the home market. In Germany and France farming is less intensive, and though farms are somewhat larger, the standard of living of the peasantry is lower.

The system of farming in Central Europe resembles this, in that live-stock farming is the basis of production, and farms are fairly large. In Bohemia and Moravia the farming system is as intensive as that of Germany, though less intensive than that of Denmark and Switzerland. As in Germany, the peasant village is a graded society, composed of large peasant farmers, employing some hired labour, the family farmer on about 20 acres, and the cottager, who is either a part-time producer or a specialist, on less than 5 acres. Before the War big estates took up a big share of the farm land, but now their share has been reduced. Though in general peasant life keeps a certain traditional form, yet the technical level is high and the standard of living good.

(2) As a contrast with this, the second type of farm organization is extensive cultivation, carried on by small peasant farms. Small-holdings under 12 acres predominate in large regions of Eastern Europe. Galicia is the extreme example of rural poverty, high farm density, and splitting up of holdings. Half the land is farmed by farms under 5 hectares, and a very large proportion of these are dwarf farms under 2 hectares (5 acres), not large enough to support a family, though they are the only source of income. A few big estates and a large number of manor farms take up 30 per cent. of the area. Politically the peasantry are emancipated, but the bulk of the population is on the verge of starvation.

In Rumania and Bulgaria small farms also predominate, but yields are higher than in Galicia, and farm densities somewhat lower, so that though technique is far inferior to the Polish, the condition of the peasants is somewhat better.

(3) The third type of farm organization, extensive farming with estate farms and land proletariat, is found only in Hungary and Western Poland, where the large estates take more than half the farm area. Medium-sized peasants are a small class; most of the farm population owns little or no land, working as labourers paid in kind on the big estates. Methods of cultivation are good, but too extensive. In Hungary the condition of

the landless labourers is bad, even as bad as that of the peasants
in Galicia, and politically they are entirely submerged.

How did these differences arise?

In the main the difference is a result of the advance of industrialization. During the nineteenth century population in every
country of Europe increased rapidly. In every region of Western
and Central Europe the increased demand for labour from
industry almost kept pace with the growth of population, so
that in each generation part of the natural increase of population
left the land. Until the second half of the century the movement was very slow;[1] not until the eighties and nineties did it
acquire sufficient magnitude to be described as the rural exodus.
In consequence, peasant farms could be handed down intact
from generation to generation; usually one child inherited the
farm, and the other children received their shares in money—
a custom only practicable where income per head is rising.

Farther east, as in Galicia, population increased, but industry
did not expand. The land had to support a bigger population;
because capital did not accumulate, technical progress was re-
tarded and the peasants had a hard struggle to maintain output
per head. The custom of real division of the land was general,
because the farm income never was large enough to pay off
shares in money. So each generation saw the farms getting
smaller and smaller. In spite of its extreme poverty, the
peasantry struggled to save, and bought up bits of land from
the capital-consuming estate owners and gradually the estates
were swallowed up by subsistence farmers. Thus growing
poverty caused excessive splitting up of land, which in turn
made economic utilization of the soil impossible.[2]

In Hungary, however, the development was different from
that of either Bohemia or Galicia; farm population increased,
but big estates remained. In the nineteenth century industrialization began and before the War was making rapid progress.[3]
However, industry did not advance fast enough to take in the
increase of population on the land, and pressure on the peasant
holdings increased. (In the mountain frontier regions it was

[1] See Chapter III (3).
[2] For an account of this process see Chapters VII and VIII.
[3] See Chapter II.

relieved by emigration.) Yet there was no splitting-up process, as in Poland: the big estates maintained their areas. The greater part of the peasantry acquired no land and lived by casual labour on the estates.

Why was there no development of peasant farming? There are probably several reasons why the big estates remained. First, the bulk of the labourers had no land or very little: they could not save, as the Polish peasants did, because their wages were paid in kind. Secondly, the very large estates were entailed. The most important influence, however, was that the land found a better market among the rich industrialists: aristocratic families could sell the estate to a capitalist who could buy, as in England, an estate and a title to go with it. Before the War, many of the estates were owned by Jewish industrialists, the 'sugar barons', like Hatvany and Harkany, or by smaller farmers, the so-called gentry, of bourgeois origin.

Thus the existing land systems were determined by the inter-action of several forces. Where political development had been influenced by liberal ideas, and where economic development created both a demand for labour in industry and a market for the products of intensive farming, the chief type of farm which was established was the medium-sized peasant farm. This kind of peasant farm prevails in Western and Central Europe. The very small farms in these regions are either part-time holdings or specialized producers: the owner of a small-holding can earn a better income by specializing than by trying to grow his own food from his few acres.

The second type, predominantly small and dwarf holdings, existed where political conditions were favourable, but economic progress slow, as in Galicia.[1]

The third type, with big estates predominating, exists where economic progress went ahead of political emancipation, that is, only in Hungary. Industrialism imposed on a feudal structure preserved the large property and prevented the peasants from acquiring holdings. Extreme rural poverty does not in itself break up big farms, unless there is no other demand for the land.[2]

In general, therefore, it is the degree of industrialization,

[1] See Chapter VII for fuller description of the land system.
[2] In its main lines the land system of Hungary is rather like the English,

coupled with political emancipation, which determines the level of the peasantry. In an industrial country the farmer has the advantage of proximity to an urban market, which can buy meat and dairy products: farming equipment is cheaper, and credit can be obtained on easy terms. Most important, in an industrial country the peasant farm can be large, because the increase of population moves into industry.

Corresponding to the differences in economic level and political status of the peasants, there are naturally great differences in their influence as an organized force in social and political life. The Czech peasants are the State-maintaining element, hard working, grave and responsible, much given to political activity and discussion. The Agrarian party directs State policy, and political power reflects itself in the peasants' attitude to political life: they are consciously responsible for State policy in relation to agriculture and are not yet a vested interest, as in Switzerland the peasants are, or over-controlled, as they are in Germany.

In Galicia the most progressive villages are as enlightened as the Czechs, and even more collectively minded. But the peasants are all on the same level of poverty and are becoming a proletariat with revolutionary tendencies. Farther east, in the provinces of Poland formerly in Russia, where there was no political activity before the War (and little since), they are still serfs in mentality: the contrast with Galicia is more in cultural level than in economic life.

A similar contrast can be seen between the peasantry in Rumania and Bulgaria. In Rumania, where emancipation has been so recent, the peasants are simply cultivators of the soil, not farmers in the sense of managers: they resent and disapprove of technical progress. In Bulgaria (and to a lesser degree in Serbia), where they can look back on two generations of independence as owners, they are enterprising and co-operatively minded, famous as market gardeners and interested in new methods. This contrast in human character and farming methods is enough proof of the significance of the reforms.

in that great social prestige and no social responsibility attaches to the ownership of land. There is, however, nothing resembling the English tenancy system.

With this observation on the character of the peasantry we reach, of course, the essential question of the value of the peasantry as a social force. The post-war land reforms greatly strengthened the peasants everywhere, transforming large numbers of labourers into owners, even, in Rumania, creating an independent peasantry. What is the nature of the communities thus created? Does the peasant community differ essentially from an urban or industrial State?

Among English historians there has always been a tendency to regret the destruction of the peasant society, apart altogether from the injustice of the Inclosure Acts, because it seemed to hold the promise of greater social equality than exists in the modern industrial system.[1] In a peasant economy responsibility for producers' decisions is more widespread than in a capitalistic economy. Hence the peasant society is thought desirable, because it produces valuable individuals. 'A State which has lost its independent peasantry is perilously near the verge of degeneration.'[2]

In addition to this valuation of peasant society there are other reasons which in recent years have given the idea of a self-sufficient society a certain influence: the extreme difficulty of adjustment to world changes in England, and the severity of trade-cycle fluctuations, suggest the danger of too great specialization, and it is natural to think that these dangers could be avoided by a simpler form of society.[3]

In actual fact there is nothing to correspond to the ideal of the peasant society as a self-sufficient whole. It is precisely when the peasant farmers are *not* self-sufficient—when they exist in an industrial State—that they develop the socially valuable special qualities, the independence and responsibility, the mental equilibrium due to knowledge of the land. These qualities are really all the outcome of a measure of success in

[1] Cf. Tawney in *The Agrarian Problem in the Sixteenth Century*.

[2] Macartney, *The Social Revolution in Austria*, p. 198.

[3] The power of the peasant society to resist an economic crisis is very frequently emphasized in recent studies of the agricultural depression; for instance, Woytinsky in *The Social Consequences of the Economic Depression*, 1937, p. 197. 'By reversing the century-old trend of evolution, and withdrawing as far as possible from the market, agricultural smallholders were better able to survive the depression than their more wealthy neighbours.' This view, as we shall see in the next chapter, is quite without foundation.

economic life, of a limited and hard-won kind it is true, but still success: and it is only when the rate of capital accumulation in a country is fast enough to allow the standard of living to rise in each generation that the struggle to live on the land can yield a measure of success.

When the peasant economy is based on subsistence farming, it seems inevitably to reach a state of high population density, coupled with capital shortage and labour intensive methods. The danger is that in these circumstances it may fail to save enough to support its population at the same level: out of its own resources it cannot provide the means of growth.[1]

This situation has fatal social effects. A land of dwarf holdings with literally 3 acres and a cow each, like Southern Poland is a nightmare of degradation and poverty. Southern Poland is exceptional: it is a society in decay, with the fertility of the soil declining. The other regions of Eastern Europe are not in this state, but as things are at present they must eventually go the same way. Their future depends on *not* remaining self-sufficient. Either they must find outlets for farm produce, or farm labour, or develop industries.

Thus, in European conditions, where land is short, agricultural self-sufficiency means, not a choice of stability in preference to wealth, but instability and poverty together.

4. EUROPE'S FARM PROBLEM

We now have a general picture of Europe's farming population, existing on different levels of economic welfare. The peasant populations with high standards of living are those which are included in an industrial economy, or supply an industrial market. Most of these markets are now shut off from foreign supplies of food: the industrial States, which normally imported foreign wheat and meat, have now cut off food imports altogether. Food prices in industrial Europe (Germany, France, Italy, Switzerland) are roughly twice the world level. The peasants in these countries are therefore in a relatively favourable position, because they have a monopoly of their internal market.

---

[1] How far the institutions of a peasant economy are responsible for the low rate of capital accumulation is a difficult question: it is discussed in detail in Chapter III (3) and in Chapter VIII.

In spite of their protected position, there is no noticeable improvement in the peasants' standard of living in recent years, since the demand from the town population does not expand; the most that protection appears to do is to maintain the farmers' share in the national income. In spite of protection, which must serve to some extent to close the gap between industrial and agricultural earnings, the movement out of agriculture continues. In Germany, in spite of high protection, there is at present even a shortage of labour in agriculture.

Decline of Agricultural Populations

	Great Britain			Germany			France	
	Occup. in agric. Million	% of total occup.		Occup. in agric. Million	% of total occup.		Occup. in agric. Million	% of total occup.
1881	1·59	12·45	1882	7·13	42·2	1906	8·78	42·37
1891	1·49	10·28	1895	7·18	36·4	Old 1921	8·66	41·58
1907	1·40	8·63	1907	8·56	34·0	New 1921	8·95	41·20
1911	1·49	8·15	1925	9·76	30·5	1926	8·13	37·95
1921	1·32	6·81	1933	9·34	28·9	1931	7·63	34·50
1931	1·19	5·69						

As labour leaves the land, it is possible to maintain the existing farms without subdivision, and there is little sign of change in the distribution of farm sizes, except a slight tendency for the medium-sized peasant farms to increase, while the smaller farms diminish. Investment in live stock and in improved equipment continues, and the productivity of labour rises. There is, therefore, no problem of rural poverty, as in Eastern Europe.

It is in the east, in the zone between the Baltic, the Adriatic, and the Black Sea, that the real problem of European farming lies. It arises because these regions are cut off from the European industrial markets; they have a rapid rate of population growth and have never gone over to intensive farming, as Western Europe has. These regions are well suited for arable farming, but in arable farming machine technique does need a large unit of operation. As we have said, up to the present the peasant farm in Europe has been well able to make use of technical improvements in grassland farming, live-stock feeding and breeding. The agricultural revolution, in its true sense, as a system of intensive cultivation for live-stock

fattening, strengthened rather than undermined peasant farming in countries of Western Europe. But for Eastern Europe the
problem of adjustment to new technique is different. East of
the Danube in Hungary, the system of intensive feeding has
never been introduced: so the mechanized methods of corn
production introduced since the War affects the power of the
small farm to compete in the world market, in a way which
the agricultural revolution never did. The change in the world
agricultural situation since 1929 will keep the price of wheat
permanently lower and will mean a permanent decline in income
for those corn producers in Europe who are not protected by
tariffs.

Adjustment seems possible in two ways: to keep the peasant
farm structure and go over to more intensive methods, or to
continue corn-growing and go in for large-scale collective farming on the Russian model. It is not, however, the technical
problem as such which presents an obstacle, but the difficulty
of reconciling technical progress with the existence of a very
dense population on the land.

To see the real significance of the economic position of the
peasant States it is necessary to look at the economic history
of the relations of agriculture to industry in the last ten years.
The question of Eastern Europe is only one aspect of the problem of how to raise the incomes of the low standard of living
countries, given the present agricultural situation.

One of the more lasting effects of the recent depression has
been the great decline in farmers' incomes in relation to the
incomes of industrial producers. It is as a result of this that
Western Europe has gone over, apparently permanently, to a
policy of high protection. In Europe it is this policy which
stands in the way of levelling up the standards of living in the
poorer countries; and the divergence in rates of population
growth will make the difference in standards more acute in
the future.

We must, therefore, examine the root causes of the present
situation in agriculture.

To return to the argument of the first section, we have
already said that the movement out of agriculture should be

regarded as a normal long-period development in any progressive society, simply because food consumption does not expand in the same proportion as incomes per head rise. Movement away from the land is a natural adjustment to a *relatively* lower level of return, even if the real income of the farmer is rising.

But the economic position of agriculture has been subject to changes of a much more sudden and violent character than should result simply from the slow expansion of demand. Since 1930 farmers have been faced with a sudden fall in income, not merely a relatively slower rate of increase in earnings, and it is this kind of sudden change which makes for State intervention to protect and subsidize agriculture.

In recent years, and in the depression of the seventies, it was the extension of cultivation outside Europe which caused the fall in prices. The present situation in agriculture is determined mainly by changes on the side of supply, not merely by the low income elasticity of demand. In the nineteenth century the main factor behind this extension of the cultivated area was, of course, heavy investment in construction goods and international lending. In the post-war expansion it was American credit policy which was responsible for the extension of agriculture in the United States, Argentina, and Canada. Because the expansion of the cultivated area was caused by credit expansion, which could not be maintained, the beginnings of long periods of depression in agriculture have inevitably coincided with the more severe general depressions in recent times, in 1873–80 and 1929–33. Owing to the relatively low income elasticity of demand for food, and the increase in unemployment in such periods, the bigger volume of food-supplies inevitably causes food prices to fall more sharply than the price of industrial products.

In both these periods of depression the gap between earnings in industry and in agriculture has widened. In the two major depressions, in the seventies and 1930's, the real wages of industrial workers rose, owing to the fall in food prices, while agricultural workers encountered a fall in income and even a contraction of employment. After the great depression in the seventies in Great Britain, wages on the land were slowly raised, as the farm labourers left the land; and it seems probable that in the decade before the War, farmers' incomes must have improved in relation to industrial incomes; there was no unusually rapid expansion of food products overseas, and farm prices remained steady. The amplitude of the fluctuation in agricultural prices in the two periods of depression has, therefore, been due to extension of food supplies, which is not, of course, a necessary feature of the trade cycle, but seems closely connected with it, in so far as capital investment in improved communications opens up new areas of supply, and has been undertaken for that purpose.

Since the price fall in 1930, the main cause of the prolongation of agricultural depression has been the stability of farm output. The total volume of world agricultural production has remained unchanged since 1929, and in consequence the fall in prices of agricultural products has been greater than it has been in industry, where falling prices have been met by contraction of output. As the farmers' share in world output increased, the purchasing power of their output decreased, and in consequence the farmers' share of income decreased also.

The maintenance of output since the 1929 depression appears to be the result of two causes: one, the structure of farming, and the other, the deliberate policy of maintaining production, practised both by exporting and importing States. Owing to the prevalence of family farming in the exporting countries, the farmer tends to meet price falls by maintaining output and reducing his income. This relative elasticity of wage rates accounts sufficiently for the maintenance of wheat output until 1934; after that year there was some contraction in output in the United States due to drought and artificial restriction, but the total world production was maintained by the expansion of output in Europe. In 1938 world wheat production increased to 114 per cent. of the 1929 level.

The decline in the aggregate income of farmer as a group has been general, affecting all countries, but has been greater in the countries which export food. In the United States the purchasing power of farmers' income is estimated to have fallen by 30 per cent. In the food-importing countries, on the other hand, State policy has maintained farm prices by import restrictions, so that the farmers' share in income has been maintained. In

Germany the farmers' share of the national income has been increased slightly, at the expense of food consumers.[1]

Technical progress in the short period brings little gain to the farmer, owing to the difficulty of leaving the land in periods of depression. Most of the immediate gain through technical advance in agriculture must have been passed on to the consumers of food, except in so far as prices have been artificially maintained by tariffs. In industry, on the other hand, it appears that in the United States there has been throughout the post-war period a tendency for the agents of production to gain directly from increased productivity per man: according to Professor Mills,[2] this tendency is in contrast to the pre-war tendency for such gains to be shared through changes in relative prices, on the one hand with primary producers, and on the other hand with consumers in general. How far the gains of the group of industrial producers are counteracted by severe unemployment within industry it is impossible to say. Even taking unemployment into account, it seems probable that the income of the world's farm population declined more than that of the industrial population. Owing to the change in the terms of trade, the industrial countries have been able to pass on to the agricultural countries much of the loss of income resulting from the contraction of the market.[3]

To counteract the effects of the price fall, the countries of Western Europe (and the overseas producing countries also) have been driven to extreme action in the form of tariffs, quotas, or direct subsidies to maintain farmers' incomes, or rather to increase farmers' shares in the national income. In so far as they have done this, they have improved the position of their own farmers in relation to that of the industrial workers, by raising the cost of living and reducing real wages. To some extent the policy of protection must arrest the movement out of agriculture. Paradoxical as it may appear, however, farm population in the West European countries with protected markets continues to decrease, and in Eastern Europe continues to increase.

---

[1] See Woytinsky, *The Social Consequences of the World Economic Depression*, I.L.O., Studies and Reports, Series C, No. 21, Geneva, 1936.
[2] F. C. Mills, *Prices in Recession and Recovery*, 1936.
[3] Woytinsky, p. 302.

It would appear to be the fact that farmers gain by high protection mainly through higher prices, and not through bigger production. (Germany with 100 per cent. protection has only achieved a 10 per cent. increase in food output.) In Eastern Europe, however, the tariff barriers imposed by the West have caused a fall in the standard of living, thus checking capital accumulation and a movement into industry, and the worse the outlook for agriculture, the more people look for work on the land.

The result of tariff policy is therefore to increase the difference in standards of living of the farm population in the importing and exporting European countries, since it maintains, and even accentuates, the differences in farm population density.

Why do the industrial States follow this policy, since it is so obviously detrimental to the interests of the industrial workers? Generally the answer given is that these States are anxious for socio-political reasons to conserve the rural population. Yet the rural population is always a minority, and (except through large landowners) rarely acts as a pressure group. In the main the reason is the desire for self-sufficiency for political reasons.

Still it is remarkable that even in democratic countries the policy of protection meets with so little opposition. Probably the reason is that the industrial workers fear the competition of very cheap labour from the land more than they object to high food prices. In England the effect of a collapse of wages on the land is not a serious threat to the wage level of industrial workers, because the proportion of farm workers is not high enough. But in Europe the farm population is larger, and if farm protection were abandoned, the influx of labour from the land would certainly lower the money wages of the town workers. If organized labour objects to a reduction in money wages more than it objects to a rise in prices (and many economists now regard this theory as axiomatic), then tariff policy is intelligible, though short-sighted, since it necessarily stands in the way of a future rise in the standard of living.

Where rural birth-rates are very high the problem is more serious. This problem can be seen in essentials in Czechoslovakia, a country which has very big differences in rural and urban standards of living, because it bridges the Historic Provinces of Bohemia and Moravia, which have a West European capital market and a West European birth-rate, and the poor Eastern provinces of Slovakia and Ruthenia, where economic and demographic conditions resemble those of Eastern Europe (though on a small scale). The industrial workers of Bohemia and Moravia find it impossible to maintain an industrial minimum wage, owing to the continuous movement of agricultural labour into industry. Consequently, the Socialist parties have agreed to the maintenance of corn and meat prices by tariffs and by the crop monopoly.

In these conditions, which could, of course, be generalized for Europe as a whole, the policy of protecting agriculture is probably less irrational than may at first sight appear from the standpoint of labour.

Thus the measures taken to maintain farm incomes and create self-sufficient food economies raise a very grave problem of adjustment between agriculture and industry in Europe itself. The longer autarchy continues the greater will be the danger to West European standards of living from the low standards of the eastern regions. For the peasantry of Europe as a whole—and it must be remembered that nearly half the peasantry of Europe lives in the eastern regions—the policy of protecting the peasant against the fall in world prices has been disastrous. Agriculture is driven to expand in these eastern regions where labour productivity is low and is even falling.

For it must be emphasized that the movement out of agriculture does not occur, except in a progressive society. If the total resources of the community, other than labour, do not expand, that is, if the rate of capital accumulation is slower than the increase of population, then labour remains on the land as population increases: more food can only be produced by more labour. Hence the movement out of agriculture is by no means an *inevitable* development (as we shall see in Chapter III); it depends on the rate of capital accumulation. Unless the society is progressive—unless incomes rise—the rural exodus cannot occur, because the movement out of agriculture into industry is not merely a transference from one occupation to another, but a process of development from a lower level of labour productivity to a higher level. Industry in general uses more capital per man than agriculture does, and the transition cannot occur unless capital is available. Therefore the longer the present situation continues, the more the standard of living in the East is likely to fall.

In Europe, therefore, a situation is arising in which it is clear that continued agricultural protection will have disastrous effects on future economic development. In any case, tariffs tend to foster production in regions of high costs, and the difference in rates of population growth will tend to make the cost divergences even greater. If the peasants were able to leave the land easily in the poorer countries, and move into industry, the effects would not be so serious; but as it is, owing to the difference in rates of population growth and the rates of capital accumulation, no adjustment can be made. The inevitable result of this disparity in incomes is that consumption of food in the low standard countries cannot expand. In consequence the world market for food products must be subject to violent fluctuations. A price fall in the world market will inevitably cause a contraction of production in the overseas countries, where output per head in agriculture is high, simply because in these countries the rate of capital accumulation is higher and the transition to industry easier. But these countries, with their big supplies of land and capital, will yet remain potentially important sources of food-supply, and will respond to any slight rise in general prices by a large expansion of output, as in fact they are doing in 1938. Their markets are, however, not likely to expand: overseas farmers supply industrial countries where the standard of food consumption is already high, and where, in future, the total volume of food consumption must decline as a result of the decline in population. In consequence, regions with very elastic conditions of supply will be connected with regions of inelastic or even contracting demand conditions. Further, of course, the populations of the exporting countries themselves will also decline, and there can be no expansion of internal food consumption.

But in Eastern Europe, on the other hand, the farm population will continue to increase, in spite of falling food prices, in conditions which preclude any improvement in farm technique,

and consumption of food per head will fall. (Its rate of population increase is now something like three times as fast as that
of Western Europe.)

5. THE POLITICAL BACKGROUND

We have considered the main reasons why the small peasant
farm predominates in Europe as a whole, and why great differences in standards of living exist within Europe itself; and
the difficulty of adjustment which tariff policy creates. The
joint effect of all these influences is to create an uncertain
political situation in Eastern Europe: the agrarian States are
poor, in relation to the west, pressure of population threatens
their standard of living, and they have been so far unable to
achieve any concentration among themselves. Can these countries find remedies for over-population on their own power,
without being absorbed into other economic units?

Since the War the main question for Europe has been the
political and economic settlement of these eastern regions,
where racial conflicts are still so acute and where economic
nationalism has done so much harm. Now, looking back at the
history of the post-war period, it seems apparent that the
division of Eastern Europe into national States is not likely to
secure either the political freedom or the economic progress
of these regions. For the peasantry of Eastern Europe the post-
war settlement meant an advance in that it gave them the land,
and experience in political life which cannot be obliterated,
even if for the time the peasants' political power is weakened.
But the growth of population presents an acute problem in the
present state of Europe: for them lower tariffs, the possibility
of migration, capital investment, are an urgent necessity.

On the one hand, they see the main hope for relief in closer
economic connexions with Germany. On the other, they see
the Russian experiment in large-scale farming as a means of
tackling the problem of over-population. How far can these
two forces, German expansion and the Russian collectivization,
be regarded as a solution for their problem?

Either would, of course, mean a change in their political
systems, and in their farm organization also. For these countries
the real problem is to find a means of reconciling economic

progress with some degree of political freedom. The immediate post-war period was a time in which it seemed as if the peasantry of Eastern Europe could at last look forward to a period of progress in political life. It must be remembered that the poverty of the peasantry of Eastern Europe is largely explained by the long period of Turkish domination and warfare. The Czech and Polish peasants alone can look back on a long history: many Bohemian peasant farms can trace their history back for two or three centuries. Farther to the east the peasants of Slovakia, Serbia, Hungary, and Rumania cannot look back on this long record of ownership, for until very recent times they cultivated the land as serfs. The burden of recultivating land, rebuilding towns, after the tide of invasion has retreated, has prevented them from sharing in the long slow development of Europe's economic life.

How far, then, is it possible to maintain the political independence of these regions? To answer this question it is necessary to look at the part which the peasantry now plays in political life. The peasant parties, whose influence in political affairs seemed so deeply rooted in the period after the War, have now lost hold, and in most of these countries are in opposition to the governments, though their organization still survives, in Poland at least, under very severe repression. Reviewing their economic and political activity, one begins to doubt whether the peasant parties—which means in reality the democratic forces—are able to deal with the land question. So long as the question meant the redistribution of the land, or the peasant against the landowner, the peasant parties played a constructive part; now that the land question means land shortage as such, it seems to have passed out of their control.

In Western Europe the part played by the peasantry in politics is relatively small. The influence of the peasantry is usually much over-estimated: it has been usual to regard the peasants as a stabilizing element, a support of the State in a conservative sense. But, in fact, in advanced industrial communities the peasants only represent a small part of the population: and what is more important, they account only for a small share of the national income (10 to 15 per cent. in France and Germany). In important decisions the farm population counts for very little as against great concentrations of industrial and financial interests.

But surely, it may be said, the extremes of agrarian protectionism, which have been introduced in recent years in France, Germany, and Italy, seem to disprove this view: surely the peasant population must dictate this line of policy? Certainly the peasant population represents voting power which no government in Western Europe can ignore, so that governments with no political sympathy for the peasants must yet maintain tariffs on food. But in general the farm population makes their influence felt through their membership of right and left wing parties alike.[1] It is in the interests of self-sufficiency that the peasantry is fostered, not because they themselves are an important pressure group.

In Eastern Europe, however, the situation is different: the peasants have played an active part in political life, both revolutionary and constructive. The peasants account for 60 to 80 per cent. of the total population, 50 to 60 per cent. of the national income, in these countries. They are, in fact, the working population, and in the immediate post-war period their aims were those of a labour movement: they aimed at democratizing the political system and redistributing the land.

To a large extent these ideals derived from their own conception of government. There it was not a question of sentimental peasant philosophies propagated by intellectuals; the post-war leaders, Švehla, Witos, Stambulisky, Radić, were genuinely peasants, and each followed his own line: Švehla as a constitutional and compromising statesman, Witos as a parliamentarian, Stambulisky the revolutionary, and Radić the mystically inspired leader; their only common ground was a great faith in the power of the peasantry to build up the new States and to maintain constitutional government. But the democracy of the new States, as Radić and Stambulisky conceived it, was to be founded on a society of small peasants, and they expected that it would take stronger root because the distribution of income was more equal than in the Western democracies.

[1] This is true of France and before 1933 was also true of Germany: at the election of 1932 the majority of the peasants in the south were still Social-Democrats. See Neil Hunter, *Peasantry and Crisis in France*, 1938.

These hopes have, of course, in very large measure been disappointed. In Czechoslovakia the Agrarian party has directed policy continuously since the republic was founded; and by uniting the Czech and Slovak and German parties on a common basis, and by its long co-operation with the Socialists, the Agrarian party can claim to have played a great part in maintaining constitutional government. Elsewhere the peasant parties no longer hold the reins: the democratic constitutions have been overthrown by reactionary governments, either semi- or complete dictatorships. How was it possible that ideals apparently so deeply rooted should turn out to be so weak?

The spread of fascism is not an explanation, for these dictatorships are not based on fascism as a doctrine: they are not inspired by any political aim, but base their power on the army and one or two groups. To describe them as fascist overestimates their strength and significance. Nor is the economic crisis an explanation: in Poland and Jugoslavia dictatorships came to power, while economic conditions were relatively good, in 1926 and 1929.

Probably the explanation is that once the land reform was carried through the peasants had no fighting programme. Their leaders represented the small peasants against the aristocracy, and once they had got the land the parties tended to become conservative, and, except in Czechoslovakia, to split up into factions, which made it easy, and even perhaps necessary, for the military forces to seize the reins.

In Poland the cause of the peasants' loss of power is more difficult to understand. Poland is a peasant country, but the peasants have not a vestige of influence on the government. The Piast party (called after an ancient Polish dynasty to emphasize its national and traditional character) was built on far more permanent foundations than the parties in the Balkans, yet it has yielded to the dictatorship, and its leader, Witos, who was Prime Minister with some intervals from 1920 to 1926, and is revered throughout the country as the peasant leader, is in exile. Probably the class division lay at the root of the failure of democratic peasant government. To Witos, an experienced and astute politician, it was clear that a very radical land reform might rouse political conflicts which might disrupt the unity of the

new State; but if his conception of the peasantry as the foundation of the restored Poland was to be fulfilled, the land reform
was essential. For this reason he planned the land reform on
evolutionary lines, transferring fixed amounts of land each year;
and he did not aim at abolishing the small gentry farmers, or
even the large landowners, entirely. This caution may explain
why his party failed to maintain constitutional government.[1]
Had the peasants seized the land at the start, the reactionary
forces behind Pilsudski could never have taken control. As it
was the *coup d'état* occurred when the land reform was half
finished.

Thus it appears to have been the class division—nowhere
more emphatic than in Poland—which proved fatal to democracy in the new State, for the dictatorship, of course, supports
itself on the big landowners, or rather on the few survivors like
the Radziwill and Potocki families, who still own great areas.
The land reform was gradually dropped, and only very recently,
under the influence of growing unrest and distress, has it been
resumed.[2] But the continuance of land reform will not satisfy
the peasants, who demand restoration of democracy and the
return of Witos. In Galicia the peasant organization has shown
itself unbreakable under severe repression, which reached its
climax in the peasant strike of 1937.

Yet elsewhere, when there was no class division, the difficulty
of maintaining democracy has been equally great.

In Jugoslavia the real cause of failure of constitutional government has been the national division between Serbs and Croats.
The Croatian peasants are united against the Serbs.[3] Yet here,

[1] Cf. W. Grabski, *Idea Polski*, Warsaw, 1936.
[2] It is characteristic of the present confusion in Polish political life that
the man responsible for resuming the work of Witos should be his opponent,
Poniatowski, an aristocrat descended from the last King of Poland, who
broke away from the Piast and leads a small radical group which favours
complete expropriation of the landlords without compensation—a much
more radical policy than that of Witos. The rest of the government are
opposed to his policy. Among the gentry farmers there are many who
detest the dictatorship and see in it the negation of the Polish ideal.
[3] In Jugoslavia the peasant movement has developed on entirely different
lines, according to the different races composing the country, Serb, Croat,
and Slovene. Of these the Croat movement is the most interesting, since it
inclines towards a philosophy of peasant life, the kind of doctrine which
is inspiring when expounded by a great political leader, as Radić was, but

too, the peasant parties still exist: as in Poland, the peasants are the only constructive forces.

In Rumania the cause of the loss of power is apparently a personal conflict between Maniu and the King. Before the War, in the Old Kingdom, Maniu led a strong peasant party (the Tsaranists), and in Transylvania Mihalache and Vajda led a nationalist party. These united after the War, and governed more or less continuously till 1929. Maniu's administration was the first serious attempt to purify Rumania of corruption. That he failed seems to have been due to the division of the party by the King's personal affairs: without Maniu's leadership the party is much weaker and seems unable to take office again.

In Hungary, of course, the situation is different. There the peasants have no political representation and never have had any organized political activity, as the Constitution, by enforcing the open ballot, excludes the possibility that a representative of the people with radical views can be returned to Parliament. In exceptional cases individual peasants have been returned as members, but are completely passive. The gentry farmers and the larger peasants (the middle-class yeoman type peculiar to Hungary) are mainly members of the Small Farmers party in opposition to the government. Though the party in no way represents the interests of the smaller peasants, still less of the labourers, in fact the policy of the party runs on much the same lines as the peasant parties in other States: in internal politics aiming at some measure of land reform on liberal lines, repudiating very strongly the Nazi movement, in foreign politics

---

sinks into nonsense in the hands of his mediocre successors. Radić's faith was that democracy can only be built up from below, from the peasant villages, since they are the citizens: feudalism and capitalism can never produce democratic society. His theories closely resembled the conceptions of Soviet rule in its early days, the producing unit—factory or village—sending its representatives to regional councils, and these sending representatives to the federal parliament. Its ideology has now become a sort of inverted Marxism: because all life comes from the soil, the peasants' job must be valued higher than that of other occupations, which should only exist in so far as they serve the interest of the peasant class. The party has no economic policy.

The Serb and Slovene movements have from the first been based on the co-operatives: the Slovenes have a very highly developed co-operative movement with four independent co-operative unions, the more important under the clerical party.

opposing the government policy of close alliance with Germany. Now the new Nazi groups are gaining much support in the countryside, by promising redistribution of the land. Hungary, it can hardly be doubted, stands on the verge of a severe social struggle: the only wonder is that it has been avoided so long. The aristocracy's fear of Nazism reflects the fear that foreign intervention may cause a social upheaval.

To look, then, at the general situation of the peasant parties suggests that the real strength of the State lies with them. They have dealt with political and economic problems with varying success. In two countries, Czechoslovakia and Bulgaria, the parties are well organized and have in fact taken the lead in political life and economic organization: they have introduced measures to control marketing (crop monopolies) and control banking through the co-operatives. In Rumania and Jugoslavia, on the other hand, the political parties have failed to produce an economic policy.

The social background has to some extent proved a difficulty for the new States. The co-operative organizations are always closely connected with political parties. Consequently, as soon as the dictatorships have come to power they have wrecked the co-operative system and done untold harm thereby, since in a peasant economy the co-operatives are the chief means of mobilizing capital. Thus the centralizing forces are weakened, and the peasants are thrown back into an individualist economy, which, as we shall see, is a fatal obstacle to economic progress.

Their present economic situation now seems to require a much stronger leadership in economic affairs than the peasant parties are giving. The land reform, and the political emancipation which preceded it, did create a type of society with a much higher degree of equality than existed before. In consequence there is less concentration of interests than there is in capitalistic countries, and fewer obstacles to reorganizing farming than there are, for instance, in England. But, on the other hand, there is no driving force which can take the initiative in improving the position of the poorer peasants, either by industrialization or by farm reorganization. Economic reorganization seems to demand more control of labour, more mobilization of capital, than the present social structure provides.

This kind of reorganization seems to require a control from above, which the peasant parties would resist. From the political standpoint, all the peasant organizations are opposed to closer connexion with Germany. Seen from Eastern Europe, the War represented a struggle between German and Slav imperialism, which ended in the defeat of both, and the victory of the oppressed nationalities in Austria-Hungary. Now that German expansion under the guise of Nazism has been resumed, the independent existence of the peasant States is threatened, owing to the weakness of their economic position, by the economic advantage which the German market offers. To them the conflict of ideologies has very little meaning: 'the Communist says, "We take the cows, but you may keep the milk"; and the Nazi, "We take the milk, but you may keep the cows." ' In fact, of course, they are right in this view: the Nazi theory makes much of the peasant, guaranteeing him his farm as inalienable property for ever, extolling him as the basis of the State, while the Communist theory regards him as a public enemy, obsolete and intransigent: but in practice the systems come down to much the same thing: both subject the peasant to very rigid control from above, in both prices and production are strictly regulated in accordance with a general economic plan, which will make ownership of land a new kind of serfdom.

There is, therefore, a dilemma: a society which really has a high degree of equality, and does give its producers a certain freedom, seems incapable of pursuing a dynamic policy. The present situation raises the question, not simply of whether the peasant farm can make use of new technical methods, but of whether the peasant form of society, with its genuine values, can be maintained. It is not so much a question of changing the scale of output as of providing the means of growth: and in the present world economic situation the peasant societies have found this a difficult task.

CHAPTER II

THE GERMAN SOLUTION

1. POPULATION AND PRODUCTION

IN all the agrarian countries of Eastern Europe the land question, in the sense of land shortage, is becoming acute. In Poland, Jugoslavia, Rumania, and Bulgaria, the situation is essentially the same, in that the population on the land is now too large to be employed in agriculture, even too large to be adequately fed by local production. Before the War the same problem existed, but on a much smaller scale.[1] Because the region was divided into countries with distinct economic interests and very different social structures, the identity of economic conditions was concealed; but now that the connexions of Eastern Europe with the west are almost broken, it emerges as an area with the same general conditions; its population is still growing rapidly, while the outlets for labour migration and the market for food are contracting.

In the industrial States of Central Europe, Czechoslovakia and Hungary, there is no land question in the same sense. Czechoslovakia has areas of great poverty and very dense farm population in East Slovakia and Sub-Carpathian Ruthenia, but these are small regions; in the country as a whole the rate of industrialization has been fast enough to absorb the growth of population on the land.[2] In Hungary rural destitution exists on a large scale, but it arises, not from excessive density, but from

---

[1] This problem, it should be emphasized, was not *created* by the division of the Monarchy. Certain areas were suffering from surplus labour supply in the pre-war period—these were mainly Galicia, Transylvania, Slovakia. Slovakia seems to have gained so far as its farm population is concerned: it has since increased only by 5 per cent., and the loss of employment in Hungarian estates must be outweighed by the increased physical output per head resulting from higher yields, and the high price of corn paid by the crop monopoly.

[2] This was true of the period before the German annexation of Northern Bohemia; now it is likely that the small agricultural core of the province which remains will have an acute population problem, owing to the loss of urban markets, the influx of displaced industrial workers, and the loss of capital equipment.

the distribution of property, and a radical measure of land reform would go far to remedy it.

In the agrarian countries, on the other hand, land shortage is the crucial question. The essential feature of the economic situation is the difficulty of maintaining output per head.

One cause of this difficulty is the contraction of international trade and the cessation of migration. The other cause is the tendency inherent in agricultural communities with a low real income per head to fail to accumulate capital on a sufficient scale to maintain output per head, because they hoard or invest in non-productive assets.

Our view of the possible remedies to be applied will largely depend on the relative importance of these two causes. An expansion of international trade in food products in Europe might alone be enough to remedy the situation. On the other hand, if the failure of production to keep pace with population arises from the defects of the land system, then the chief hope of recovery will be in reorganizing farming, on collectivist lines, with the object of correcting the tendency to over-invest. To take the most pessimistic view, it is possible that neither of these courses offers any hope of improvement. In Poland, for instance, it is said that there are three possible adjustments to the present situation: (1) mass migration; (2) mass industrialization with the use of foreign capital; and (3) mass starvation. This view implies that these countries cannot do anything on their own power to improve their economic situation, and that improvement can only come from without. This view we must now examine.

To estimate the extent of the decline in output per head is very difficult. In the first place it is necessary to compare the increase in population with the increase in production, and for this purpose the statistical data are defective. Figures of the farm population exist for Czechoslovakia, Hungary, and Bulgaria, not for Poland, Rumania, or Jugoslavia; and for these last three it is necessary to base an estimate on the rural population. (For Jugoslavia even this is not known, but as we have good statistical data for Bulgaria we can assume that its conditions are similar.)

However, the general direction is clear. The rate of growth of the farm population in Eastern Europe has been uniformly rapid in the post-war period: in 1931 the number on the land was everywhere much greater than it was in 1921 or 1910. In Western Europe, of course, the development has been in an opposite direction; since the end of the nineteenth century and in the post-war period farm populations have continued to decline. In Central Europe the development has been similar to that of the West. In Czechoslovakia since 1921 the number on the land has declined by 280,000 or 6 per cent.; the proportion of farm population declined from 40 per cent. in 1921 to 32 per cent. in 1931. There has been a very rapid decline in the numbers on the land in the western provinces of Bohemia and Moravia, partly compensated for by the increase in Slovakia (a 5 per cent. increase) and Ruthenia, where the rate of growth of farm population in the years 1921–31 was about the same as that of the farm population in Eastern Europe—about 18 per cent. In Hungary the farm population has increased very slightly, by 50,000 or about 1 per cent. The movement into industry has continued, though not so rapidly as before the War. The proportion of farm population in 1930 fell to 50 per cent. of the total as compared with 55 per cent. in 1920.[1] Thus though both Czechoslovakia and Hungary have regions of dense population and rural unemployment, these two countries do not suffer from agricultural over-population in general. Industrial expansion takes a proportion off the land at a rate which is comparable to that of Western Europe in the last ten years. The rate of total population increase in these countries is similar to that of Western Europe.

In the agrarian countries, on the other hand, the rate of increase of the total population is faster, and the growth of the farm population has very nearly kept pace with it. The proportionate decline of the agricultural population has been very slight: indeed it has almost kept the same proportion as in the pre-war period.[2]

[1] In both these countries there has been an increase in the *working* population on the land: the reduction in the total is due to the changing age composition of the population; an increase of 8 per cent. has occurred in Czechoslovakia, and of 14 per cent. in Hungary as compared with the pre-war period (1910).

[2] Wazaroff, 'Die Bevölkerung Bulgariens', in Molloff, *Die sozialökonomische Struktur der bulgarischen Landwirtschaft.* In Bulgaria from 1887 to

Unfortunately there are no reliable statistics going back before the War, except for Bulgaria. These show that the farm population increased from 1910 to 1935 by about 40 per cent., and from 1920 to 1935 by 24 per cent.—almost as fast as the total population. This rapid rate of increase is due to abnormally high fertility rates in the period before the War.

In Poland the farm population increased by about 15 per cent. from 1920 to 1935, and as the total population in 1920 appears to have been slightly less than in 1914 it can be supposed that roughly 15 per cent. represents the growth since the pre-war period. Although the rate of natural increase is now only two-thirds as high as it was before the War, the decline in the rate is exactly compensated for by the decline in migration: about one-third of the natural increase in population migrated in the pre-war period, and this outlet is now closed.[1] Thus the increase in farm population is largely due to the check to migration.

In Jugoslavia and Rumania it can be assumed that the rate of growth has been almost as fast.

To compare the increase in production with the increase in population it is necessary to take the pre-war figures for comparison with 1928–32 and 1933–7, as in the immediate post-war period conditions were abnormal and grain production was much below the pre-war level. Taking the level in 1909–13 as the base period, grain production has decreased by 20 per cent. in Rumania, increased by 14 per cent. in Poland, 20 per cent. in Jugoslavia, and 24 per cent. in Bulgaria. Thus in Poland and Rumania production has certainly not kept pace with population growth, nor in Bulgaria, though there the disparity is not large. The case of Jugoslavia is doubtful, because the statistics are defective.

1926 the proportion of rural population hardly changed: in 1887 it was 81 per cent. and in 1926 79·4 per cent. By 1934 it had fallen to 78·5 per cent.: about a quarter of the natural increase of the population on the land moved to the town from 1926 to 1934. Farm population in 1926 was 74 per cent. of the total as it was in 1910, and now must have fallen to 72 per cent.

In Poland the proportion of farm population to total population fell slightly, from 63·8 per cent. in 1921 to 60·6 per cent. in 1931; in Rumania (the Old Kingdom) rural population fell from 79·2 to 77·2 per cent., in the same time.

[1] See Szulc in *Ekonomista*, i, ii, 1936, 'Zagadnienie przyrostu ludnosci w Polsce'.

Growth of Farm Population in Eastern Europe

	Total Population (millions)					Farm Population (millions)				
	1910	1920	1930	1935*	1935 in % of 1920 (1910)	1910	1920	1930	1935*	1935 in % of 1920 (1910)
Czecho-slovakia .	..	13·6	14·7	15·2	112	..	5·4	5·1	4·9	92
Hungary .	7·6	8·0	8·7	9·05	113 (119)	4·2	4·4	4·5	4·5	103 (108)
Poland (1921 & 1931) .	..	27·2	31·9	33·4	123	..	17·3	19·3	20·2	115
Rumania .	..	..	18·0	18·95	..	..	..	13·0	..	..
Jugoslavia	..	12·0	13·9	14·85	124	..	..	9·8	..	..
Bulgaria .	4·3	4·8	5·7	6·15	128 (143)	3·1	3·4	4·1	4·3	123 (137)

* Estimated.

Cereal production in Eastern Europe
million quintals
(Potatoes as ⅛ of corn crops)

	1909–13		1923–7		1928–32		1933–7	
	Average	%	Average	%	Average	%	Average	%
Czecho-slovakia .	65·10	100	60·154	92·4	75·147	115·4	72·303	111·1
Hungary .	57·83	100	55·317	95·7	57·971	100·2	63·152	109·2
Poland .	158·24	100	148·594	93·9	172·772	109·2	181·101	114·4
Rumania .	129·70	100	91·785	70·8	112·719	86·9	103·544	79·8
Bulgaria (1908–12).	24·00	100	20·393	85·0	28·565	119·0	29·773	124·1
Jugoslavia (wheat and maize only)	57·00	100	48·232	84·6	58·307	102·3	68·051	119·4

To take the other branches of production into account is very difficult. Live stock per head has certainly declined, as there is only a slight increase as compared with the pre-war period.

For Bulgaria an index of agricultural production has been calculated covering all field production. This shows that the volume of production had increased in 1930-4 by 36 per cent. as compared with 1908-11, and had therefore almost kept pace with the growth of farm population. But Bulgaria's position is exceptionally good: the whole of the increase has come from the industrial crops, tobacco, and the oil plants. The country has been able to maintain its income by more intensive cultivation and by turning to industrial crops.[1] Corn output per head, however, has not been maintained and if live stock were taken into account, output per head would have fallen.

In the rest of the agrarian countries there is no sign that other lines of production have increased more than by a very small amount. We can conclude that output per head has fallen by a small amount in Poland, and by 30 per cent. in Rumania. The decline in output has not caused a proportionate decline in consumption, because a larger proportion of the crop is retained for home consumption, and a smaller proportion exported. In Rumania and Poland cereal consumption has declined slightly.

Changes in the crops grown show the effect of population growth on the standard of living. Maize output in Rumania and Hungary, and potatoes in Poland, have increased by about 20 per cent. These are more intensively cultivated crops, producing more calories to the acre, but showing a lower standard of nutrition. If live-stock production had increased in those regions, the bigger output of maize and potatoes would mean an increase in the output per man; as it does not, the crops must be grown for food; the increased output of maize is a sign of growing poverty.

Thus we can conclude that even before the general depression these countries were struggling to maintain the income per head of their farm population.

This situation implies that in the post-war period these countries did not increase their productive efficiency at all, or only very slightly. Their inability to do this is, of course, a sign of inadequate capital accumulation, since in the grain-exporting countries overseas the rate of increase in output per man owing to changing technique has been very rapid indeed. Even in

[1] Tchakaloff, *The National Income of Bulgaria 1934-35*, Publications of the Statistical Institute for Economic Research, 1937, No. 2.

Western Europe, where there has been no fundamental change like mechanization, output per man has increased very fast.

On top of these conditions came the price fall of agricultural products, beginning in 1929. The purchasing power of farmers' incomes fell, and their share of national income declined in all food-exporting countries. Even before the changes in income levels due to the world market price fall, the disparity between incomes in industry and agriculture in the agrarian countries was abnormally large. The peasants in Eastern Europe already suffered from the tariffs imposed on food exports by the Danubian food-importing countries, so that the terms of trade were turning against them before 1929. At that time the income per head of the farm population was equal to roughly half the income per head of the town dwellers. (Of course the difference in social structure must be borne in mind; the non-agricultural population is small, and a large part of its income is based on monopoly profits, representing the earnings of a small class of capitalists. Wages alone in industry and agriculture could not show such a large divergence.)

The depression meant a much greater adverse movement in the terms of trade. In 1935 exports from these countries had fallen in value about 50 per cent. as compared with 1929. Bulgaria's farm income reckoned in purchasing power of industrial goods fell about 35 per cent.

Since 1929 the disparity of incomes has rapidly increased. This effect can be shown very clearly in the case of Bulgaria. In 1926 the *rural* population represented 80 per cent. of the total population and took 60 per cent. of the total income; in 1934 it took 78 per cent. of the total population and 50 per cent. of the income. The ratio income per head of the rural and urban population changed from roughly 1 to 3 to 1 to 4. (In 1926 the average income per head of rural population was 6,908 leva, compared with 19,760 leva per head of urban population; in 1934 it was 3,307 leva compared with 16,986 per head of urban population.[1])

Thus while the amount of physical output per head was tending to fall slowly, its purchasing power fell very sharply.

This sharp fall in relative incomes is a result of the change in

[1] Tchakaloff, op. cit.

world conditions, the increased productivity of agriculture overseas, and clearly the only way in which adjustment to the change
can be made is by a reduction of the number of people engaged
in agriculture, above all in corn growing. Only if the peasants
could move into industry, or into other branches of food production for which the demand is more elastic—such as fruit,
vegetables, oil plants, and industrial crops—is there any hope
of arresting the decline in the standard of living.

But this adjustment is extremely difficult. In industrial countries the problem is not generally understood. In England the
opinion is very commonly held that 'the peasant' can stand a
good deal in the way of wage reduction, because in the event
of a price fall he can live off the farm. This sort of assertion
is made owing to the habit of regarding peasant agriculture as
somehow outside the scope of the economic laws which determine the activity of commercial farmers. The view that peasants
do not suffer ignores the effects of capital accumulation and the
growth of population; it is true that a peasant on a largish farm,
with a reserve of savings and with a small family, can contract
for a time his purchase of industrial products without serious
suffering. But the peasant holding in Eastern Europe is a small
area of land and must be shared out among a number of children
in each generation. In some regions the limits of subdivision
have been reached already. Moreover, the maintenance of output depends on maintaining the capital: in all regions except
the very remote the crisis drove the peasants deeper into debt,
and forced them to sell more farm produce rather than less.
(This result can be shown to have occurred in Bulgaria.) Contrary to general belief, peasants in Eastern Europe, except in
the remote regions, are far from being subsistence farmers: even
in Bulgaria 35 per cent. of the farm output is sold on the market.

In consequence of the fall in income per head the rate of
capital accumulation is checked; there is not a sufficient volume
of savings—or at least it cannot be mobilized on a large enough
scale—to stimulate industrialization. The fact that labour is
getting cheaper does not stimulate the growth of industry in a
peasant region, any more than it does in a depressed area.
Population growth as such does not cause the transition to industrial society.

The result is that in all these countries there is now a large body of surplus labour on the land: surplus in the strict sense that it could leave the land without reducing the volume of production, not surplus merely in the sense that it could be unemployed if production were mechanized or otherwise improved.

2. TRADE AND TARIFFS

Every change in the European economic and political situation in the post-war period has worked against the agrarian States of Eastern Europe. First came the extension of the wheat areas in the overseas producing countries; then the fall in agricultural prices, and the long depression, and finally the closing of the markets for food by extreme forms of protectionism in Europe.

These changes have been disastrous, because they have destroyed the development of agricultural specialization in Europe itself. Before the War the large industrial countries (France, Germany, Italy, Switzerland, Belgium, and Holland) were still largely self-sufficient, importing not more than one-fourth of their total food requirements, but their dependence on food imports was increasing. Specialization was developing: the countries with highly organized peasant farming—Denmark and Switzerland, Holland and Belgium—were rapidly expanding their exports of dairy produce, meat, and vegetables, and the countries of Eastern Europe, with big estates and extensive farming, were expanding corn exports.

Before the War importing Europe (that is, Europe excluding Russia and the Danube basin) produced 285 million quintals, or two-thirds of its food supplies, and imported 114 million quintals, 70 million from overseas, and 40 million from Russia. Another 20 million was exported from the Danube States, equal to about a quarter of their production. In the post-war period up to 1930 the level of exports from the Danube remained at about half the pre-war level. Europe's dependence on overseas supplies increased, and the Danube's share declined.

The following table shows the change in the relative importance of the Danube States as wheat exporters, since the War, and the alteration in their position in the last two years as a result of German economic expansion.

By 1930–1 the Danubian countries had recovered their pre-war production, and almost reached their pre-war level, in 1931 exporting 18 million quintals. But this prosperity was short

World Production of Wheat
(in million quintals)

	World Production ex. Russia	Europe ex. Russia	per cent.	Europe ex. Danube and Russia	per cent.	Danubian countries	per cent.
1909–13	822,606	370	45	285	35	85	10
1925–9	997,100	368	37	284	28	83	8
1930–4	980,100	413	42	328	33	85	9
1935	970,300	428	44	366	38	82	8
1936	957,100	403	42	299	31	104·3	11
1937	1,037,000	420	40	322	32	98.2	9

World Trade in Wheat
(in million quintals)

	World net Exports (including Russia)	Exports from four Main Exporters	per cent.	Danubian Exports	per cent.	European Net Imports	per cent.
1909–13	144	70	49	19	13	114	79
1925–9	175	160	91	7	4	143	82
1930–4	155	126	81	9	6	136	88
1935	128·3	113	87	12	9	85	66
1936	129·5	115	89	15	11	75	57
1937	—	88		9		—	

lived: from 1932 onwards, as a result of the policy of autarchy, market after market closed against them. In 1932–4 Rumania, Bulgaria, and Jugoslavia dropped out of the market altogether as wheat exporters. All food exports were equally affected: exports of cattle, pigs, meat, and eggs all fell by about 50 per cent. By 1934 importing Europe had increased its production to 350 million quintals, and had cut down imports to 90 million; of which two-thirds went to Great Britain. The continental countries had cut down imports to almost nothing.

No improvement came till 1936 and 1937; as a result of the good harvest of 1936 and the clearing agreements with Germany wheat exports suddenly recovered their 1931 level. As a result of the clearing agreements, the Danubian countries in 1937 regained their pre-slump level in exports of corn, pigs, and meat, but exports of cattle and eggs remained below the 1931 level. Poland has not shared in this improvement and of all the East European countries has suffered most through the policy of autarchy.

The following table shows the change in the main food exports in the last ten years: owing to the improvement in 1936–7, the 1933–7 average exports of meat has been maintained at the level of 1928–32, but exports of cereals, cattle, pigs, and eggs are less.

Partly owing to clearings with Germany, and partly owing to the expansion of export trade in new lines, the quantum of exports in 1936 reached its pre-depression level in Hungary, Jugoslavia, and Bulgaria. According to the calculations in the *Review of World Trade* in 1936 Hungary's exports increased to 130 per cent. of the level of 1927, Jugoslavia's to 98 per cent., and Bulgaria the same. Poland and Rumania had not recovered their pre-depression level.[1]

But owing to the price fall, the purchasing power of these exports is very much lower. The terms of trade have moved against all agricultural countries since the depression; the price of their exports in terms of imports has fallen some 30 per cent. Thus even if the quantum of exports has recovered to its pre-slump level, these countries have not recovered their previous position.

Most of the expansion which has occurred has come through increased trade with Germany. In the last two years there has been a great change in the direction of trade. Even before the initiation of the German Four-Year Plan for the economic penetration of these regions there was a tendency for trade to change

[1] To make calculations of the change in the quantum of trade for these countries is difficult owing to the shift in importance of the different export commodities due to the price fall. This change is most striking for Bulgaria. Before the War cereals accounted for 66 per cent. of her exports, fruit for 2 per cent., and tobacco for 1·3 per cent. Now, in 1931–5 cereals represent 18 per cent. of her exports, fruit 10 per cent., and tobacco 41 per cent. Rumania's main export is no longer wheat but oil. The quantum indices for these countries can be found in the League of Nations *Review of World Trade*, 1936, Annex I, 'Price and Quantum Indices of Imports and Exports.'

its direction, away from the Danubian markets. From 1930 onwards Austria and Czechoslovakia, which had been the chief

Cereal Exports from the Danube States

(wheat, wheat flour, and maize)

(millions of quintals)

			1909–13	1928–32	1933–7
Hungary	.	.	11·5	7·8	6·4
Jugoslavia	.	.	3·3	5·1	6·5
Rumania	.	.	23·2	12·9	11·5
Bulgaria	.	.	5·6	2·5	1·9
Total	.	.	43·6	28·3	26·3

Other Food Exports from Eastern Europe

			Cattle, thousand head		Meat, thousands of quintals	
			1928–32	1933–7	1928–32	1933–7
Hungary	.	.	94	79	15	73
Jugoslavia	.	.	104	68	58	80
Rumania	.	.	87	44	54	23
Bulgaria	.	.	12	13	0	14
Poland	.	.	20	10	508	447
Total	.	.	317	214	635	637

			Pigs, thousand head		Eggs, thousands of quintals	
			1928–32	1933–7	1928–32	1933–7
Hungary	.	.	169	162	95	95
Jugoslavia	.	.	248	235	240	130
Rumania	.	.	107	175	132	89
Bulgaria	.	.	2	9	168	156
Poland	.	.	705	168	497	236
Total	.	.	1231	749	1132	706

markets for all Hungary's food exports, and took about one-third of the exports of the other States, followed the example of the rest of Europe and raised tariffs to almost prohibitive levels. In 1934 the value of food exports from the four Danubian exporting countries to the two importing countries fell to 33 per cent. of their 1925 level, whereas food exports to the rest of Europe fell only to 45 per cent. Most of the decline in inter-Danubian trade was due to the tariff war between Hungary and Czechoslovakia.

The main change came in 1936; Germany's share in the trade of these countries doubled, as a result of Dr. Schacht's visits to the capitals of South-Eastern Europe. Until that time the exchange clearings system had simply been a measure of exchange control, aiming at maintaining the stability of the over-valued mark by taking imports only from countries which had already bought German goods. By 1936 it was clear that though this method had succeeded in cutting off the import surplus, it could only do so by reducing the volume of trade. To get raw materials it was necessary to sell German goods on more favour-able terms, or to bring about an unofficial depreciation of the mark. Under the clearings system Schacht concluded agreements under which these countries could buy German goods at special rates, fixed for every transaction, which meant a depreciation of the mark by 30–50 per cent.

From the German standpoint these agreements are extremely advantageous in that they enable Germany to buy goods at low prices, on specially favourable terms.

But for the countries of Eastern Europe the method of extending trade through clearings has disadvantages. It has led to the accumulation of credit balances in Germany which they cannot use to buy goods from other regions. It is in fact a system of tied markets aiming at bringing these regions under German control. In fact, under the trade agreement these countries are definitely committed to turning over their agriculture to produce 'industrial plants', cotton, flax, soya, which Germany would otherwise have to buy in the world market.

Since the annexation of Austria, Greater Germany controls 40 per cent. of the trade of these countries. Its buying power will now be greatly strengthened.

Will the extension of German economic control relieve the economic situation in Eastern Europe? On the face of it there appear to be great prospects: the 90 millions in the agrarian

States can gain by access to the 80-million market of Greater Germany: they will gain too by the investment of capital in roads, irrigation, by cheap supply of artificial manures. The Danube States can easily dispose of their corn surpluses: Germany's annual imports before 1931 amounted to 20 million quintals, that is, the same amount as Danubian corn surpluses. It is the background of rural poverty which gives momentum to Germany's policy of expansion in the East.

But it is important not to exaggerate the scope of this change. For Germany expansion to the East is all important, as it means self-sufficiency in essential foods, in many raw materials, and in oil. But for Eastern Europe the German market may not be wide enough. Owing to population pressure it will be impossible for the peasants in Eastern Europe to arrest a decline in the standard of living unless they can get a big expansion of their export trade in products which realize a high value to the acre; the privilege of supplying Germany with their pre-slump corn surpluses at unfavourable rates of exchange will not fundamentally change their economic position.

The normal adjustment to the fall in corn prices would be to intensify live-stock farming, by retaining maize to feed to pigs and poultry, or specializing on new lines. Signs of this sort of adjustment are noticeable in Hungary and Bulgaria, which have both taken up new export commodities with some success. Bulgaria's exports of grapes have increased from 12,000 quintals to 300,000 in the last four years, and Hungary has doubled its poultry exports. In part this is due to good marketing organization in Bulgaria, but most of the gain is due to the expansion of demand in Great Britain, the only market which can buy 'luxury' foods in great bulk.

What the agrarian states need is access to markets with rising standards of living which will take meat, poultry, eggs, and vegetables in large quantities at high prices. In Germany, so long as the country follows a policy of autarchy and investment in armaments, this rise cannot occur on a sufficient scale. The fact that it is the industrial raw materials (cotton, flax, &c.) which Jugoslavia is to cultivate under the trade agreements shows that the main aim is to make Germany self-sufficient in raw materials which would otherwise have to be bought in the world market (and might be bought more cheaply, since natural conditions in the Balkans are not favourable).

It must not be concluded, therefore, that German economic control over these regions provides a complete remedy for the present situation, even though it offers these regions a wider market. Closer economic connexions with Germany are not likely to relieve the problem of the two countries with the gravest problems, Poland and Jugoslavia, and will not provide an adequate market for the products of intensive agriculture unless real wages in Germany rise and Germany's industrial development is resumed at a very rapid rate. This is unlikely to occur, since the rapid industrialization in the post-war period was due entirely to the investment of foreign capital in heavy industries. Before the war the rate of industrialization in Germany was conditioned by the expansion of lending to overseas countries, international migration, and the growth of world trade. The great increase in the standard of living in the second half of the nineteenth century and the early twentieth century in Europe could never have occurred without the expansion of agriculture, providing both food and raw materials, in regions outside Europe, and in that expansion Germany shared. If Germany's trade outside Europe does not expand, the prospects of employing the farm population of Eastern Europe at a higher standard of living are not very great.

Germany can, of course, expand its demand for labour in agriculture. For the 1938 harvest Germany proposes to take 100,000 seasonal labourers from Italy and Eastern Europe. But this shortage of labour in agriculture is only created by the tariffs, which give agriculture a monopoly of the internal market.

But so long as the agrarian States have no other outlet, it is obvious that the need for closer connexions with the German market will remain very acute. At present the danger is that they sacrifice political independence for relatively small advantages in the economic sphere. This danger could once have been avoided by the formation of a Danubian or East European Federation. The scope of the wider markets opened through the union itself would not have been very large; but if such a union could have succeeded in uniting the industrial countries, Czechoslovakia and Hungary, with their higher rate of capital

Direction of Foreign Trade in Eastern Europe

	Hungary			Rumania			Jugoslavia			Bulgaria			Poland		
	1929	1933	1937	1929	1933	1937	1929	1933	1937	1929	1933	1937	1929	1933	1937
millions of national	1·039	391	589	28·960	14·171	30·965	7·922	3·378	6·272	6·397	2·846	5·020	2·813	960	1·196
...ds of metric tons	230	154	203	589	731	804	444	244	380	26	36	57	1·753†	1·082†	1·250†
	%	%	%	%	%	%	%	%	%	%	%	%	%	%	%
.	42·1	38·2	41·0	37·0	17·2	27·2	24·1	35·6	35·2	42·5	45·1	47·1	41·7	23·3	18·4
.	11·7	11·2	24·1	27·6	10·6	20·1	8·5	13·9	21·7	29·9	36·0	43·1	31·2	17·5	14·5
.	30·4	27·0	16·9	9·4	6·6	7·1	15·6	21·7	13·5	12·6	9·1	4·0	10·5	5·8	4·9
.	6·9	8·6	12·3	7·7	9·2	7·4	24·9	21·5	9·4	10·5	9·7	4·2	1·4	2·6	4·5
.	16·4	7·3	3·5	6·2	4·8	8·4	5·4	10·8	7·9	4·8	3·5	5·5	10·5	5·0	4·3
.	12·3	9·4	8·7	8·6	8·3	12·9	15·9	8·4	7·5	11·0	2·0	2·3	5·3	3·4	2·7
.	22·3	36·5	34·5	40·5	60·5	44·1	29·7	23·7	40·0	31·2	39·7	40·9	41·1	65·7	69·1
.	3·6	8·0	7·3	6·4	15·4	9·0	1·3	2·7	7·4	1·6	1·8	13·9	10·2	19·2	18·3
.	1·2	4·5	2·1	4·5	12·4	5·9	4·0	2·2	5·4	5·1	3·3	1·6	2·2	5·5	4·1
.	4·0	5·2	5·0	..	..	2·7	2·2	3·3	..	2·1	5·2	..	1·4	1·5	1·8
.	1·1	1·5	2·9	0·2	0·2	1·5	1·6	1·9	4·6	1·7	1·1	3·8	1·1	1·7	8·4
millions of national	1·064	313	476	20·628	11·742	17·896	7·595	2·883	5·234	8·325	2·202	4·927	3·111	827	1·254
...ds of metric tons	559	148	284	92	39	59	139	66	92	42	19	27	424†	196†	307†
	%	%	%	%	%	%	%	%	%	%	%	%	%	%	%
.										20·8	44·4	58·2	33·1	21·9	19·1

accumulation, with the purely agrarian regions, the prospect of capital investment would have been hopeful. The main function of such a union would have been to create greater security for international capital, and the greater tariff concessions it could obtain.

Throughout the post-war period, the political differences between the East European States stood in the way. Czechoslovakia's own farming interests resisted closer connexions with the east. Hungary, though strongly opposed to German aggression and to Nazism, has been hindered from effective action by the fear of the violent class struggles which the future must hold. Czechoslovakia, Jugoslavia, and Rumania are united mainly by their opposition to Hungary. Yet there are forces in the present situation which might provide a basis for closer unity: in Poland, Jugoslavia, and Rumania the peasant parties remain constant elements in the political situation, opposed to the pro-German leanings of their governments, and yet apparently incapable of seizing the reins, because the development of economic relations with Germany seems the only course now open.

3. Possible Remedies

What remedies can be suggested?

The extension of the market from German expansion will not offer these countries markets on favourable terms. It is clear from the existence of surplus population and the low standard of living that what is necessary is to produce more to the acre, not merely to sell more. Better markets for eggs, poultry, fruit, and vegetables are more important than better markets for corn. Germany, at least for the present, by her policy of fostering corn production keeps the prices of primary foodstuffs high and so prevents an increase in the consumption of these goods.

No remedy can be found except reintegration with the economic life of industrial Europe. At best corn exports are only a small proportion of their total output, and as their population increases they should retain more of it. But to produce more, greater efficiency in farming methods is necessary.

Assuming that there is some reduction in the tariffs on food products and that wider markets can be found, will it be possible for these countries to change their farming system enough to employ their surplus population and to raise their standard of living? There are apparently two ways in which the situation can be attacked:

(i) An intensification of farming, coupled with tariff reductions.

(ii) Industrialization, either by means of foreign capital or as part of a collectivization policy aiming simultaneously at farm reorganization and industrial expansion.

Obviously it is in the direction of better farming that the easiest change will come because it would be compatible with the present social structure. This is an important consideration, for there can be no doubt that the family farm system does satisfy the social ideals of the peasantry. The post-war agrarian reforms, by giving the peasant access to the land, created a social order which satisfied the peasants' aspirations. Either industrialization or collective farming would bring into existence a new social order in which most of the farm population would become paid workers; and towards this sort of change the peasants feel real aversion.

But to see how much farm reorganization can be expected to do we must look in greater detail at the causes and extent of rural poverty in these regions.

CHAPTER III

OVER-POPULATION

1. WHAT IS OVER-POPULATION?

TO appreciate the effect of the fall in income we must
examine the effect of high population density. The difficulty of adjustment to the changed world situation really
arises because the decline in output per head, not in itself very
large, has occurred in conditions in which output per head was
already very low.

This low productivity of labour is a result of high population
density together with shortage of capital. A high density of
labour on the land need not, of course, in itself indicate a low
output per head. There are regions of Western Europe where the
land is also densely settled, and yet the standard of living is not
lower than in other regions where population is spread thinner
—for instance, Belgium and the Rhineland, the Swiss lowlands
and the south of France. But these are regions with special
cultures—the olive and the vine—or regions where farming is
highly capitalized. Where capital can be invested in farming,
the density of labour is of very little significance; intensive use
of capital to the acre accompanies the intensive use of labour,
and output per head is high. In Eastern Europe, however, the
land is really the peasant's only capital, except his working
live stock: the land has to support twice or three times as
many people as in Western Europe, with less capital equipment.

Consequently, output per head is lower even than a comparison of land per head would suggest. For comparison with
the agrarian states it is better to take countries in Central rather
than Western Europe. In Bohemia and Western Hungary the
amount of land per head is 2 hectares (5 acres), the average
yield 16 quintals to the hectare (12 cwt. to the acre), while in
Eastern Europe the average land per head ranges from 1 hectare
to 1·2 hectares (2½ to 3 acres), and the wheat yield amounts to
10 quintals to the hectare (8 cwt. to the acre). Thus in Eastern
Europe the corn output per head cannot be more than one-third

of the output in Central European countries, where the farm population attains an adequate standard of living.[1] (Even within the agrarian countries there is, as we shall see, no correlation between high yield and high density. On the contrary, it is the regions of poor soil, remote from communications, that are more densely settled, the rich plains that are relatively sparsely settled.)

Here some digression as to the meaning of over-population is necessary, to avoid misunderstanding of the sense in which the term is used in this and following chapters. It is not, of course, accurate to describe as over-populated any country with a high density of farm population, a low output per head, and a non-mechanized method of cultivation. To give the term any meaning it must be supposed that the size of the population itself causes the wage per head to be lower than it would be if the population were smaller. In this sense a country is over-populated if wages fall, because the supply of labour increases faster than the other productive resources of the community.

In Western Europe, and in general in countries with a capitalistic economic system, there can be no question of over-population, because there is no long-period tendency for wages to fall. In fact, most economists tend to regard a rise in the productivity of labour as a normal long-period development. The problem which they seek to explain is why economic expansion—the growth of the productive resources of the community—proceeds unevenly and is broken by periods in which part of the labour and capital resources are unemployed. 'The only situation of which we have any knowledge in a capitalistic society is one in which total investment is growing at a fairly rapid rate',[2] and it is taken for granted that this rate will be more rapid than the increase in population.

Of course, this long-period development is taken for granted mainly because in the nineteenth century productive resources did expand, in the form of new land and new capital equipment, at an extremely rapid rate. The prophecies of Malthus were not fulfilled, because the growth of population was accompanied by changes in the technique of industry requiring

[1] See Chapter IV for more detailed comparison of standards of living.
[2] Knight, 'Capital, Time and the Interest Rate,' in *Economica*, 1934.

large capital equipment and heavy investment, and through this investment it was possible to develop new regions for agriculture.

In these conditions it was inevitable that agriculture in Western Europe should contract, for two reasons: first, because as income per head rises, the proportion of income spent on food necessarily declines, and second, because the new sources of supply could produce much cheaper. As we have already said, in general in a progressive economy, agriculture will always tend to occupy a smaller proportion of the community's productive resources: as incomes rise, the demand for housing, clothing, and services will increase more than in proportion to the rise in income, the demand for food less: and in consequence, demand for labour in these industries increases, causing a relative increase in wage rates which will attract labour to move out of agriculture into better-paid occupations. Probably if the change in demand were the only factor working there might be only a *relative* decline in the importance of agriculture; but in the nineteenth century there was not only a relative but an absolute decline in the numbers employed on the land, due to the opening up of new sources of supply. Hence in Western Europe there has never been any problem of population pressure.

But in Eastern Europe, and in Asia, we see an entirely different development. Industrialization has made little progress. Population continues to increase rapidly, without much increase in capital resources, and consequently must be employed on the land. As the marginal productivity of labour falls, income per head falls also. Low wages on the land do not cause the development of industry, if the capital resources of the community are not increasing. Poverty in some regions of Eastern Europe has driven the peasantry to start industries of a non-capitalistic kind (e.g. the numerous small home industries of Slovenia working for export), or to specialized agriculture of a labour intensive kind (the migrant Bulgar gardeners); but it cannot drive them to institute mechanized or capitalistic industry.

Why should the line of development be different? It is no answer to say that the system of production and distribution is not a money economy; this is true only of very remote regions.

To answer this question it is necessary to point out that the direction of economic development in Western Europe has been conditioned by a rapid rate of capital accumulation, which there is no reason to regard as normal, although in fact certain types of economic theory do tend to think it self-evident that the capital equipment of the community will always be maintained.[1] There cannot, however, be any real grounds for thinking that a community will always tend to save enough to maintain its output per head, or to increase it. Indeed, the most recent developments of interest theory suggest that far from a high rate of capital accumulation being normal or necessary, there is a constant tendency for the economic system to run down, through the tendency to hoard. Without entering into this controversy, it can be asserted that the modern theory of interest does not suggest any reason for regarding over-population as abnormal. For over-population only means that the capital resources of the population fail to increase fast enough to maintain output per head: it would be equally accurate to speak of a shortage of capital, since it is not the growth of population itself which causes the fall in wages, but its disproportionate growth. All discussion of the meaning of an optimum population remains vague, simply because it is not realized that it is in reality the rate of capital accumulation which is the subject of discussion, and not any level of population density.

It must be concluded that any country with a rapidly increasing population may reach a state of such low productivity that

[1] This is true of the Austrian theory of capital. The basis of this theory is the doctrine that a rise in the rate of interest can stimulate an increase in savings. Accordingly, if population increases, wages fall, and the price of capital goods rises: the rate of interest rises because capital goods are scarce in relation to labour. The rise in the rate of interest will cause an increase in the volume of savings. Thus it would follow that an increase in population could never cause a continuous fall in wages: an increase in population would simply mean that more saving would occur. On this theory, the experience of Western Europe in the nineteenth century must be regarded as normal, that of Asia and Eastern Europe as abnormal. Hayek's treatment takes it for granted that as a long-run phenomenon capital consumption will not attain a rate which will exceed the simultaneous formation of new capital ('Kapital-aufzehrung', *Weltwirtschaftliches Archiv*, Juli, 1932). But other theories of interest, above all that of Keynes, deny the connexion between the real productivity of capital and the amount of saving done. If the amount of saving is not directly related to the productivity of capital, then it follows that a rise in the rate of interest due to population growth need not cause an increase in the supply of savings.

the decline in output per head cannot be arrested, because low wages are not sufficient inducement to cause capital investment in industry. How far the rate of capital accumulation in Eastern Europe results from the kind of social institutions—from peasant society—and how far from the special difficulties of the post-war period, it is difficult to say.[1] At any rate there is now much surplus labour on the land.

Must the state of falling output per head necessarily lead to under-employment?

If, as population increases, the area of land and the capital equipment remain the same, output per head must fall, but it need not follow that labour is unemployed. In fact, of course, a change to more labour-intensive methods is in progress—more maize and potatoes are cultivated in order to give more employment at lower wages. But—and this is a point which is often overlooked when it is asserted that over-population does not cause unemployment—the limits of labour intensification are quickly reached when no addition to capital can be made.[2] For instance, to cultivate the soil in Rumania with more labour alone would, under present conditions, probably bring in a negative return, so easily is soil fertility affected by drought. With additional capital investment in irrigation more labour could be used per acre, but, as things are, capital is not available.

Consequently land shortage may easily mean unemployment if the qualities of the land do not make more intensive cultivation practicable. Physical conditions may set a fairly clear limit to the amount of additional labour which can be employed: in maize-growing regions the possibilities are greater than in the north, where climate is cold and soil poor. In these conditions an increase in population means redundant labour. The traditional idea of the peasant as a worker weighed down by cease-less toil is a picture based on industrial conditions; in countries where capital is cheaper the small farmer can invest in any

[1] The influence of peasant ownership on investment is discussed in Chapter IX.

[2] Cf. A. M. Carr Saunders, 'The Growth of the Population of Europe' in *European Civilization*, vol. v, Oxford, 1936: 'Unemployment is, therefore, not a necessary consequence of excessive numbers: in fact the only necessary consequence of over-population is avoidable poverty.'

direction, and over-work in consequence. But in Eastern Europe under-employment is the great evil. Its cause is inadequate capital accumulation, coupled with soil conditions which do not favour labour-intensive methods.

Thus, to say that a region is over-populated means simply that the working population is excessive, with reference to a certain technique of cultivation, which must be taken as fixed as things are. In this sense it is perfectly sensible to make calculations of the labour requirements of certain crops, and to compare them with the actual density of agricultural population in order to ascertain how many workers are excessive. This was the method used by the school of agricultural economists in Moscow before the War, for analysis of Russian conditions, and now used in the calculations made for Poland and Bulgaria. To take an example: if the system is maize and wheat cultivation, or rye and potatoes, with some live stock and extensive grazing, but no dairying or root crops, one could conclude that the limits of employment are roughly 30 active population to the 100 hectares of farm land,[1] or 60–70 total farm population, and beyond this limit the country is over-populated. But it is the superfluity with reference to a given system which is essential. In the words of a Bulgarian economist: 'If I see five sheep with three dogs and two men, I call that over-population.' Understood in this sense, it cannot be doubted that there really is over-population in Eastern Europe as a very widespread though localized phenomenon.

Whether this condition necessarily means that the fertility of the soil will be gradually exhausted depends, apparently, on natural conditions. In Poland the fertility of the soil is certainly being exhausted, but in Bulgaria yields are maintained. If real income continues to fall, it is evident that these conditions may lead to capital consumption and a decline in the fertility of the soil.

---

[1] 'Farm land' is used as a basis for calculating rural density throughout this chapter, since to calculate population density with reference to total area is misleading, owing to the large proportion of forest in E. Europe. Farm land covers the whole area used for agricultural production, i.e. arable, gardens, meadows, and pastures, and excludes uncultivated land and forests. Where pastures are mainly rough grazing, as in the Balkans, they are excluded.

2. WHAT LEVEL OF DENSITY INDICATES SURPLUS POPULATION?

The fact that redundant labour exists on the land need not necessarily mean that a country as a whole is over-populated: for labour is only superfluous with reference to a given system, and if the farming system could be changed, or if industry could expand, this surplus labour could be absorbed. Leaving, for the moment, the question of how far the labour supply in the land would be superfluous with a different system, we must estimate the extent to which labour on the land is superfluous under conditions as they are now.

To estimate the extent to which surplus population exists it is necessary to determine a standard of rural density which corresponds to the labour requirements for a certain farming system with a certain technical level. On the face of it, this may appear a difficult task, but in fact over-population appears in such a crude form that it is easily recognizable; in the over-populated districts, such as Galicia, the existence of surplus labour is very evident. The simpler and more uniform the methods of production, the easier it is to estimate how much labour is excessive.

Over Europe as a whole, the level of rural density rises, broadly speaking, from north-west to south-east. Great Britain has the sparsest farm population and the largest area of farm land per head of farm population, followed by, Denmark, Sweden and France. Central Europe (Germany, Switzerland, Austria and Czechoslovakia) has higher densities. At the other side of the map lie the most densely populated regions (regarding farm density only) of Eastern Europe, Poland and Rumania with about 75 farm population to the hundred hectares of farm land, Bulgaria with 82, and Jugoslavia with over 100, the highest density of farm population measured in relation to farm land.

If we compare the two extremes, Denmark and Bulgaria, it appears that in Denmark labour requirements for field crops (cereals, potatoes, and roots), measured in labour hours, are roughly half what they are in Bulgaria;[1] that is, the cultivation

[1] Cf. Egoroff, 'Die Arbeit in der Landwirtschaft', in Molloff, *Die sozial-ökonomische Struktur der bulgarischen Landwirtschaft.*

of these crops needs twice the amount of labour in Bulgaria, because the methods of production are less mechanized. But the actual density of the working farm population in Bulgaria is more than three times as high, and one could conclude that something like one-third of the rural population are in excess of the labour requirements, even though no machinery is used in cultivating crops.

However, Denmark is a corn importer, and its methods of production are highly capitalistic: its farming system is very different from that of Poland or Rumania.

A better standard of comparison for Eastern Europe is the farm density in Hungary and Czechoslovakia, which have farming systems based on arable cultivation of corn crops with some live-stock farming, but have no intensive dairying. In these regions the farm density is roughly 30 farm workers to the 100 hectares of farm land, and 60 farm population to 100 hectares of farm land. This represents 1·7 hectares, or 4 acres per head. This may be regarded as corresponding to the labour requirements of this type of farming. In Eastern Europe farm densities are roughly one-third higher, ranging from 42 to 56 workers per 100 hectares of farm land, and 70 to 100 farm population per 100 hectares farm land; this represents from 1 to 1·3 hectares, or 2½ to 3·2 acres per head.

As compared with farming methods in Czechoslovakia and Hungary, the methods of production in Eastern Europe are more labour-intensive; less machinery is used; but, on the other hand, the crops sown are not intensively cultivated. Labour requirements are on balance less; and on this basis it would be reasonable to assume that over Eastern Europe as a whole one-quarter to one-third of the farm population is surplus, and that the proportion is higher in certain districts, of which Galicia is the most important.[1]

Calculations of surplus population have been made for Poland

---

[1] Poniatowski (*Przeludnienie wsi*, 1936) comes to the conclusion that one-third of the population of Poland was superfluous in 1930 (and about half in Galicia). Oberländer (*Die Übervölkerung Polens*, 1935) calculates that different amounts of labour are necessary per hectare, according to the intensity of production, allowing 3 hectares in the west, 4·5 in Eastern Poland and Galicia, 5·5 in East Poland and Białystok. This gives a surplus population of 42 per cent. for the whole of Poland.

and Bulgaria[1] with reference to labour requirements, which show that the proportion of surplus labour amounts to about one-third. Bulgaria has a higher degree of density of population in relation to arable land than Poland, but as the intensive

Density of Farm Population, 1931[2]

Country	Farm population (000's)	Farm area 1,000 ha.	Farm population per 100 Ha. farm land	Farm population per 100 acres farm land
Czechoslovakia .	5,101	8,475	60·2	24
Hungary . .	4,470	9,576	59·0	24
Poland . .	19,346	25,589	75·6	31
Rumania . .	13,060	17,407	75·0	30
Bulgaria .	4,165	5,110	81·6	33
Jugoslavia .	9,768	9,445	103·4	42

crops are relatively more important, this result may be accepted as showing that more or less the same conditions exist in South-Eastern Europe, as in the districts north and south of the Carpathians. If Bulgaria, with its well-organized and specialized agriculture, is to be regarded as over-populated, Jugoslavia certainly is, and Rumania also, in certain districts.

If we take a density of 70–5 farm population to the 100 hectares or roughly 3½ acres per head, as indicating over-population, all

[1] A similar calculation has been made for Bulgaria by P. Egoroff (in Molloff, *Die sozialökonomische Struktur der bulgarischen Landwirtschaft*, Berlin, 1936, p. 152), which shows that only 63 per cent. of the available labour force is utilized—roughly about one-third is superfluous, as in Poland.

[2] For this table it has been necessary to calculate the number of population dependent on agriculture or farm population, as distinct from the rural population, for Rumania and Jugoslavia, as these countries have no census of occupations.

In Jugoslavia the census does not even classify the rural and urban population; the agricultural population has been estimated as 70 per cent. of the total population, which corresponds to the ratio in Bulgaria, for which country occupational statistics are available.

In calculating the farm area of Jugoslavia rough grazing is excluded from farm land as its value is very low. If included the farm area would be 50 per cent. larger.

For Bulgaria there are as yet no figures for the farm population in 1931. The farm population has been calculated by assuming that the ratio of the farm population to the rural population is the same as in 1926.

For Czechoslovakia, Poland, and Hungary the figures are taken from the Census of Occupations.

Poland except the west and the east, all Rumania except South
Bessarabia, the Dobrogea, and the Banat, can be considered
as too densely populated, all Jugoslavia except the Danube
Province, and all Bulgaria. Exceptionally high densities exist in

Amount of Land per head of Farm Population in Eastern Europe, 1930–1

	Ha.	Acres			Ha.	Acres
Czechoslovakia:			*Rumania:*			
Bohemia	1·9	4·7	Old Kingdom	.	1·3	3·2
Moravia and Silesia .	1·7	4·2	Transylvania	.	1·3	3·2
Slovakia .	1·5	3·7	Bessarabia	.	1·5	3·7
Ruthenia .	1·2	3·0	Bukovina	.	0·9	2·2
Total	1·6	4·1	Total	.	1·3	3·2
Hungary:			*Jugoslavia:* Provinces:			
West Hungary .	1·7	4·2	Vardar .	.	0·9	2·2
The Great Plain	1·7	4·2	Verbas .	.	1·2	3·0
North Hungary	1·5	3·7	Drava .	.	0·6	1·4
Total .	1·7	4·2	Drina .	.	1·1	2·7
			Danube	.	1·4	3·4
Poland:			Zeta	.	0·8	2·0
Central Provinces	1·3	3·2	Morava	.	1·0	2·4
Eastern Provinces	1·7	4·1	Primoria	.	0·7	1·7
Western Provinces	1·8	4·5	Sava .	.	0·9	2·2
Southern Provinces .	0·9	2·3	Total	.	1·0	2·4
Total .	1·3	3·3				
Bulgaria: .	1·2	3·0				

Southern Poland (Galicia), the hill districts of the Old Kingdom
of Rumania and Transylvania, the Bukovina, Jugoslavia (except
the Danube Province, which has demographic conditions like
those of Hungary), in Bulgaria and also Ruthenia, the small
province in the extreme east of Czechoslovakia.

The densely populated districts are not those with the richest
soil or with the more favourable market conditions: on the
contrary, it is the mountain districts and the poorer soils which
show the densest concentrations. This is, of course, a situation
which would not be found in Western Europe, where the fact
that a region is densely populated only shows that it pays to
utilize the soil more intensively. But in Eastern Europe the

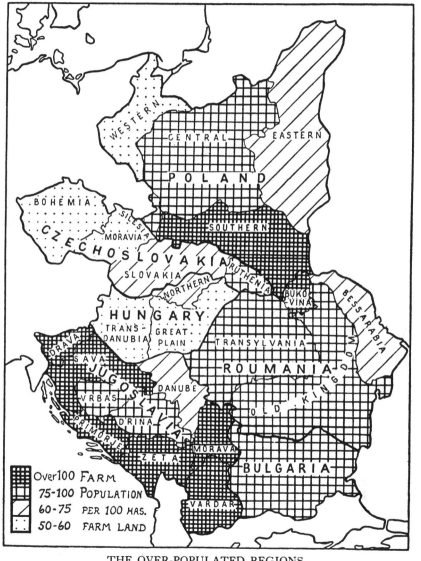

WESTERN

CENTRAL   EASTERN

P O L A N D

BOHEMIA

SILESIA

MORAVIA   SOUTHERN

C Z E C H O S L O V A K I A   RUTHENIA

SLOVAKIA   BUKO-
                                            VINA   BESSARABIA
NORTHERN

H U N G A R Y   TRANSYLVANIA

TRANS-   GREAT
DANUBIA   PLAIN   R O U M A N I A

DRAVA

SAVA
        JUGOSLAVIA   DANUBE
VRBAS   OLD KINGDOM

        DRINA

PRIMORJE

ZETA   MORAVA

                B U L G A R I A
VARDAR

Over 100 FARM
75-100 POPULATION
60-75 PER 100 HAS.
50-60 FARM LAND

THE OVER-POPULATED REGIONS

figures of density are significant simply because land is the chief form of capital, and the less land a peasant has the poorer he is.

Of course there are differences in the farming systems of the agrarian countries. Labour requirements are much greater for

Arable Land per Head of Farm Population

	Hectares	Acres
Hungary . . .	1·2	3·0
Czechoslovakia . .	1·1	2·8
Rumania . . .	1·0	2·4
Poland . . .	0·9	2·3
Bulgaria . . .	0·9	2·2
Jugoslavia . . .	0·7	1·8
U.S.S.R. (1928) . .	1·0	2·4
,, (1935) . .	1·2	3·0

the intensive cultures, like the vine or vegetable and tobacco. But to make calculations on this basis would not much affect the final result.

Probably the best measure of population density is the amount of arable land per head. This is the standard which the peasants themselves use, regarding 1 hectare of arable land per head as the minimum guaranteeing a subsistence level. By taking this standard, the relative position of the countries is not much affected, but it is useful because it permits comparison between Eastern Europe and Russia, where 'farm land' is difficult to classify owing to the great areas of rough grazing.

The results of using this standard are as in the table above.

3. Causes of the High Density of Farm Population

Why is it that in Eastern Europe the bulk of the population is still on the land, and continues to increase, while in Western Europe the agricultural population is a small part of the total population and continues to decline, in spite of agricultural protection?

In Western Europe as a whole the proportion of the total population engaged in agriculture is now very much lower than it is in Eastern Europe, amounting to about 20 to 30 per cent. of the total population, as compared with 50 to 80 per cent. in the agrarian countries. In Eastern Europe the number of farm population to the acre is higher also, in many regions even twice as high (apart from specially intensive regions like Belgium).

The explanation of the development of Western Europe is, of course, as we have said, the high rate of capital accumulation, and the development of foreign trade. As the trade of Western Europe with the rest of Europe expanded, the industrial countries increased their imports of food: wages in industry rose, while incomes on the land fell, and as population grew the workers on the land moved into industry. Thus the decline of town population is for these countries a sign of rising real income per head, due to the increased productivity of labour.

Generally speaking, the countries with a relatively small farm population are the countries with the highest standard of living, both in the towns and on the land. In Western Europe there is no close connexion between the *proportion* of population in agriculture and the *density* of the population on the land, because the rate of total population growth has been different: France, for instance, has a higher proportion of agricultural population, but a lower density of farm population, than Germany: Belgium has a lower proportion on the land than Denmark, but a higher density of rural population. But apart from a few regions, with very special conditions, the density of farm population is in Western Europe everywhere lower than in the east, because since the seventies, at least, if not earlier, industrialization has been advancing rapidly enough to take most of the increase of the rural population off the land.

But the contrast in economic development goes back even farther than the seventies; even at the beginning of the nineteenth century the industrial development of Western Europe was far more advanced than that of the east. Although large-scale capitalistic development of industry had not begun (except in England, where the density of total population was of course highest), a relatively dense concentration of population already existed at the beginning of the nineteenth century on the western fringe of the continent—that is, in the north of England, the north of France and Flanders, the Rhine up to Lake Constance and Switzerland. After England, Flanders showed the greatest density in Europe, with 120 inhabitants to the square

kilometre. A group of secondary industrial centres (mainly tex-
tile industries) existed in Central Germany and in the adjoining
provinces of Bohemia and Silesia, where a densely settled
peasantry was engaged in home industries. In the course of
the nineteenth century these areas declined in relative importance as the great concentration of industry in Western Germany grew and grew.

In all these regions, from the beginning of the nineteenth
century onwards, industry expanded and drew on supplies of
labour from the surrounding country-side. Eastern Europe,
then as now, lay outside the area from which population could
be drawn: population was much sparser, and there was no real
pressure on the soil: in consequence it was not drawn into the
orbit of western industrialization, as far as labour supply was
concerned.

As the total population of Western Europe grew, from the
middle of the nineteenth century onwards, the towns of Western
Europe began to buy supplies of corn from the Eastern Plains;
they could not support their population by the production of
their own surrounding regions, even by using more intensive
methods of cultivation. Had the overseas supplies not been
available, Western Europe and above all, England, would have
been forced to rely increasingly on the European sources of
supply, which were dear, though produced with cheap labour,
owing to the high cost of transport. In consequence the industrial development of Western Europe would have been hindered
by the high price of food production in terms of industrial
products, had there been no extension of corn production overseas.

Indeed, it seems possible that the greater part of the rise in
real incomes in Western Europe was due to this expansion of
corn production. Throughout European history the rate of
increase of production of corn had never much exceeded the
growth of population, and for centuries the output per man had
increased very slowly; until the technical discoveries of the
eighteenth century increased yields, increased food production
meant extending the area of cultivation, not using new methods.
The technical discoveries in agriculture in the eighteenth century greatly increased the productivity of labour, but barely

enough to keep pace with the growth of population. In the first half of the nineteenth century in England there appears to have been no marked rise in real incomes, owing to the high level of food prices.

Through the investments in railway transport the relationship between population and production of food was changed; suddenly vast new areas were brought into cultivation—and for the first time world corn production began to increase much faster than world population. In the twenty years 1860–80 the population of the United States increased by 100 per cent., its corn production by 300 per cent. Thus it had great surpluses for export, as no other country ever had before. When prices fell, about 50 per cent. in the twenty years, the terms of trade changed in England's favour and real wages rose; farm wages fell in England, corn production contracted, and the farm population began to decline. To some extent all Western Europe shared in this development. Eastern Europe, however, lost in the process, because the demand for its corn declined, its transport costs were not much reduced by steam transport, and consequently Austria-Hungary and Russia were obliged to borrow to develop their railway systems, without the prospect of high returns such as the overseas countries had. Thus the main cause of the contrast in rural density has been the rapid industrialization of the west. In the economic history of the nineteenth century Eastern Europe did not amount to more than a footnote.

Towards the end of the nineteenth century another cause began to operate: in Eastern Europe the rate of population increase became much faster. In the nineties Bulgaria and most of the Balkans, Ukraine, and Poland had exceptionally fast rates of increase. Consequently migration only served to relieve the growing pressure on the land. By the end of the nineteenth century the rate of increase of the total population in Western Europe was slower; owing to the expansion of industry, the farm population was either declining or increasing very slowly: there was no important increase in the density of rural population after 1880. In Eastern Europe the rate of total increase was more rapid and the progress of industrialization very slow; by 1914 in these regions the farm population had everywhere reached a higher density than that of the west, and since that time the difference has increased.

In the densely populated rural regions of Central Europe, formerly included within the Monarchy, the main reason for the high farm density is that they began the nineteenth century already rather densely settled, and population continued to increase at the 'normal' European rate during the nineteenth century. Industrialization was fostered by government policy in some provinces, such as Bohemia, discouraged in others, such as Galicia, with the result that the rural population in these two provinces to-day lives on very different levels. In the regions where industry did not develop, the bulk of the increased population remained on the land. At the same time the rate of increase was more rapid in these provinces: in the second half of the century the rate of increase of population in Galicia was rather faster than it was in Bohemia, 39 per cent. increase in the years 1870–1925, as against 25 per cent. This rate of increase was not, however, abnormally fast. The real disaster for Galicia was not an abnormally fast growth of population, but the slow progress of industrialization in a province which already had a high density at the beginning of the century. Conditions were similar in Slovakia (then North Hungary), Croatia (then part of West Hungary), and Transylvania.

In the Balkans, and the eastern provinces of Poland formerly included in Russia, over-population is mainly due to the rapid rate of population growth. As we have said, at the beginning of the century the Danube Plain in Hungary and Rumania, the Balkans, and the provinces of Polesia and Wolhynia were almost empty, but in the second half of the nineteenth century the rate of population growth accelerated. In the years 1815–70 the population of these regions increased by 100 to 300 per cent., partly, no doubt, in the Danube Plain by migration from the hills.[1]

This rapid increase in the population of Russia and the Balkans began (so far as can be judged) after the middle of the nineteenth century.[2] For a time this increase could be met by

[1] Cf. Haufe, *Die Bevölkerung Europas*, Berlin, 1936.
[2] Kuczynski, *The Balance of Births and Deaths*, vol. ii. The net reproduction rate in Russia in the nineties was 1·65; Congress Poland had a slightly less

taking more land into cultivation, because Eastern Europe was only half cultivated at the beginning of the nineteenth century. This explains why the growth of population did not result in an excessive supply of labour in agriculture at an earlier date. For a long time, population could increase without causing a fall in income, for new land was available, even if little technical progress had been made. This extension of the area is still continuing in Jugoslavia and Bulgaria, though only poor soils are now available.

The growth of population must have been largely independent of any rise in the standard of living. Some historians have attributed the rapid increase of the population in Russia to peasant emancipation; but in general there seems no explanation for the rapidity of the rate, from the economic standpoint.

Thus the present high density in Bulgaria, Rumania, Jugoslavia, Eastern Slovakia, Ruthenia, and Poland is due to an abnormal rate of increase of total population.

Looking back over the nineteenth century we can see the cause of Eastern Europe's difficult development. First, at the beginning of the nineteenth century, it was very little industrialized compared with the west. In the Austro-Hungarian Monarchy state policy checked industrial development in some provinces, encouraged it in others. In the Balkans and in Russia population began to grow at an abnormal rate. Then, as Western Europe experienced a great expansion in demand for its industrial products, in return for cheap supplies of food, the demand for corn from Eastern Europe declined. The end of the nineteenth century and the beginning of the new brought some improvement, owing to migration to overseas countries. But in the post-war period the markets were closed together; the density of rural population continued to increase, though the market for food produce was contracting.

The natural rate of increase of the population in these countries has fallen sharply since 1930, owing to the decline in the birth-rate. Since the pre-war period the birth-rate has fallen

rapid rate of increase than the rest of Russia; in the Ruthenian Provinces (now the eastern voivodships and part of the southern voivodships) the rate was abnormally fast. In Bulgaria the rate of increase was even more rapid than in Russia; the net reproduction rate was 1·82 in the nineties.

very rapidly in Bulgaria and Poland, from 41 in Bulgaria in 1909–12 to 30 in 1934; in Poland from 37 to 26·5 in 1934. This is due to a decline in fertility, and also to a reduction in the numbers of women of child-bearing age, as a result of the decline of births during the War. But the fall in the birth-rate will only mean that the population on the land continues to increase at a slower rate; as the population continues to reproduce itself, there can be no reduction of the total population from this cause.

THE STANDARD
OF LIVING (1)
Peasant farm
of 8 hectares

CZECHOSLOVAKIA
SOUTH BOHEMIA

Rye harvest on farm of
5 hectares

CHAPTER IV

THE STANDARD OF LIVING

WE have already pointed out that there is no single peasant standard in Europe, any more than there is a single standard for the urban worker. The chief line of contrast lies between Eastern and Western Europe; and there is a greater difference between the standard of living of the farmer in Switzerland and Poland than there is, for instance, between the standard of living of the farmer in Switzerland and England. Between the two extremes of Switzerland and Transylvania (see illustration facing page 18), there is a wide range of peasant communities, existing on several different levels.

To see how great the difference in income levels is we must make a broad contrast between the gross income of the peasant family in the West of Europe and in the East, that is, between regions of intensive and extensive farming. The chief factors which influence gross income are, of course, the greater physical output per acre and the higher price of the produce in the west: the type of farming is more intensive, owing to climatic conditions and the proximity of the urban market, and also, of course, to the higher level of prices due to tariff protection.

For the purpose of rough comparison we can divide peasant farms in Europe into three main income groups: the dairy producers, the meat producers, and the extensive corn-growers. The dairy producers include the farmers of Switzerland and Denmark, Holland and parts of Germany, who farm very intensively; they supply urban markets, with high standards of living, and buy artificial manures and feeding-stuffs in large quantities.

The meat and corn producers are the peasants in large regions of France and Germany, Czechoslovakia and Western Hungary, where farming is less intensive and is protected from foreign competition by tariffs and quotas.

The third group covers the farms of Eastern Europe in general, where wheat and maize, or rye and potatoes, are the main product and live stock is relatively unimportant.

To bring out the difference in output per hectare between

these types of farming we can use the farm accountancy figures published by the Rome Institute of Agriculture, showing gross income per hectare. These show a gross return per hectare of over 1,000 francs in Switzerland, 350–500 in Germany, Denmark, Holland, and Scotland, about 200 in Austria and Hungary, and under 200 in Poland.

Gross Return and Family Farm Earnings, 1934–5
(in gold francs per hectare)

	Gross Return	Family Farm Earnings[1]
Switzerland	1,061	177
Denmark*	397	143
Scotland†	372	132
Holland	439	78
Germany*	489	68
Austria	216	60
Hungary	194	48
Poland	123	52

* Peasant Farms.   † Dairy Farms.

(International Institute of Agriculture, Farm Accountancy Statistics for 1934–5. Rome, 1938.)

Although, of course, the accountancy results only relate to a small number of farms, and do not show the level of income attained by the farm population as a whole, yet they serve to indicate the range of difference in the value of output per hectare, or the gross return. In the countries with higher gross returns per hectare, farm income per hectare is also higher, though not higher in the same proportion, because as cultivation is intensified, the return to capital and labour declines. The countries with more intensive cultivation not only have higher farm incomes per hectare, but also much higher farm incomes *per head* of farm population, since the farm density is much lower.

The level of farm income in Poland, 52 gold francs per hectare (roughly £1 per acre) must mean a very low money income per head, since there are only 1·3 hectares per head of

[1] Family farm earnings, or farm income, is the income which remains after all the costs other than the labour of the farmer and his family have been deducted; it represents 'the sum which the farmer could have spent on his needs without decreasing the farm capital'.

THE STANDARD
OF LIVING (1)
Western Hungary.
German village
Vemend, with one
child system

farm population. From the farm accountancy results it is possible to get a rough indication of the difference in farm earnings per head by comparing the cost of labour per day; in Switzerland it amounts to 1·47 gold francs, in Czechoslovakia to 0·60, and in Poland to 0·13 gold francs. At best, the Polish farmer can obtain a money income per head equal to one-third of the income of a German peasant, one-sixth that of a Danish peasant.

Of course, the money value of farm income is never an exact indication of its purchasing power. But the comparison of money incomes tends to underestimate the difference in real incomes, comparing Western Europe with the East, because in the agrarian States the purchasing power of farm produce is much lower than it is in the industrial countries, so that if purchasing power were taken into account the difference would be greater still.

What, however, does this low level of money income mean in terms of food, housing, and clothing? In the agrarian countries there has been a decline in physical output per head and in the purchasing power of farm produce since 1929, so that there must necessarily have been a fall in the peasant's standard of living. In some regions the peasantry have been reduced to destitution, in others, sections of the population can still live on a fair standard; and the first thing necessary in discussing the effects of recent changes is, of course, to find a way of measuring incomes in different regions for the bulk of the farm population, and to draw a poverty line which corresponds to the peasant's own ideals of economic well being.

In Eastern Europe this means simply to ascertain where the food supplies are sufficient, i.e. to ascertain where the average output per head is sufficient to feed the population from harvest to harvest. In Poland a rich village is one which has bread all the year round. In Rumania and the southern regions the question is a little more complicated, since maize is more plentiful and there is less actual corn shortage: but the test can be the same.

The simplest way of making the calculation is to calculate the average physical output per head in each of the provinces. Of course, such a calculation only furnishes a rough guide to the variation in income, but it may be used to bring out the contrast in levels of income which are due to differences in population density and farming systems. Unfortunately for a general comparison it is only possible to use corn output per head, because statistics are inadequate. In Western Europe, of course, meat and milk are more important than corn production, and if they were included the level of output per head would appear much higher. Still in a mixed farming system the corn output does reflect the productivity of labour in general. (Switzerland must be omitted altogether from the comparison, since grazing plays such a large part in its farming system.)

The table on p. 84 is an index of output per head for the countries of Central and Eastern Europe. Only the cereals index is based on actual figures: the milk and meat figures are estimates based on the number of animals, and are given to show that the meat production is never enough to offset the low cereals output.

The map shows the level of cereals output per head of farm population in all European countries (except Switzerland and Austria, which are predominantly meat and milk producers). In Europe as a whole we can distinguish three levels of productivity, which correspond to three different standards of living:

1. The first level is that of the rural communities which exist in predominantly industrial countries and sell the bulk of their produce. This includes the whole of Western Europe, Great Britain, Germany, Denmark, and the Western half of Czechoslovakia, which show a level of over 20 quintals per head, owing to their high yields and low farm density.

France, with its smaller yields, shows a considerably lower level, just over 12 quintals per head.

A level of output comparable to that of France is attained by Western Poland, Transdanubian Hungary and the Plain, and the Danubian Province of Jugoslavia (the present Dunavska banovina, which covers fertile regions in the former Voivodina and Banat). These rich districts are either those with an industrial market and an intensive agriculture—such as the western provinces of Poland, from which there was a strong movement of labour to German industry in the pre-war period; or districts with a relatively sparse population and a rich soil, such as the Banat and Voivodina districts.

THE STANDARD OF LIVING (2)
Czechoslovakia, Central Slovakia

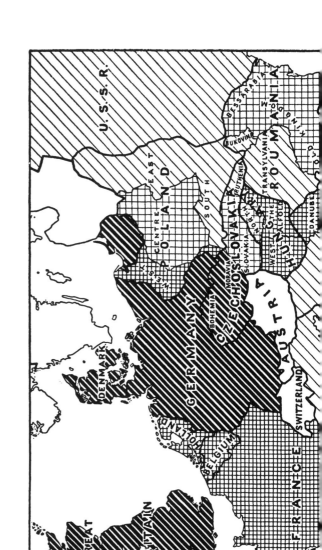

Production per head of Farm Population, 1928–32

	Cereals*	Meat	Milk	Total
Czechoslovakia:				
Bohemia	21	9	14	44
Moravia and Silesia . . .	19	6	12	37
Slovakia	10	2	5	17
Ruthenia	3	1	4	8
Hungary:				
West Hungary . . .	14	6	4	24
Great Plain	13	4	2	19
Northern Hungary . . .	9	3	2	14
Poland:				
Central	11	2	4	17
Western	19	6	9	33
Southern	5	2	4	11
Eastern	7	2	3	12
Rumania:				
Old Kingdom	10	1	2	13
Bukovina	4	1	2	7
Transylvania	7	1	2	10
Bessarabia	10	1	1	12
Jugoslavia (1929–32) Provinces:				
Danube	17	4	2	23
Sava	6	2	2	10
Drava	2	1	3	6
Drina	8	2	1	11
Verbas	6	2	2	10
Zeta	3	1	2	6
Morava	7	1	1	9
Vardar	5	1	2	8
Primoria	3	1	1	5
Bulgaria	7	1	2	10

* Including potatoes as ⅛ of 1 quintal of cereals.

Where rural poverty exists in these regions, it arises from income distribution, not low productivity. About two-thirds of the farm output is sold.

2. Second, the regions where the average output is sufficient, about 10 quintals of cereals per head, and there is no shortage for those who have the average. But because the average is a minimum, all those who have less than the average amount per head (the numbers will be estimated later) must go short of food. About one-third of the farm output is sold, in Rumania about one-half.

THE STANDARD OF LIVING (3)
Slovakia. *Bardejov market*
Rumania. *Liberal party meeting at Campulung*

This group includes the regions with rather denser population and lower yields, Central Poland, Slovakia, the Old Kingdom of Rumania, and Bessarabia. The standard of living is low as regards the consumption of industrial products, yet can be regarded as adequate, so far as food is concerned.

3. Finally, there are regions with less than 10 quintals per head, which stand out as poverty-stricken, in the sense that the bulk of the population is inadequately fed. Yet although the food supply is inadequate about one-quarter of the farm output is sold, in some quarters one-third.

This group includes areas with different kinds of farming systems: in Poland the southern and eastern provinces; in Rumania the province of Transylvania; in Jugoslavia, Croatia (now known as the Sava Province), Bosnia, now the provinces of Drina and Verbas; and the Vardar Province (N. Serbia). Bulgaria's position is probably rather better than it appears, as these were years of bad harvests: 1930–4 would give a better result. Further, the production of industrial plants of high value is increasing. The country is so much divided into small valleys with special cultures that the general average probably tells little.

There are few areas with even less than 500 kg. per head. These are Ruthenia, the Dalmatian coast (Primoria Province), South Serbia (the Vardar Province), and Montenegro (the Zeta Province). These are regions where the peasants do not live mainly from agriculture; they are shepherds with patches of land in the valley for maize. Slovenia (the Drava Province) is a poor province where much of the population works in forests and in domestic industries.

The big difference between the West European industrial zone and the other countries shows that the most important factor in determining farm output per head is proximity to the market, or rather inclusion in an industrial economy. Hungary and Western Poland have higher incomes for this cause also, though they have now been cut off from their old markets. In the other regions, almost entirely agrarian, the main factors influencing output are the density of the population and soil conditions. As we have seen in the preceding chapter, on the basis of labour requirements, a farm population over 70 to the 100 hectares of farm land means that there is some redundant labour; and if yields are below 10 quintals to the acre this density also means that there is food shortage (70 to the 100 hectares of farm land roughly indicates 1 hectare of arable land per head). Thus the poverty of these regions is due both to land shortage and low yields. In Poland, and to a lesser extent in Rumania, the two are connected—yields are falling owing to the pressure on the land.

To what extent do the figures of average output per head reflect the average income, i.e. how far does the distribution of land ownership affect the distribution of income?

This can be estimated by considering the distribution of land between different classes.[1] In the Balkan regions, Serbia, Bulgaria, Old Rumania, the distribution of income is very equal. Bulgaria probably has the highest degree of equality. The average farm size is 5 hectares, the same as in Czechoslovakia and Switzerland, but the dispersion round the average is very close; there are hardly any large farms.

In all these countries there is a class of landless labourers with much less than the average income per head. This class is largest in Hungary: according to the census of 1930, 43 per cent. of the agricultural population were landless labourers, or possessed less than 1 acre of land. About one-quarter of the total are labourers who have no continuous work, as distinct from the labour permanently employed and resident on the big estates. On the average these labourers work 150 days in the year, at a wage of 3 pengö per day per man and 2 pengö per day per woman. Their average income (including the value of the houses) amounted to 183·4 pengö per year in 1930–1; since then wages have fallen to 1·30 pengö per man, so income per person amounted to 90 pengö per year (which would purchase 270 kg. of bread). Thus about one-quarter of the population earn a starvation wage, though the average output per head in Hungary is high.

On the big farms of Hungary living conditions are as bad as in the worst districts of Poland, owing to the income structure, rather than to the method of farming or the density of population.

Even in the countries mainly under small farms there is a big class of landless labourers. In Jugoslavia an inquiry carried through in 1932 showed that the average family income of the labourers with little or no land had an income per man-

[1] See Chapter VIII.

THE STANDARD OF LIVING (4)

Rumania. Hateg region in
Transylvania.
*Home spun and woven linen
and wool, home tanned shoes
and sheepskins*

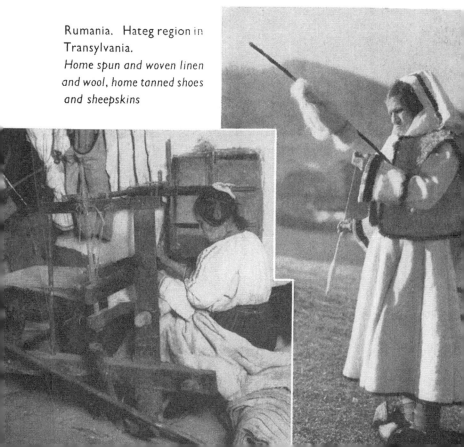

day of 5·71 dinars—about 6*d*., or about 1*d*. per head—roughly equal to 2½ kg. of bread per day. Unfortunately, the Jugoslav statistics are very defective and give no estimates of the numbers without land or with very small holdings; but observation shows that in the over-populated districts this level of income must be fairly general. Till Christmas or till March they can supply their own need for bread; and afterwards eat their goats, wild grasses, weeds, to exist till the next harvest.

In Poland most dwarf peasants, i.e. those with less than 2 hectares, have incomes below the average income per head; the class represents about one-third of the total number.

Thus, in consequence of the low productivity of the land, and to a lesser degree as a result of the inequalities in land owner-ship, there is widespread food shortage, even starvation, for certain periods of the year.

The first cause, low productivity of the land, is the reason for destitution in the districts with less than 8 quintals per head output—Southern Poland, a great part of Jugoslavia,[1] Bulgaria, Transylvania, Sub-Carpathian Ruthenia. In all regions of genuine subsistence farming, the farmer does not produce enough to subsist. In Poland the time before the harvest has a special name, the *przedmowek*, which has come to mean *the hungry months*. Of course, even in these regions there are small sections of the community which by reason of favourable market position or by owning more land than the average can earn higher incomes; but these are only exceptions.

The second cause, distribution of income, is responsible for destitution in the districts where crop production amounts to something like 10–12 quintals per head. Here the supply of bread crops is adequate for the bulk of the population, but because the average is a low one those of the population who do not attain the level must go short of food. In Congress Poland the dwarf peasants—perhaps 20 per cent. of the whole—do not earn enough. In Rumania it is difficult to say what the pro-portion is, as there are no figures to show land distribution.

Of the total peasant population of Eastern Europe of 60 millions probably about one-fourth do not produce enough to

[1] See Memorandum submitted to the League of Nations Nutrition Com-mittee: *Les Régions passives de Yougoslavie*.

satisfy their need for food, in the sense of bread. These are roughly distributed as follows:

3	millions in	Southern Poland	(50 per cent. of the total)				
1½	,,	Central Poland	(25	,,	,,	,,	)
2	,,	Eastern Poland	(50	,,	,,	,,	)
1	,,	Hungary	(25	,,	,,	,,	)
0·15	,,	Slovakia	(15	,,	,,	,,	)
½	,,	Ruthenia	(80	,,	,,	,,	)
1½	,,	Bulgaria	(30	,,	,,	,,	)
2	,,	Transylvania	(50	,,	,,	,,	)
½	,,	Old Kingdom of Rumania	(25	,,	,,	,,	)
3¼	,,	Jugoslavia	(33	,,	,,	,,	)

15¼ millions

(a) NUTRITION

In the first group, the industrial regions, the food supply is adequate both in quantity and quality. Good diets with sufficient animal proteins are general among the peasants in Bohemia and among the richer peasants in Transdanubian Hungary; in these regions the majority of the peasants eat meat regularly three or four times a week. Supplies of pig meat, poultry, eggs, vegetables form a normal part of the diet. Bread is wheat and rye. Coffee and sugar are consumed every day.

In the second group, although corn production is adequate, the diet of the peasants cannot be regarded as satisfactory, if we consider the standard of food from the standpoint of adequate nutrition—adequate in the sense not merely of providing enough energy, but a balanced diet with a correct proportion of proteins, fats, and carbohydrates.

In the Plain districts the chief feature of diet is the high consumption of grain and fat, with little milk. In the Hungarian Plain, the Danube district of Jugoslavia, and the Rumanian Banat, this diet is adequate. The main foods are fine wheat bread, bacon fat, vegetables, and poultry, and the paprika, which supplies the vitamins lacking in the food. This is the diet of the rich and medium peasants; that of the landless worker is of course mainly bread, and is not adequate.

In Hungary the consumption of proteins is higher than in Rumania, although the same high quantity of carbohydrates is consumed. The diet of the medium-sized peasant is rich in

THE STANDARD OF LIVING (4)

Rumania. Transylvania. *Funeral in Meria, Hateg region*
Bukovina. *The meal on the grave*

proteins of animal origin. The consumption of fats by Hungarian peasant families is also much higher than that in Rumanian villages owing to the bigger production of pig fat. Similar consumption habits can be seen in the Banat among the German peasants, whose store-rooms always contain enormous vats of lard. In the Hungarian Plain eggs, chickens, and fruit are plentifully consumed by the larger peasants but not by the poorer.

Probably the worst type of diet is the Rumanian. It consists almost entirely of *mamaliga* (maize pudding) with very little consumption of meat, no consumption of milk in most families, and very few eggs, vegetables, or poultry, though these are produced.

In consequence of this uniform feeding the health condition of the peasantry in Rumania is very bad. The infant mortality rate is 18 per hundred, the highest in Europe. Diseases of malnutrition are very prevalent: 80 per cent. of the children suffer from intestinal parasites. Out of 500 consultations in one village organized by the Sociological Institute of Bucharest over 50 per cent. had diseases due to starvation or to malnutrition, mainly general debility, rachitis, gastro-enteritis, pellagra, anaemia, and goitre.

In Rumania and Hungary the deficiencies of diet are mainly due to the type of farming pursued; the specialization on corn production means too little variety in the produce. In these districts the diet which the peasant family can attain is determined by the number of live stock rather than by the area of the farm. Consequently the diet of Poland in the central districts is from the nutritional standard rather better than that of Rumania, because almost all farms keep a cow; on the majority of peasant farms in Rumania no cow is kept.[1] In Hungary there are peasant farms of 10 hectares which should be large enough to maintain a family, and yet, owing to extensive cultivation and shortage of live stock, the protein supply is poor. In the mountain districts,

[1] A powerful influence on the consumption habits of the population is exercised by the Church both in Poland and Rumania. About 170 days in the year are fast-days on which no meat may be eaten. Consequently the peasant is inclined to regard extra consumption of eggs or meat as morally unjustified and will not attach much importance to increasing his own consumption.

on the other hand, there is shortage of bread, while the milk supply is adequate. The deficiencies are due to the small area of the farm and the poor yields of corn.

In the third group, food is inadequate both in quality and quantity. The typical diet of the mountain regions is that of Ruthenia and Galicia: rye bread, potatoes, sour milk, cabbage,

Annual Consumption per consuming unit in kilograms

	Broniszów (Galicia) 1928	Slovakia 1928	Sub-Carpathian Ruthenia 1928	Bohemia, Moravia, & Silesia 1928
Wheat, rye flour . .	328·0	253·80	269·40	279·62
Potatoes . . .	682·0	246·00	366·00	186·14
Cabbage and green vegetables . . .	81·1	..	..	..
Cream cheese . .	20	4·26	2·59	5·02
Milk	366·1	327·03	346·00	416·50
Butter and fats . .	17·4	15·71	9·48	21·31
Sugar	0·5	18·00	3·90	28·42
Meat	2·0	31·62	17·70	47·84
Eggs (number) . .	10·0	131·00	134·60	224·05
Poultry . . .	..	11·42	6·92	10·40
Fruit	..	47·72	27·20	60·82

and dumplings of potato flour. Poultry, eggs, and meat are never eaten on the farm. In Galicia only about half the peasants can eat their own pig: he must be sold to buy necessities.

The table above shows the contrast between the average consumption per unit in three poor regions and that of the good regions in Czechoslovakia.

The main points of difference between the good diet and the poorer diets is the higher consumption of all foods in Bohemia, excepting flour, which is only slightly higher, and potatoes; the consumption of meat is twice or three times as high, the consumption of milk about 25 per cent. higher.

To improve the diet of large sections of the population it is necessary to diversify agricultural production in the plains; in the mountains the food-supply is inevitably inadequate; and only with a much smaller number on the land could it be made satisfactory from the nutritional standpoint.

RUMANIA (OLD KINGDOM)
Peasant housing in poor village of Stanesti

In the Balkan countries, since the depression began, special action is undertaken to relieve the starving. In Croatia, and many regions of Jugoslavia, free meals are given to all school children; many of the richer Bulgarian villages have also organized regular free meals.

(b) HOUSING CONDITIONS

The housing conditions of the peasant population are not directly determined by the physical output of corn, as their food-supply is. Often the best agricultural districts have worse housing conditions than poorer regions, because in mountain districts the supply of building materials is cheap; but in the areas of black earth soil, which are richer from the point of view of output per head, there is a shortage of timber. Rumanian peasants in the poor hill districts of Muntenia and Oltenia inhabit well-built houses of remarkable comfort and beauty, whereas those on the rich soil of the Danube Plain and Delta live in small mud huts, though the output per head of corn is much larger. Housing conditions in the fertile Hungarian Plain are noticeably bad, in relation to the farm production of the district, owing to the shortage of timber.

Another factor, apart from income, which makes for good housing accommodation in poor districts, is the existence of surplus labour. In Poland in spring, in the long intervals of field work, the peasant families re-thatch the roof and white-wash the walls for Easter. Everywhere much new building is in progress, and most of all in the poorer villages of Galicia and Congress Poland.

In the industrialized regions, of course, rural housing is good. Compared with the spacious two-storied peasant houses of Switzerland and Southern Germany, the Central European peasant house is small and not so well built. But though it is always a one-storied building, its rooms are as a rule larger, better lit, and better ventilated than English farm cottages.

In Bohemia the peasant house usually contains at least three rooms. The house, the gate, and farmyard wall are whitewashed a dazzling white once a year. Nearly all have slated roofs: a very few have thatch or shingle. The houses are all in good repair and are well kept. The rooms are well lit by double windows, have clean wooden floors, furnished with unpainted wooden furniture locally made. All the houses have an indoor water-supply except some of the very small farms; but indoor sanitation, or a sink in the kitchen, is very rare. One-third of the Czech farms have water laid on; two-thirds are supplied with electrical current.[1]

Housing conditions in Hungary vary, owing to the land tenure system and the shortage of timber; in Transdanubia, where wood is plentiful, the houses are large and well built as in Bohemia; in the Plain houses are small and usually the floor is bare earth. The best conditions can be seen in South Hungary and the Banat.[2] Hungarian peasants regard a wooden floor as a sure sign of prosperity. On the Great Plain, in the rich valley of the Tisa, even large peasant houses with 15 hectares of land have no wooden floor, or at most a floor in the bedroom and not in the kitchen. A sample investigation made by Dr. Heller of 1,000 peasant houses shows that only 22 per cent. of the peasant families have wooden floors.[3]

As regards water-supply and sanitation, the Hungarian level is low. Wells are usually shared by two or three houses. It is very rare to find water laid on. Even in Hungarian provincial towns it is usual to find no water-supply; and on the Plain it is possible to find large peasant farms with a bathroom but no water.

In the Old Kingdom of Rumania housing conditions are surprisingly good. Peasant houses are more like villas: they are two stories high with a wide balcony, covered with vines running round the second story, and with three or four rooms in addition to the kitchen. The houses give the impression of comfort, since home industries are highly developed; the beds are covered

---

[1] See the Czechoslovak Census of Agriculture, *Czechoslovak Statistics*, vol. lxxxvi, 1932.

[2] A custom which seems peculiar to South Hungary and the Banat is the construction of a very large house mainly for purposes of display. In the Rumanian Banat it is usual to find German houses where the family is living in one room in a large four-roomed house; the other three rooms are large and lofty, with wooden flooring and furnished densely with town-made furniture, but are hardly ever entered by the family.

[3] István Heller, 'Magyar Gazdák Szemléze', *A cseledek és falusi népünk-lakasviszonyai.*

WESTERN HUNGARY
PEASANT HOUSING
Big peasant farm of
20 hectares,
Dobrököz

Medium peasant farm
of 16 hectares
exporting
lucerne seed

Farm of 6 hectares
fattening pigs

with linen sheets and woollen blankets, the floors with woollen rugs which are produced at home. This is mainly true of the districts in the hills and the borders of the Plain. In the Plain itself and in Bessarabia building materials are scarce and houses are built of mud with one room and kitchen only, of the same type as in the Ukraine.

In the poorer regions overcrowding is fairly common. The Czechoslovak Census of Agriculture shows the number of rooms per person, and thus the extent of overcrowding.[1] Though these figures relate to one country only, they serve to bring out very clearly the contrast between three regions with very different standards of living: Bohemia, typical of industrialized agriculture; Slovakia, a somewhat over-populated region, representative of East European conditions (which is, however, as a whole, much less densely populated than Galicia); and Ruthenia, representing the primitive and destitute. According to the census, over five people to one room are found in one-quarter of the Slovakian farms, one-third of the Ruthenian, and only one-tenth of the Bohemian.

However low the standard seems to be, the primitive wooden huts of Slovakia and Galicia have advanced from something still worse—the 'smoke house' (like the 'black house' of the Hebrides), which prevailed everywhere in the nineteenth century. All the houses now have a big clay stove and chimney. Formerly the house had no chimney; the fire-place was on an open hearth in the middle of the living-room, and the smoke seeped out through cracks in the roof. These houses are very rare now in Galicia and Slovakia, but are almost universal still in the southern districts of Croatia, the district Lika, which is one of the most over-populated agricultural districts in this region. The typical house there has two rooms: the kitchen, which has no window, only a door in the opposite walls leading outside, and an inner room with a tiny window and no floor. In the poorest houses the cattle are housed in the same room. These conditions are probably the worst in Eastern Europe, bearing in mind that they are in an agricultural district in contact with civilization, and not isolated, as Bosnia.

[1] 'Recensement des exploitations agricoles, 1930', *Czechoslovak Statistics*, vol. cxv, III, Part 4, Table 20.

In the eastern frontier districts of Poland, where conditions are typical for White Russia, housing is primitive and sordid. Extreme overcrowding exists because there is no subdivision of the farm; when the children marry they continue to live in their parents' houses. In the village illustrated the average number inhabiting one room is seven people. In some houses 12 or 15 people are living, and in one 24. These rooms are low, with ceilings not more than 7 feet high, with tiny windows which do not open. The only furniture is the stove, a rough table, and benches round the walls, covered with sheepskins.

The prevalence of peasant ownership has a very marked influence on housing standards.

Housing conditions of the agricultural labourers on the estates in Poland and Hungary are as a rule inferior to those of the peasant, comparing the classes, of course, in districts with similar agricultural conditions. The investigation made by Dr. Heller[1] for Hungary shows that for a sample covering 1,186 houses the small peasants had better living conditions, and were less overcrowded, than the permanent farm servants or the landless day labourers. In all classes 70 per cent. of the houses had two rooms; but the housing space for the peasant families was larger as the families are smaller: housing accommodation was better, as regards windows, kitchens, earth-closets, and wooden floors, among the class of small peasants than among the other rural workers. The reason is that the peasant is accustomed to invest savings in his slack periods in repairing and building, and young couples build a house at the back of the farmyard, whereas the labourers' houses remain overcrowded, and no new building is done.

Both in Western and Central Poland and Hungary the permanent workers on the estates live in barracks adjacent to the farm buildings. These are one-storied buildings with a row of dwellings side by side. Each family has as a rule only one room and kitchen. In Western Poland these buildings are well built and well kept up, but in Central Poland and the south they are in a bad state of repair. In Hungary the condition of the buildings depends on the prosperity of the estate, but even on some of the better estates they are in a bad condition, the floors are of earth and the houses are falling to ruin.

HUNGARY. FARM LABOURERS' HOUSING
Cave cottage at Tibbolddaroc
Estate labourers' barracks

The worst housing conditions in Europe, in view of the good level of agricultural technique, can be seen in the villages inhabited by the agricultural proletariat in Northern Hungary, where the labourers live in caves; their earnings have long been too low to build new houses; they have dug holes in the sandstone rock, bricked up the entrance and made cave-dwellings; families of eight and nine children can be found living in degradation even greater than in the poorest eastern parts of Poland. In villages of the same district, where the land is better distributed, the housing standard of the peasants is noticeably much better.

(c) CONSUMPTION OF MANUFACTURED GOODS

Since the crisis there has been a general decline in the consumption of industrial products. Where the purchase of manufactured goods is confined to necessities like salt, shoes, and ploughshares, the effect on the standard of living has been very severe.

The regions can be roughly divided into the same three classes. In countries like Bohemia with industrialized agriculture, the range of industrial goods purchased corresponds in the main to that of the working class in Western Europe, though the goods are inferior in quality: peasants buy regularly coffee, sugar, beer, tobacco, all clothing, shoes and stockings, china and enamel ware for the kitchen, a tiled stove, complete sets of furniture made by the local carpenter, and they subscribe to the party newspaper. Clothing is good though plain. In most regions of Hungary clothing is bought, but the style is the traditional peasant type among women. The equipment of the house also follows traditional lines; pottery is village made.

In the poorer regions, Slovakia, Transylvania, Galicia, a good deal of the clothing is produced at home from wool and flax, woven into coarse white serge for short overcoats or linen for shirts. Men and women wear the high boots, children go barefoot. In these regions the purchase of manufactured goods is confined to tobacco, oil for lamps, matches, an occasional cooking-pot, salt; coffee and sugar are rare luxuries.

Farther to the south, in Rumania and Bulgaria, all clothing

is made at home, often in good fabrics and with great skill. Shoes are made of bark or leather by village craftsmen. Flint and steel are used instead of matches; pig's fat and ashes make soap.

In one direction, boots and shoes, there has been a marked rise in the standard of living in recent years, in the countries where the Czech firm Bata has its factories (Czechoslovakia, Jugoslavia, and Rumania). The price of these standardized goods brings them within the reach even of the poorest peasants: for 3s. the peasant can get a pair of heavy rubber shoes, for 8s. a pair of leather boots. Bata has skilfully adapted the product to the market, producing very heavy rubber boots for farm work, and for the Balkans rubber shoes imitating the traditional Turkish slipper. The low prices of the goods mean a big rise in real incomes.

CHAPTER V

THE EFFICIENCY OF THE FARMING SYSTEM

1. CZECHOSLOVAKIA AND WESTERN HUNGARY

CLASSIFICATION OF REGIONS

W E must now investigate the prospects of increasing the efficiency of the farming system. Over-population in Eastern Europe, as we have seen, simply means that a large proportion of the present labour-supply is redundant with the present system of cultivation. But why should we regard the farming system in these countries as fixed? Those who are familiar with the very far-reaching changes in farming methods in England in recent years, or indeed, in commercial farming everywhere, may naturally ask why these countries do not reorganize their farming. If the farmers can double crop yields they could double the food-supply, and there would not then be any serious problem of food shortage.

But the belief in reorganization neglects certain features of farming conditions in Eastern Europe. It must be remembered that the low yields do not prove bad methods; the average wheat yields which are usual in Eastern Europe are slightly higher than the average in the countries of large-scale farming—the U.S.A. and U.S.S.R., the Argentine and Australia. Consequently the results of farming in these countries really set no standards for the farm populations of Eastern Europe: to use their land in the American or Russian way would only be compatible with the higher standard of living if about three-quarters of them could leave the land. It is true that there are regions where yields are bad because methods are backward; but in most of Eastern Europe the yield is low because soil is cultivated which, with the present resources of the world, ought not to be cultivated at all as arable land, and need not be, if the farm population of these countries were free to move.

To increase the yield per acre the kind of farming which they must imitate is that of Western and Central Europe, which gets a big output per acre of a variety of different products.

But it is only countries with access to an industrial market which show very high yields, or countries which practise high protection; the farming system of Western Europe is a highly peculiar thing, depending, in the first place on the climate and the high rainfall which favours the production of grass and root-crops; in the second place, on the urban market with its high standards of living. A review of the different conditions will show how far it would be possible to raise the standard of living by better organization, or by better farming methods, to the level of the peasantry in regions of intensive cultivation.

To bring out the contrast between farming systems east and west we should draw a farming frontier, east of which live-stock farming is little developed.

The line which divides the regions of intensive and extensive live-stock production can be drawn across Central Europe; on one side of it is Germany, the Western half of Czechoslovakia, and Hungary west of the Danube; and east of it the Hungarian Plain, Slovakia, Jugoslavia, Rumania, and Central Poland. West of this line live-stock feeding forms the principal source of income in most types of farming: genuinely intensive feeding without much bought feeding-stuffs is indicated by a density of 70 horned cattle per 100 hectares of agricultural land (30 to 100 acres). (Where feeding-stuffs are bought the density may easily reach 100 cattle to 100 hectares.) This type of farming is characteristic of Switzerland, Austria, and Southern Germany, and of the western provinces of Czechoslovakia; in fact it prevails everywhere in the Western European industrial zone in connexion with dairy production. It cannot be found anywhere in Eastern Europe, because it needs both favourable market and climatic conditions.

In Eastern Europe the density of live stock per hectare is never anything like as high as this, even under the most favourable conditions, though there is some variation between the regions owing to the difference in climate.

The following tables show the broad lines of division. The figures for average yield of corn crops and live-stock density per 100 hectares are given for Western Europe to show the contrast. Within Western Europe itself, there are two levels of intensity, measured by yields and live-stock density: that of the countries with intensive dairy farming, Denmark, Switzerland, and Holland, and that of the countries with some intensive regions, but in general a more extensive system, Germany and Great Britain.

As compared with this standard of intensity, there are roughly

Crop Yields, 1930–4

	Quintals per hectare		Cwt. per acre	
	Wheat	Rye	Wheat	Rye
Holland . . .	28·8	21·5	23·0	17·2
Denmark . . .	28·7	17·5	23·0	14·0
Switzerland . . .	20·6	20·3	16·5	16·2
United Kingdom . .	22·3	16·9	17·8	13·5
Germany . . .	21·5	17·3	17·1	13·8
Czechoslovakia:				
Bohemia . . .	18·9	20·0	15·1	15·9
Slovakia . . .	14·4	13·5	11·5	10·8
Total . . .	15·9	17·5	12·7	13·9
Poland:				
Western . . .	17·8	13·9	14·2	11·1
Southern . .	9·3	9·6	7·4	7·6
Total . . .	11·7	11·2	9·3	8·9
	Wheat	Maize	Wheat	Maize
Hungary . . .	13·0	16·4	10·4	13·1
Rumania . . .	8·9	10·9	7·1	8·7
Jugoslavia:				
Danube Province .	11·9	20·4	9·5	16·3
Vardar Province .	8·6	9·3	6·9	7·4
Total . . .	10·0	14·5	8·0	11·6
Bulgaria . . .	11·6	12·2	9·2	9·7
U.S.S.R. . . .	7·3	8·5	5·8	6·8

three levels in Central and Eastern Europe. One is a level of intensity comparable to that of Germany and Great Britain: this is attained in the western provinces of Czechoslovakia and Poland, with yields of 14–15 cwt. to the acre and a cattle density of 25 to the 100 hectares of farm land. Then there are regions of lower intensity with yields of 10–14 cwt. and a cattle density of 15 to the 100 acres, represented by Western Hungary and Slovakia; and a still lower level with yields 10 cwt. to the acre and less, and a cattle density of 10 cattle to the 100 acres. This low level is typical of Eastern Europe in general.

The dividing line is clearly marked by the course of the Danube

Live Stock in Relation to Farm Land, 1934

	Per 100 hectares		Per 100 acres	
	Cattle	Pigs	Cattle	Pigs
Holland (1932) . .	102	86	41	35
Denmark (1932) . .	92	148	37	60
Switzerland (1932) .	111(74)*	64(42)	45(30)	26(17)
United Kingdom . .	64	18	26	7
Germany . . .	65	81	26	33
Czechoslovakia:				
Bohemia . . .	71	51	29	21
Slovakia . . .	32	33	13	13
Total . . .	52	40	21	16
Poland:				
Western . . .	41	51	17	21
Southern . . .	46	21	19	9
Total . . .	36	27	15	11
Hungary:				
West Hungary . .	31	55	13	22
Great Plain . .	17	36	7	15
Total . . .	23	40	9	16
Rumania . . .	25	17	10	7
Jugoslavia . . .	28	22	11	9
Bulgaria . . .	32	20	13	8

* Excluding Alpine grazing.

through the middle of Hungary: Western Hungary has a cattle density of 14, the Great Plain only 7. Rumania, Jugoslavia, and Bulgaria carry only 10–12 cattle to the 100 acres, and about two-thirds of these are working oxen, and are not used for the production of meat and milk. East of the Danube the typical small farmer keeps a couple of oxen, or a horse and one pig; a large proportion of farms keep no cow or pig at all. In Poland most peasants keep one cow, but a large proportion cannot afford to eat their pig.

From the tables it is apparent that over Eastern Europe as a whole, farming methods are much less intensive than in the

CENTRAL EUROPEAN LIVE STOCK
Lipitzaner horses, Detva, Slovakia
Rumanian peasant cows
Mangalitsa pigs, Hungary

west, measured either by yield per acre or by number of live stock kept. This difference is due to two factors: the distance of the market for live-stock products, and the dry climate. Nowhere east of Austria is there a developed dairy industry. Live-stock fattening with intensive arable cultivation is practised in Central Europe. East of these regions live-stock feeding is extensive, using mainly maize for pig fattening in the Plain regions and in Poland potatoes.

The difficulty of live-stock production is a great obstacle to capital accumulation. To raise a cow or pig means that the peasant can invest in a very liquid form of capital, which at the same time replaces the fertility of his fixed capital, the soil. But in Eastern Europe the live stock are used mainly for working the soil and barely earn their keep, and the peasant has no way therefore of gradually adding to his capital, except by purchasing more land.

Apart from the effects of tariffs and transport, the cost of producing meat is high in most of these countries, because natural conditions do not favour pasture farming or root growing. Still there are regions where meat production could be much increased. Given a more favourable market for meat, vast supplies of pigs would be available now from Poland and Hungary. So far as milk is concerned, expansion is limited by the cost of transport.

Thus we can make a broad general distinction between farming conditions in Eastern and Western Europe, mainly on the basis of differences in rainfall.

To classify the extensive farming regions in Eastern Europe there are three factors which must be taken into account: rainfall, soil, and climate.

Combining these factors, it is convenient to distinguish two main kinds of region in the zone of extensive cultivation:

1. (a) Regions with good soil (the black earth) and dry climate. These are the Hungarian Plain; the adjoining district in Jugoslavia known as the Danube Province or the Voivodina; the Rumanian Plain, and North Bulgaria. These regions lie south of the vine limit which means that the climate is suitable for fruit and vegetable production; they suffer from drought, and the chief means of increasing

the fertility of the soil would be irrigation. The farm population density is low in Hungary (50), much higher in Rumania (75).

(*b*) Farther to the south are regions in Serbia and Bulgaria with similar soil conditions in the valleys, but a warmer, even sub-tropical climate. These regions resemble the first class in that their main problem is drought. But they differ in that there is no uniformity of soil conditions: much of the grazing land is barren mountain and almost worthless. Farm density is very high (90) in Bulgaria.

2. (*a*) Regions with poor soil and dry climate. Most of these regions lie north of the vine limit. The soil is part of the podsol area, and the climate dry, though not excessively so. The farm density is high (80) in Central Poland.

(*b*) Regions with poor soil and wet climate. These include Galicia (part of which, however, has good soil, the good Carpathian loam, even a little black earth in the east), Transylvania (poor acid soil), Bukovina, East Slovakia, Ruthenia, Croatia (Sava Province), and Jugoslavia south of the Sava. These are all over-populated.

INTENSIVE REGIONS: (i) WESTERN CZECHOSLOVAKIA

As a first step, to get a standard of comparison, we should look at the type of intensive farming which exists in countries of Central Europe where the technical level is good and the standard of living adequate. As an example of these conditions, South Bohemia and Western Hungary can be taken. These are both regions of good farming, but provide a complete contrast in the size of farming units. Bohemia, a highly industrialized region,[1] is mainly a country of large and medium-sized peasant farms; the farms of 25–75 acres, which would be regarded in England as largish small-holdings, take up 40 per cent. of the total farm area. Western Hungary, by contrast, is a region of big farms, and enormous latifundia (such as the Esterhazy estates, with 250,000 acres); over 50 per cent. of the land is farmed in units over 150 acres in size.

[1] See Introduction.

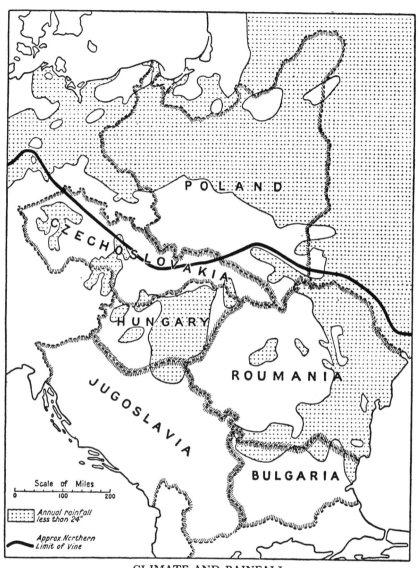

CLIMATE AND RAINFALL

These regions where agricultural production could be intensified by irrigation are
the shaded areas in Hungary and Rumania; these dry districts are roughly the same
as the regions of black earth soil. North of the vine line there is little scope for
intensification

The two regions have similar natural conditions: a high rain-fall (over 24 inches in much of the area), good clay and loam soils. Rotations are practised systematically and artificial manures are used.

The regions also have a similar system of land utilization, with the greater part of the land under arable (70–80 per cent.). The Czech system, however, is much more intensive; cattle are generally stall-fed on hay, roots, sugar-beet pulp, as in Central Germany and Switzerland. In Western Hungary extensive grazing still plays a part, and every village has its common pasture; at sunrise the cowherd, the swineherd, and the goose-herd walk down the village street blowing horns to collect their flocks, which then move off in batches to the pasture, returning at evening, each pig and goose scattering unhesitatingly to its own farmyard.

With this system, live-stock density in Hungary is necessarily lower, only 31 head of cattle to the 100 hectares, as compared with 70 in Bohemia: yields are also lower, 13 quintals of wheat against 18 in Bohemia. The pig density is the same, 50 to 100 hectares; but the type of pig is different: the Czech are light-weight pigs, for pork and bacon, and the Hungarian are lard pigs, the heavy curly-haired mangalitsa, fattened up to 200 kilo-grams, mainly for export. Thus a typical Czech peasant farm of 8 hectares will keep 5 or 6 head of cattle, and feed 4 pigs: a typical Hungarian peasant farm of 14 hectares will keep only 4–5 cattle, but fatten 7–8 pigs.

In both provinces output per man is high, as might be ex-pected with highly capitalized farming and a low density of farm population. The average amount of land per head is 2·0 hectares in Bohemia, 1·7 in Western Hungary, a result partly of the movement off the land, partly of slow population growth in recent years. In Bohemia, owing mainly to the high live-stock density, the physical output per man is roughly double what it is in Hungary.

Owing to the large size of the average peasant farm, the Czech villages show a high level of mechanization. Sowing and reaping are done by hand on the smaller farms, by machines on the medium and larger, though binding is done by hand. Of the two regions, Bohemia is more highly mechanized as to reaping

CZECHOSLOVAKIA, SOUTH BOHEMIA
Typical peasant farms
Autumn ploughing

and drilling machinery. Hungary, as might be expected in a region of large farms, is better equipped with ploughing machinery, usually the old-fashioned steam ploughs. However, not all the Hungarian big estates, by any means, use machines; some even plough with oxen and wooden ploughs. On the Czech peasant farms, on the other hand, horses are mainly used for ploughing, but for other work machinery is general: almost all farms have a small threshing-machine driven by an electric motor, a clover cutter, and a machine for hulling corn. The stables are frequently badly ventilated and small, but usually fitted with water and electric light. One-third of the Czech farms have water laid on; two-thirds are supplied with electrical current. On the larger peasant farms the stables are well built and fitted with automatic water-filling troughs. All farms have milk separators. Manuring is the weak point; there are no containers for the manure and no pumps for the liquid manure. The cultivation of the meadows is neglected; nothing is done to improve grazing.

In Bohemia the money value of farm output is much higher. Corn prices in Czechoslovakia are maintained by the State crop monopoly, and the Czech peasant now gets two or three times the price of wheat received by the Hungarian peasant; thus his higher standard of living is to some extent due to State intervention, though probably only to a small extent, as the prosperity of the region dates back long before corn prices were artificially raised. In South Bohemia, still largely an agricultural region, milk is not sold except in the regions close to towns.

The Czech peasant standard is well up to the West European level. Owing to the lack of a milk market the money income of the Czech peasants in South Bohemia is generally lower than that of Swiss or South German peasants on farms of the same size. As, however, the majority of the farms have a larger acreage than the South German or the Swiss, the actual standard of living of the peasant population is not very different from the German or Swiss standard. Consumption of industrial goods is lower, housing space probably less, than they are in Germany; the consumption of bought foods, coffee, sugar, beer, is probably lower also. The food standard in Bohemia, however, is good, and in view of the greater degree of self-sufficiency, perhaps has more variety than that of the German peasant—geese, cheese, eggs, fruit, vegetables, and mushrooms are generally consumed. Milk with a very high fat content is a staple food, usually consumed as sour milk (*kysela*), with bread or in soup with potatoes—a very usual meal. Soup with vegetables, bread, dumplings with meat (the national dish) are the chief dishes. Butter is eaten with bread (which never happens farther east); bread is rye, baked at home, and ground by the local miller from the peasants' own flour. Meat is eaten once or twice a week; in winter there is the pig, on Sundays a fowl or beef. Coffee is made—a sure sign of wealth in rural communities.

Housing reaches a high standard; construction is good, and the old farm-houses follow a traditional style. Clothing is always bought, ready-made or made by the village tailor or dressmaker: shoes are, of course, Bata's football boots or rubber Wellingtons.

Though it is a peasant standard of living, in the sense that there are no town habits of consumption, no cars, and very few radio sets, it is a good standard, measured by the real necessities—food, water, and electricity.

There is little sign of the 'vanishing world', as a Czech sociologist has described peasant life, no peasant dress, or special style of furniture, no dialect. Though there is a class of peasant employers, there is not any perceptible class division: the workers are not a separate class but are young and unmarried, sons of smaller peasants, or emigrant Slovaks. Only 5–6 per cent. of the total number of farm workers are hired labourers. The distribution of land ownership is so general that village life has a genuinely democratic character. There is no social gulf between the farm with 4 hectares and the farm with 20.

INTENSIVE REGIONS: (ii) WESTERN HUNGARY

In Western Hungary the basis of the farm system is wheat: live stock is relatively much less important than in Bohemia. Consequently the region has been hard hit by the crisis: and the only adjustment apparent is the greater production of lucerne for seed. This is mainly exported to Germany.

NORTH HUNGARY
TAKTAHARKANY ESTATE
(4,000 hectares)

Drilling

Steam ploughing

Hungarian oxen

Sugar-beet train

As to the management of the great estates, it is difficult to generalize. Some, usually the manor farms, are managed on much the same lines as those of the peasants—simply maize and wheat cultivation with subsidiary feeding. On farms of 500–1,000 hectares (1,200–2,400 acres)—very large farms by English standards—the buildings are primitive, with no permanent flooring, and the feeding quite unsystematic. On one good dairy farm, a specialist and prize-winner, sheds had only earth floors with no feeding gangway and no water laid on. Artificial manures are little used, even on big farms. A fairly low level of technique is general among the gentry farms, the name being adopted from England, meaning farms from 500 to 1,000 hectares, farmed by their owners, a large class.

The latifundia owned by the aristocracy are managed in very large units by permanent officials, for the most part with a technical education. The owners themselves rarely reside on the estate. These enormous farms are worked on traditional lines, keeping up a good standard, but not adjusting production to market changes. Some of the estates are extremely conservative, using wooden ploughs and merely living on the fertility of the land.

Others are exceptionally progressive. Such work as that of Manninger, director of the estates of Prince Montenuovo at Németbóly, near Pécs, experimenting scientifically on a big scale, puts the function of the big farm in a new light. Most big estates in Hungary have steam ploughing equipment for deep ploughing, which is considered essential to conserve the moisture of the soil, drought being the main cause of crop failure. This belief has been challenged by Manninger, who has undertaken revolutionary experiments in wheat cultivation. The principle of these new methods is the abandonment of ploughing entirely; instead, the soil gets several harrowings, which conserves moisture better. This new method is based on the recent discoveries on capillary attraction, which have been applied by Manninger to evolve a technique of dry farming for Hungarian conditions. The method implies a big reduction of cost: it would allow the scrapping of most of the steam ploughing machinery in the country, which has been regarded as the *ne plus ultra* of technique. Steam ploughing is roughly three times as costly as ploughing with oxen, and twice as costly as ploughing with tractors. Manninger has also been responsible for the breeding of the famous Bankut wheat, equal to the best Canadian hard wheat, and now generally cultivated all over Hungary.

These new methods of technique and new types of wheat designed for the Hungarian climate are now being generally imitated by bigger farms, an argument for large-scale operation as a means of carrying scientific research into practice.

Against the big estates it can be argued that the entire farm system depends on the existence of casual labour for work at the peak periods of the year, and this labour exists only because the land is unequally distributed. Actually, many of the big estates keep reaping machinery, but, in view of the distress prevailing among the land proletariat, the government in recent years has requested the landowners not to use it. In fact, to use labour is cheaper, since the whole gang of casual labourers cuts the harvest for $\frac{1}{10}$th or $\frac{1}{13}$th of the corn crop with no payment in cash. For sugar-beet the employment of casual labour is essential.

The unequal distribution of land and the low intensity of cultivation causes unemployment among the casual labourers.[1] These labourers come from densely settled regions of extreme poverty and destitution in County Zala, and from County Borsod in Northern Hungary. Roughly a quarter of the population lives below the subsistence line. The condition of the workers on the estates is much dependent on the farm owner; on some estates they are well housed and fed, on others the regulations of the contract are evaded—wages are paid in bad corn, in raw spirits, or by the provision of poor land for the potato patch.

The condition of the peasants, i.e. the medium-sized peasants of 12–29 hectares, who take up perhaps 10 per cent. of the area, is good—not so good, size for size, as in Bohemia, as yields are lower and markets more remote, but none the less their income provides an adequate standard of comfort. House water-supply and electrical current which, as we said, are usual in Bohemia, are here almost unknown.

[1] See Chapter VIII (2) for further discussion.

WESTERN HUNGARY, KOPPANY IN BAKONY HILLS
Peasant cattle grazing
Pigs leaving for pasture

The best peasant villages in Transdanubian Hungary are those of the German settlers. In the Bakony hills, in counties Tolna and Baranya, these have achieved a good standard, dependent, as in the Banat, on large farm units and family limitation for some generations back. They carry more live stock to the hectare than the big farms, but cultivate the land equally well. They are well organized in milk co-operatives. Villages of this type are Véménd and Tevel (see illustration). Farms in these villages average 15 hectares in size, the original unit of settlement in the eighteenth century. Such farms keep 2 horses, 2–3 cows, 2–3 young cattle to feed to a weight of 500 kilograms, 6–7 pigs for fattening to a weight of 100–150 kilograms, selling 3 or 4 and eating the rest. In addition, they sell milk and eggs. Little corn is sold, usually only a few quintals of wheat. Some of the larger peasants, with farms of 25 hectares, specialize in lucerne production for seed and in horse and cattle breeding. Lucerne is the basis of their field system, taking one-third of the area, and has increased in recent years.

The good standard of living in both these regions, it is apparent, depends on live-stock farming; on the maintenance of fairly large peasant farms, i.e. of at least 15 acres in size; and on a low population density due to rapid industrialization.

Thus the conditions under which peasants can attain a good standard of living are as follows:

1. Corn yields of 15–20 quintals per hectare.

2. A cattle density of 30 to 60 per 100 hectares.

3. A farm population density of 50–55 to the 100 hectares.

This combination of factors of production gives a corn output of 20–30 quintals per head and a meat output of 5–9 quintals per head; the total output of corn, meat, and milk per head amounts to 25 quintals in Hungary, 50 in Bohemia (see table in Chapter III).

Now, even taking the lower level of intensity of cultivation, that of Hungary, for comparison, it gives an output per head more than 100 per cent. higher than that of the poorest regions of Eastern Europe, and about 60 per cent. higher than that of the better-off regions like the Old Kingdom of Rumania and Central Poland. To raise the standard of living in these countries to an adequate level, output per head must be increased by at least 50 per cent. in the better-off districts, and by 100 per cent. in the poorer districts. An increase of this scope for the poorer districts is certainly out of the question.

In general the technical change is impossible, owing to natural conditions, which prevent the development of livestock production. Farming of the intensive West European type depends on the use of root crops and green crops in an arable rotation. These crops serve as the food supply of the live stock and, at the same time, are the means of replacing soil fertility. The whole system depends on the maintenance of soil fertility with organic manure. In Eastern Europe this type of mixed farming (in essentials the same as the English system) does not exist. Yields are only half as high, live stock less than half as many to the acre, while farm density is about 50–80 per cent. higher.

There are, however, greater possibilities of advance in some regions than in others. In the regions east of the Danube and south of the Carpathians there is no regular rotation—maize succeeds wheat year after year, and no systematic use of organic manure or root crops. In Western Europe, of course, soil fertility would long ago have been exhausted on these methods. But because the soil of the Danube Plain is the exceptionally rich black earth with a high nitrogen content, it produces fair yields even with bad methods (though now the yields begin to fall). Low yields in these regions are due to bad farming. The fertility of the soil could be restored, and yields increased, by the introduction of lucerne.

In Poland, on the other hand, rotations with leguminous crops are practised; indeed, without high farming the poor, sandy soil would produce very low yields. As regards the methods. of field cultivation, Polish farming in the western and central regions is as advanced and intensive as in Western Europe. But the farm system is one-sided: the soil is too poor and the climate too dry to favour roots; in consequence there is a shortage of feeding-stuffs, and the density of live stock is only half what it is in Bohemia, though slightly higher than in Hungary. Artificial fertilizers are used to make good the deficiency of organic manures; but they are now too costly. The farm system is as intensive as that of Western Hungary, but a much larger farm population lives on the land.

Thus there is a marked contrast between the regions, Hungary and Rumania with good soil and bad farming, Poland with good farming and bad soil.

For the future economic development of these regions, soil and climate are determining factors, and each region must, therefore, be surveyed with reference to its natural conditions.

CHAPTER VI

THE EFFICIENCY OF THE FARMING SYSTEM

II. THE DANUBE PLAIN IN HUNGARY, RUMANIA, AND BULGARIA

THE regions of black earth soil and its different varieties are Hungary (the Great Plain or Alföld); the Banat (now in Rumania); the former Voivodina (now known as the Danube Province of Jugoslavia); the Old Kingdom of Rumania, together with Bessarabia and Dobrogea; and North Bulgaria. Parts of Serbia have somewhat similar characteristics.

In all these regions the soil is excellent, and no amount of bad farming has yet destroyed its fertility. But the whole region labours under the disadvantage of a very dry climate, which causes big fluctuations in yields, and occasionally a crop failure.

1. THE HUNGARIAN PLAIN

The Hungarian Plain is Europe's Corn-Hog Belt, or rather, the region which should be the Corn-Hog Belt if European regions could specialize fully. The greater part of the vast expanse is under corn: wheat and maize, alternating without fallow or green crops. Root crops, clover, and lucerne are not generally cultivated, though now lucerne is being introduced by the big estates and the more progressive peasants. Wheat is grown for sale and export, and generally for home consumption also. Maize is sold if the prices are high; if low, it is fed to lard pigs. Cattle are bred on small farms and sold to big estates where they are fattened on hay, lucerne, and sugar-beet pulp.

But live-stock production is not important; the cattle density to the 100 hectares is only 16 head, most of which are the big white oxen used for farm work. Owing to the low live-stock density, little manure is used: only 19 per cent. of the arable land gets a dressing of stable manure, only 7 per cent. gets artificials. In spite of the low level of cultivation, yields have been maintained.

The great obstacle to raising the corn yield (the average

THE HUNGARIAN PLAIN

Typical 15 hectares farm, producing pigs, maize, and poultry

wheat yield in 1930–4 was only 13 quintals) is the drought which occurs one year in four and causes great fluctuation in output. Not only is the rainfall low, but the evaporation is very fast. Irrigation could do much to improve yields and would enable farmers to grow more intensive crops.

The weakness of the farming system is its low intensity and conservatism. Most small farms of 15 acres or less continue on the old lines, relying mainly on the sale of corn, keeping a couple of horses, or oxen, 10–20 pigs, and 50–100 head of poultry.

Cultivation is getting more extensive. There has been a big decline in the number of live stock per acre and per head of agricultural population since the pre-war period. In the Alföld, horned cattle have declined from 23 head per 100 hectares in 1911 to 16 in 1930, and from 111 to 64 per 100 farm workers in agriculture. Pig production has declined also. This must be due to the influence of big estates as well as to tariffs, since in other States live stock has increased since the pre-war period. At the same time maize production has increased, about 20 per cent.—an ominous sign of intensification on peasant farms and a fall in the standard of living, since it is not being fed to live stock.

On some farms in the Southern Alföld the beginnings of intensification can be seen. This can be attributed partly to the relatively greater importance of big peasant farms of about 50 hectares (120 acres) in this region. Many of these in recent years have begun to produce fruit and poultry as subsidiary to wheat, and to give up pig fattening. Round Oroshaza and Bekescsaba, where there are export centres, poultry feeding is beginning on a large scale and standardization is being introduced. In recent years Hungarian poultry exports have increased to three times the pre-war level, and now amount to the same value as wheat exports. Most of this production is concentrated in this district, and the result can be seen in a better standard of living. Fruit is concentrated mainly round Szeged and Kecskemet, and output is also expanding rapidly. In general, however, ignorance of proper methods is a great drawback and planting is usually undertaken only with advice from a technical expert, whose services do not seem to be sufficiently organized.

As regards organization, the Hungarian peasants of the Plain are far behind the Bulgarian and Polish, not to mention the Czechs. This lack of organization is no doubt due to the divergence in interest between large and small farms. The big farmers are concerned only to maintain wheat prices and do not turn to new lines of production.

The social conditions of the Plain are highly peculiar. Unlike the rest of the European country-side, it is settled in isolated farms. This type of settlement goes back to Turkish times: during the Turkish occupation the peasants took refuge in the towns, forming the extraordinary conglomerations of town-villages in the Plain. After the Turks left they emerged and built cottages on their land, but continued to live part-time in the towns. To-day the vast stretches of the Plain are covered by big estates (40 per cent. of the area) and thousands of little scattered homesteads, the '*tanya* world', on the outskirts of the villages. Though the farms are attached to a village or a town administration, actually they may lie fifteen or twenty miles away from it: big stretches of the Plain have no villages at all. The towns of the Plain, Bekescsaba, Oroshaza, Hódmezövá-sarhely, are villages in fact and appearance, without drainage or water-supply, and with a parish administration, though in size they are towns with a population of 10,000 to 30,000. Even the largest towns are half villages. Szeged has a population of 140,000 and half of the inhabitants are peasants. There is therefore no village life of the ordinary kind: for instance, the County of Bekes has a total area of 640,000 hectares with only 28 villages, each containing on an average 11,800 inhabitants and having an area of 22,840 hectares. This gives peasant life its special characteristics.

In spite of the crisis, and in spite of the low technical level, these small farms in the Southern Plain make an impression of crude plenty: there is no organization, order, or comfort, but every little farm-house is hung with vines, its garden is thick with pumpkins, poppies, sunflowers, and tomatoes, twice their English size; its drying shed bursts with maize cobs; fat pigs, turkeys, and geese wander about in the stubble, strings of crimson paprika hang under the eaves; earth and sun seem to produce all this without much human assistance. The house is

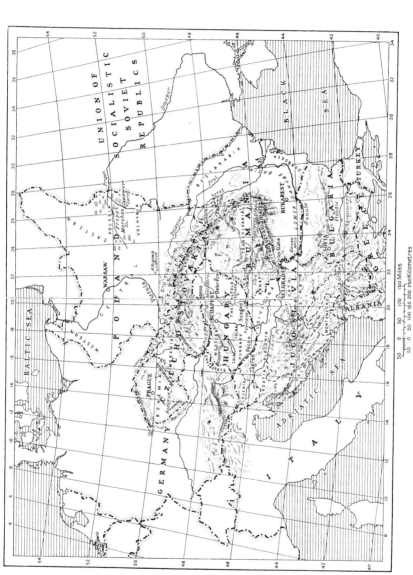

EASTERN EUROPE

Physical and Political Features, showing the regions and villages described

neglected, with an earth floor, and has low rooms stuffed with bedding and pottery; the water-supply is the primitive well with its long well sweep.

The fact that under this system a section of the peasants has an adequate standard of living is due to the low farm population density (57 farm population to the 100 hectares farm land). But the land is unequally distributed: though the medium-sized peasants are well off, there is acute poverty among two large classes—the small tenants on the land belonging to the towns, and the villagers in the Nyirség (near Debrecen). On the outskirts of the towns labourers rent land from the municipality, and owing to the prevalence of unemployment bid up rents, and begin to farm without capital and paying high rents. Round Debrecen and Szeged these settlers can be seen living in temporary shacks of clay, with a few hens and pigs. In the northern villages of the Nyirség the soil is poor and yield low: the condition of the peasant labourers is among the worst in Europe. The houses are low thatched huts with one room, and the population, which contains Slovak and Ruthene elements, lives on the verge of starvation, as seasonal labourers on large estates which cannot employ them full time.

2. THE BANAT AND THE VOIVODINA (IN RUMANIA AND JUGOSLAVIA)

These regions are the islands of prosperity.

The southern half of the Hungarian Plain (in its geographical meaning), which now lies outside the frontiers of the present-day Hungary, in Jugoslavia and Rumania, has prosperous and progressive agriculture. The technical level is much higher than that of the Plain district in Hungary (the Alföld) and that of the Old Kingdom of Rumania, though soil and climate conditions are much the same. These districts were the former provinces of the Banat and the Voivodina, now divided between Jugoslavia and Rumania. (The Rumanian part of the Banat is the counties of Arad and Timiş between the Tisa, Timiş, and Mureş; the rest of the Banat and the Voivodina are now included in Jugoslavia as the Danube Province.) For Jugoslavia and Rumania the possession of a part of this rich region is of great importance, for it was the granary of the Old Monarchy, producing the finest wheat and heaviest maize crops in Europe. In these provinces the amount of arable land per head—3·9 hectares—is about four times the level of the other provinces of Jugoslavia and Rumania; yields are about 60 per cent. higher.

The main reasons for its prosperity are: first, the black earth soil; and second, the systematic colonization of the area in the eighteenth century in medium-sized peasant farms. In 1718, when the Turks ceded the province to Austria, the Plain was barren and depopulated; the Hapsburgs settled it with Germans, Rumanians, and Serbians, not anticipating the growth of national feeling. Holdings of 15 to 20 joch were given (8–10 hectares), then, as now, an adequate size for a family to feed itself. The Swabian stock has kept itself apart from the surrounding population, and, by limiting the size of the family, has maintained the size of the original holdings intact. The Rumanians appear to follow the same custom. In the pre-war period wheat prices were good, farms were large, and in consequence the general standard of living is comparable with that of Bohemia and Germany, and better than that of the Plain region in Hungary.

The type of farming is extensive, as in the Hungarian Plain, and too dependent on wheat and maize; but rotations are more advanced, machinery is more general, yields of wheat and maize are high; in the Rumanian Banat wheat is 12 quintals to the hectare, and in the Danube Province, 11½; maize 13 in Banat, and 20 in the Danube Province.

As regards change in production, the region is no more progressive than Rumania or Hungary; live-stock density is about the same as in the Hungarian Plain, less than in the Old Kingdom of Rumania. In the Rumanian Banat, though the general level of technique and the standard of living are undoubtedly very high for Central European conditions, there is an ever-increasing landless population.

3. RUMANIA: THE OLD KINGDOM

In Rumania the same conditions exist as in Hungary: good soil, frequent drought; but the methods of cultivation are worse than in Hungary. In the Old Kingdom of Rumania the type of cultivation on the Plain is the most primitive and extensive

RUMANIA
Fibis in the
Banat
Live stock on rich
peasant farms

imaginable; agriculture means simply cultivation of wheat and maize with very little subsidiary production. No rotation or fallows are practised. Wheat succeeds maize year after year, and lucerne is rarely introduced. If maize is not planted immediately after the frosts cease, it cannot escape the drought of July and August; hence early planting is absolutely necessary, but yet it is often delayed and the crop is lost in consequence.

In the Plain district there is an absolute uniformity in methods of cultivation; it is sufficient to describe the method of production in one village to illustrate the technical weaknesses of this type of farming over the whole country.

This village, Goicea Mica, is situated in the County of Dolj, near Portaresti, a few miles from the Danube, and has a population of 2,458 people and 645 families. The arable land amounts to 2,138 hectares, 0·88 hectare per person and about 3·3 hectares per family.

The whole area of the village is under corn and looks like a single big farm, as all peasants sow the same crop on their individual strip side by side, just as they did when they worked the land as share-croppers before the agrarian reform. Year after year wheat alternates with maize with no green crops and no fallow.

Most of the processes of cultivation are done by hand. The village owns four drilling machines and a few threshing and winnowing machines. Ploughing is done by ox teams or by double teams of oxen and horses. The main defect of cultivation is that the autumn ploughing is neglected entirely; the stubble remains in the fields for the animals to graze on until the following spring. Very little live stock is kept.

The great weakness of peasant farming in all these dry regions, the high proportion of working animals and shortage of productive live stock, is very evident here. The larger farms of 5 hectares carry one horse or a couple of oxen, four or five sheep, and one pig. At least one-third of the peasants have no cow and the smaller peasants no draught animals. In this village the amount of live stock is lower than it is in the country as a whole, perhaps owing to epidemics.

There is no method of utilizing the animal manure: it is frequently burnt as fuel or used to build pigsties. Systematic feeding of the live stock is unknown; oxen and pigs are fed simply with maize stalks and cobs; sheep are grazed in the summer by the Danube. The cost of maintaining the working animals is low, so the peasants do not try to cultivate lucerne. Epidemics among pigs are very frequent, and in consequence few are kept.

The surprising thing is that the land produces any crop at all with this system. Yet the black earth soils are so rich that this type of cultivation can go on producing a yield of 8–14 quintals per hectare (with violent fluctuation due to drought). But yields are gradually falling off. In the County of Dolj (much above average for Rumania, where yield is 10 quintals per hectare) wheat yields have declined from about 16 quintals in the pre-war period to about 13 at the present time.

As farms do not vary much in size, the gross income can easily be calculated: from 3·3 hectares the income would be 40 to 50 quintals of maize and wheat, of which about 30 quintals of wheat is sold, and the maize retained for consumption by the family and the farm live stock. Thus the system only *can* exist with a very low standard of living; unless the chief food was maize, the peasants could not produce enough cereals to feed themselves and the oxen and horses.

This system of farming requires heavy application of labour at certain times, mainly for hoeing the maize (which must be done three times), and in the harvest; but for long periods in the year peasants are not working at all. Under a system of this kind the size of farm obviously has very little importance; it is characteristic of Rumania that as soon as a peasant gets more land than the minimum required for family subsistence, he rents out the remainder on a share-cropping system, dividing the crops half and half between himself and another peasant who works the land. In this village three or four peasants who are grain merchants are the only rich peasants of the village.

The remarkable feature of this very primitive type of cultivation is that field work is carried out along very uniform lines, as if the peasants were working under orders. All field work is done at roughly the same time in the same way, and yet there is no co-operation or social organization at all in the village. Consequently technique suffers from the absence of machinery

RUMANIA, Goicea Mica in the Old Kingdom
Primitive irrigation.   Ploughing on the black earth soil

which could get the sowing done early. Delay in sowing the maize and wheat is frequently the cause of the failure of the crop, because it does not reach maturity before the dry season. To maintain the yield it is absolutely necessary to select early ripening varieties and to plant immediately after the frosts cease.

Given better methods of cultivation, which would imply mainly the use of machinery and greater uniformity in seed or sowing, the yields of wheat and corn ought easily to be raised by 50 per cent. It should also be possible to improve the efficiency of live-stock production by injection against disease and by introducing lucerne as a green crop for feeding. There is, however, no possibility of intensifying live-stock production very far in this climate. But the real need of the region is irrigation, rather than any improvement in methods. The development of vegetable production could be easily undertaken if the land were irrigated. A few peasants have, in fact, constructed a very primitive water wheel to irrigate part of the village fields, which produce very heavy crops of tomatoes and melons. (See illustration.)

In the villages of the Danube Plain in Rumania there is no acute pressure of population on the means of subsistence as there is in Poland, simply because the soil is rich and the yield good in spite of the bad methods of cultivation. But the one-sided cereal production is a grave danger to the health of the peasant. In most villages there must be increasing difficulty in employing an increasing population at the same standards so long as these methods are adhered to. The danger is that under the present methods yields will continue to decline. To prevent this from occurring a system must be introduced which will compel a better utilization of the soil and more variety of cropping.

In the Carpathian foot-hills bordering on the Danube Plain the population density is higher and the standard of living much lower. The farming system is the typical Balkan mixture, each farmer keeping a few sheep on remote pastures, cultivating a patch of maize, vines, or plum trees in the valley. In these conditions much larger differences of income exist; a type of capitalist peasant arises who owns the processing equipment —vats for storing brandy, wine cellars, or primitive wooden machinery for wool combing. In these villages a very large proportion of the peasants own less than 1 hectare of land; 40–50 per cent. of the families have no cow or goat. As to actual food shortage, the poverty of this region is perhaps not as great as in Poland or Transylvania, but as the diet is exclusively maize the condition of the people appears far worse. The diet is responsible for prevalence of gastro-enteritis, goitre, and rickets; 80 per cent. of the children have intestinal parasites; the rate of infant mortality is high, and brutal methods are used to cause abortion.

4. BULGARIA

In Bulgaria agriculture is partially highly intensive, producing crops of high value to the hectare, such as grapes, tobacco, and vegetables; partly extremely extensive, even nomadic in character. Indeed, it is more gardening and grazing than agriculture in its usual sense. One and the same farm can combine both types of farming, working a plot in the fertile valley and keeping sheep in the barren hills.

North Bulgaria, between the Balkans and the Danube, has more or less the same conditions of labour and production as Rumania: maize and wheat cultivation by primitive methods on small farms. The system suffers from the defects which have already been described, the excess of working horses and the low standard of machine and manure technique. But the peasants in Bulgaria are far more enterprising and progressive than the Rumanian:[1] the co-operative movement is well developed, with banks in every village and the greater part of agricultural sales under its control. Lucerne is being introduced more generally, and cattle breeding improved more rapidly, than in Rumania.

South of the Balkans and north of Rhodope, agriculture takes on the characteristic Balkan character. There are two regions

---

[1] This is true of the peasants as a class; by contrast, the leaders of the Bulgarian peasant parties are mediocre politicians, while the Rumanian peasant parties have produced men of high ability and character.

RUMANIA

Goicea Mica. Typical 5 hectares farm growing wheat and maize

of intensive agriculture, South-West Bulgaria (the tobacco and rose region) and the Plovdiv valley, the centre of the vine-growing and vegetable region. Over the whole country, in all regions, small farms predominate; though the average size is not lower than in Czechoslovakia or Switzerland—an average of 6 hectares to the farm—the distribution round the average is much closer than in any country of Eastern Europe. There are no large farms and the dwarf holdings are not over-important (17 per cent. of the number under 2 hectares as compared with 33 per cent. in Poland). Roughly one-third of the total *area* is taken by each group of farms (not properties): 2–5 hectares, 5–10 hectares, 10–30 hectares, and only 5 per cent. over 30 hectares. The custom of renting land is widely prevalent among smaller holdings, as in Rumania. The distribution of ownership has remained more or less unchanged over the last fifty years, though there is now a very clearly marked tendency to increase the number of properties in the two smallest size groups.[1]

As typical of farming conditions in South-Eastern Bulgaria, a Thracian village may be selected, for which special results from an agricultural survey are available. This is Brestovitza, a village specializing in grape production in the district of Plovdiv, at the foot of the Rhodope mountains. It is above the average in income, since it produces the high-quality dessert grapes for export, which arrive in England in October.

The district has the typical red soil and dry uncertain climate; it suffers frequently from drought. The density of farm population is high, only 0·7 hectare per inhabitant and 3·4 per family. All the holdings are small and are distributed as follows: up to 2 hectares, 12·5 per cent.; 2·5 hectares, 42·2 per cent.; 5–7½, 22·5 per cent.; 7·5 to 10, 11·5 per cent.; and 10–15, 11 per cent. Of the land belonging to the village, 30 per cent. grows corn, 10 per cent. is fallow, 52 per cent. is vineyard, 5 per cent. industrial plants, the remaining 2 per cent. gardens and meadows.

In view of the large area under vines, the working live stock is excessive—195 oxen and 25 working cows, 657 horses and

[1] Zagoroff, 'Die Grundbesitzverhältnisse in Bulgarien', in Molloff, *Die sozialökonomische Struktur der bulgarischen Landwirtschaft.*

330 asses and mules—a total of 1,207 working animals for an area of 2,816 hectares, or 44 to 100 hectares. The producing live stock are very few, only 13 cows, 1,916 sheep, 4,002 poultry; 360 households had no producing live stock.

Compared with the rest of Bulgaria, the village is relatively advanced in mechanization. Of the total number of ploughs, 670 were iron and 180 wood—in the country as a whole, wooden ploughs still outnumber the iron. Threshing is partly done by machinery and partly by oxen treading out the corn, as in Jugo-slavia.

The rotation followed in most of the country is wheat alternating with fallow; but in this region a three-year rotation has now been introduced: maize has been sown on part of the fallow land and the industrial crops are cultivated on the rest of the fallow. In all Bulgaria about half the harvest is threshed by machine: the existing number of machines is enough to thresh the whole crop, but they are not fully utilized, partly because their owners often exact too high a price from other peasants.[1] This excess of machinery is, as we shall see in Chapter VIII, a common feature of peasant agriculture.

From the experience of this village it is possible to draw a conclusion of very far-reaching significance: that is, that the intensification of labour in the direction of production of high-value crops, such as grapes, creates a demand only for seasonal labour at very low rates of pay. Though this region has carried intensification to extreme lengths and represents the highest level in the country, the change in production has not been sufficient to absorb the surplus population, and probably could not do so.

Though progress has been made, intensification of new crops has not gone very far in Bulgaria as a whole. Most of the special crops have long been cultivated. In recent years the industrial plants have increased, taking up 4·3 per cent. of the total area; vineyards have increased slightly and rose gardens declined; fallow has declined from 20 per cent. of the cultivated area to 12 per cent., and so has the area under communal pasture.

[1] To avoid exploitation the Ministry of Agriculture has fixed a percentage of the crop as the charge for using the machine.

Thus the conversion to more intensive types of agriculture is only now beginning, and it is doubtful if it can go much farther. The main reason is the risk of specialized production for a small farm: unless the peasant has much more security for the market of a new product than he has now, he will continue to produce corn. The main cause of uncertainty is the tariffs on these goods. To give an instance of how tariff policy can prevent the swing over to new methods: in the Plovdiv region factories have recently been built to can tomato and strawberry pulp for export, and to do this land has been irrigated with water from an electrical power-station in Rhodope, which was constructed at a high cost with foreign capital. Now tariffs have been imposed by Great Britain on tomatoes and strawberry pulp, the market for the goods is lost, the cost of continuing the power-station cannot be met, and the plant works only to one-third of its capacity. Given wider markets the possibility of expanding this type of production may be quite large, though most of the land must be used for corn, but at present the risk is too great.

In every line of agriculture the government makes efforts to raise the technical level; the service of agronomes is well developed; the breeding-stations work wisely, aiming at raising the standard of the home-bred bull, and are supported by live-stock co-operatives. But in spite of good organization, milk and corn yields are still low, and no great advance can be seen in mechanization.

Does this good organization appreciably affect the level of farm income as compared with countries where organization is weaker? On the basis of the output-per-man calculation, farm income in Bulgaria appears lower than in the Old Kingdom of Rumania.[1] This is because the Old Kingdom has a lower density of population and the index shows cereal crops only. If all crops were included, the position of Bulgaria would be better. Organization has not done much to raise the standard of living, which remains low: in many things the Bulgarians keep to the old Turkish ways, refusing to sleep in beds or sit on chairs. But the great merit of the co-operative system is that it stimulates the change over to other types of product,

[1] See Chapter IV.

and mobilizes the peasants' savings for corporate investment. Yields are increasing, and output per head probably is maintained. By contrast with Rumania, it appears that organization can make an appreciable difference to the rate of development, even if it cannot raise the standard of living in the short period.

CHAPTER VII

THE EFFICIENCY OF THE FARMING SYSTEM

III. POLAND, TRANSYLVANIA, JUGOSLAVIA SOUTH OF THE SAVA

1. POLAND: CENTRE AND EAST

MOST of Poland—except Galicia—is part of the great podsol area which stretches across Europe from Eastern Germany to Northern Russia (see map on p. 103). This soil is very poor in humus and only produces good yields with heavy application of artificial manures and green crops ploughed in.

This kind of farming is practised, with very high yields, in East Prussia and Pomerania, but in Germany the high yields are due to the tariff, which makes heavy artificial manuring profitable. In the parts of Poland formerly included in Germany the farming system is now much less intensive than it was before the War, and yields per head have declined.

In Central Poland agriculture is concerned entirely with rye and potatoes, with pigs only as potato eaters. Owing to the unsuitability of the climate for roots, cattle feeding is not general: the cattle density is lower (35 per 100 hectares) than in Central Europe, though higher than it is in the dry regions of Hungary and Rumania.

Considering the use of artificial manure yields are not high, amounting to 12–16 quintals to the hectare. Because the peasant farms buy less artificials than the estates, their yields are lower as a rule by about 20 per cent. On this farming system it appears that the peasant farm is at a disadvantage, since the fertility of the soil seems to depend far more than it does elsewhere on artificial rather than organic manure. Live-stock density is much higher on peasant farms, 45 to the 100 hectares against 25 on the large estates.

Both on big farms and small the same rotation is followed:
(i) potatoes with clover;
(ii) oats or barley with clover;
(iii) clover or lupines;
(iv) rye or wheat.

The bad climatic conditions necessitate keeping many horses for field cultivation (14 horses to 100 hectares is the density of the central districts). This is characteristic both of large farms and peasant farms; no ploughing machinery is used, either on estate farms or on peasant farms; on estate farms, and to some extent also on peasant farms, sowing and harvesting machinery is used. Power-driven machinery is used only for threshing.

However, though there is very little difference in methods of cultivation on estate and peasant farms, the disposal of the crop is quite different, the large estates selling crops, the peasant feeding them to live stock. In the more progressive villages, both try to achieve a type of farming which is suited to their size, the big farm planting crops with a high seasonal demand for labour, the peasants attempting to increase live-stock production and to spread their labour requirements, but with very poor results.

The distribution of property is much more equal in Congress (Central) Poland than in the western provinces. The farm density is high; 81 farm population to the 100 hectares of farm land. In these central districts the medium-sized peasant farms of 5–20 hectares take 45 per cent. of the total area. There are very few larger peasant farms, like those in Bohemia.

Both the peasant farms and the larger farms can do little to intensify production, for neither live stock nor dairy farming is profitable. Probably some improvement in milk production could be made by better feeding, and by better use of the green crops, but there is no real foundation for the development of dairy production. Of course, crop yields could be much increased by heavy applications of artificial manures, but with present prices this is wholly impracticable and likely to remain so. Both large and small farms are severely affected by the price fall of rye and have gone back to a less intensive method of cultivation. Both will be forced in the future to give up rye cultivation as much as possible, and to specialize in other products; but the soil is not really suitable for anything but rye and potatoes, and could not support its present population with any other crop. The big farms have attempted to increase their income by cultivating special crops, but this is only possible

POLAND
CEPCEWICZE. NEAR SARNY IN POLESIA
Over-crowding. Small cattle. Sandy soil

when they possess small areas of good land; otherwise the soil is not suitable. Fruit production is not likely to be profitable for long owing to the limited internal market.

The standard of living is noticeably much higher than in Galicia; the houses of the larger and medium-sized peasant are large and well built, but the housing and food standards of the village as a whole is low compared with that of the Bohemian peasant. The peasant on 6 hectares cannot attain anything like the level of the Czech peasant. Like the solid peasant class everywhere they adhere to a sort of traditional dress, but buy it in the towns; the light blue chauffeur's cap, the short fur-lined coat, and high leather boots. They look down on the seasonal workers from Galicia, or on the 'Polesiuk' who drives his oxen on foot to sell in Central Poland from the eastern provinces 200 miles away. But the poorer peasants who work on the estates and larger peasant farms live in great misery.

In the eastern provinces of Poland, Polesia and Wolhynia, there is still less prospect of better farming. These regions cover two types of soil: the southern part of Wolhynia, adjoining the black earth region of Rumania and Russia, and a great area of sand extending north to Nowogrodek and south to Sarny, round the basin of the Pripet. Most of this land is either too wet or too dry for cultivation, and without drainage on a large scale cannot support its present population. The average rainfall is about 550 mm. Forty per cent. of the area is under marsh, forest, and peat bogs. Most of the arable looks like pure sand. In these regions the peasants' life is a struggle for existence on a poor soil in a grim climate, with nothing to relieve its misery and its monotony. The villages are vast conglomerations of low wooden huts, with one room lit by a window a foot square; the room contains little besides a stove and rough benches, covered with sheepskins which are crawling with lice. The level of cultivation is the lowest possible: so primitive that manure is spread on the fields by hand. The chief crops are rye, potatoes, followed by fallow. Of the farm land 60 per cent. is arable, 40 per cent. is poor pasture.

Live stock per hectare is sparse, though the amount per head of population is higher than in Galicia, but the cows are minute, scarcely bigger than the lean wild pigs.

Compared with Galicia, the density of population is low, and the farms are larger, with 7·5 hectares as the average, which is large enough as a rule, but in spite of this the area is to be regarded as over-populated because yields are low and the land only half cultivated. Often farmers have too much land to cultivate with their live stock. One farm of 10 hectares which was visited only cultivated 7, as 3 cows and 2 oxen did not produce enough manure. A sign of growing poverty is the gradual destruction for fuel of the forest belonging to the peasants. Most of the forest land in these districts belongs to the big estates. The larger manor farms and the estates seem to exist on the same level of technique as the peasants, and maintain a very low standard of living: old aristocratic families with names famous in European history live with less comfort than the poorest peasant in Germany. Bread is barely sufficient, and potatoes are also scanty. As members of the Orthodox Church, they keep fasts for twenty weeks in the year, eating only bread and fish oil.

No industrial products (except vodka) are bought. Linen is woven at home, shoes are plaited bark. Even matches are not bought; flint and steel are used.

The main problem is the improvement of the pastures which form about half of the total area and are at present mainly bog and marshland. Far-reaching schemes for improvement are necessary to drain the Pripet basin, but as this would involve co-operation with Russia it may be regarded as out of the question, since there is a tendency to regard the marshes as a natural frontier against Bolshevism. (In fact, this opinion is baseless, as the bulk of the population of these districts is Ruthenian and antagonistic to the Polish Government; its revolts have been subdued with great cruelty.)

Apart, however, from such costly schemes there are possibilities of improvement which have been investigated by the Farm Institute at Sarny. The drainage of the swamps and treatment with kainite and phosphates caused an immense increase in the yield at a very low cost. With this treatment yield of pastures can be increased from 2 quintals of rye to 20 or 30.

It is possible to see the effect of these methods in the villages adjoining the institute, where they have been applied to their pastures, and large areas have been drained with wooden pipes at very small cost.

For political reasons, credits are given by the government to enable peasants to undertake these changes, but the remoteness of the district makes the return very low. No practicable improvement can succeed in increasing productivity of the soil enough to feed its existing population.

2. POLAND: SOUTHERN PROVINCES (GALICIA)[1]

Galicia has better natural conditions than the rest of Poland; much of it is the good Carpathian loam, and the climate is wetter. Here the farming system is more intensive, the livestock density is higher, about 45 cattle to the 100 hectares; the crop system is good in that rotations are known and practised. But yields are lower, amounting to 9 quintals as compared with 12 in Central Poland, and are falling.

Yields in Southern Provinces of Poland

	Quintals per hectare		
	Wheat	*Rye*	*Potatoes*
1909–13	11·7	11·3	110
1931–5	9·2	9·7	100

About half the area is under corn crops, a quarter under meadows and green fodder crops, and less than a quarter potatoes and roots. The rotation followed shows signs of population pressure. On peasant farms it is usually as follows:

(i) Potatoes with farmyard manure.
(ii) Barley and oats.
(iii) Clover—twice cut.
(iv) Wheat.
(v) Rye.
(vi) Oats or winter barley.

[1] Conditions in Bukovina resemble those of Galicia, though the population is more primitive.

Thus the soil is used three years in succession for corn with inadequate manure.

A sign of the shortage of green fodder is the very general practice of sowing two crops in one year, either a corn crop which is cut green in May, or lupines, which are cut and followed by potatoes and turnips.

The weak point of these farms is use of manure. The potato crop always gets a heavy dressing, 400 quintals to the hectare, or 50 peasant cartloads, but it is mainly straw with little value. Very few of the farms have proper pits for manure and very few make use of the Swiss liquid manure cart which could be of great benefit in these conditions. So backward is the practice in this respect that it has been recently proposed to pass a law compelling the correct conservation of manure.

In many districts milk marketing is well organized on a co-operative basis. The average yield of the cows in the best villages is 1,200 litres per year, a good level. Special banks for savings exist in connexion with the co-operative marketing societies: the co-operatives are on a sound financial basis and even in the depression have built mills and dairies out of their profits.

In some of the villages communal pasture still exists; in others it has been divided up long ago. Another defect of the farming system is the state of the pastures, which are overstocked and entirely uncultivated. On the initiative of Professor Włodek of Kraków, a movement has begun to form co-operatives to control the pastures, limiting the right to pasture cattle, and requiring a rent in liquid manure for each animal pastured.

Examples of over-average peasant farms in the most advanced villages near Lancut can be given to show the very high proportion of live stock to the area of the farm, and the excessive number of workers.

    I. Village of Handzlówka:
        (i) Farm with 9 acres; 1 horse, 4 cows, 1 heifer, 4 calves, 4 workers.
        (ii) Farm with 2 acres; 2 cows, 3 workers.

    II. Village of Albigowa:
        (i) Farm with 3½ acres; 2 cows, 1 heifer, 1 worker.
        (ii) Farm with 5½ acres; 3 cows, 1 horse, 10 pigs, 16 hens, 6 workers out of family of 10.

(iii) Farm with 9¼ acres; 2 horses, 1 foal, 6 cows, 1 fat pig, 1 sow, 1 boar. (The farm buys hay.) 4 workers. Sells 10 quintals wheat.

(iv) Farm with 4¼ acres; 2 cows, 1 heifer, 1 horse, 2 pigs, 2 workers.

The numbers of workers are those who are living permanently on the farm and have no other occupation. Each of these farms will grow a great variety of crops in very small quantities; a few buy in hay. The majority of the farms have 1 cow and 3 or 4 acres of land.

The distribution of land of the members of the co-operative in Handzlówka is typical. The 960 owners were divided as follows: under 2 hectares, 545; 2–5, 368; 5–20, 45; and 2 priests' holdings.[1]

The big farms in this district are shrinking steadily year by year, selling off land at high prices to the neighbouring peasants. In methods of production the bigger farms differ only slightly from the peasants, sowing more sugar-beet, for which they have quotas, and keeping fewer head of cattle to the acre. Yields of corn are higher and milk yields are roughly twice as high as on peasant farms. Big farms use no ploughing machinery, though drilling and reaping is always done by machinery. Very few of the big latifundia now remain, with the exception of the big estates of Lubomirski and Potocki, who have succeeded up till now in keeping 'off the list' for division under the land reform, by planting fruit-trees on a large scale.[2] The food wages on the estates appear to be adequate, being fixed by minimum wage contracts, but the housing conditions of the labourers (who live in the villages) are very poor and worse than those of the peasants, who keep their homes in good condition and rebuild frequently.

[1] Similar distribution exists in the village of Broniszów, of which a monographic study has been made (J. Fierich, *Broniszów*, 1928).

	Distribution of live stock			
	1 cow	*2 cows*	*3 cows*	*4 cows*
1–3 hectares . .	26	2	1	0
3–6 ,, . .	7	39	7	1
6–10 ,, . .	0	9	10	3
over 10 ,, . .	0	2	1	2

[2] See Chapter VIII.

Nowhere is the field chess-board so chaotic. For over a century the holdings have been continuously subdivided up among families, the farms getting smaller and smaller and the small pieces of land more and more scattered. The original unit called the *lan*, corresponding to the English hide, can be seen in the long narrow strips of land now split up into 20 or 30 pieces, some of them no more than 10 feet square. Thus a peasant who has 5 acres of land, a very typical size, would have 1 acre of potatoes, 1½ of rye, 1 of oats, ½ of wheat, ½ of clover, ¼ of barley, and ¼ of vetches. These small pieces are spread out in 20 or 30 places, some as much as two or three miles from the village.[1]

Thus the farming problem here does not arise from lack of technical knowledge but from the layout of the land, and the division into small areas, which cannot possibly be economically utilized, and even these defects are of minor importance beside the inevitable cause of declining yields, the too intensive corn cropping. Pressure of population makes it inevitable that this amount of corn should be grown, and prohibits any attempt to combine the farms into larger units. The peasants in these villages are clearly living on the verge of destitution, with their 3 acres and a cow as their only source of income. In their outlook, their co-operative organization, and their revolutionary political views they are a civilized proletariat rather than a peasantry. Poverty is universal; there is no rich peasant class. Consequently, there is a higher degree of social equality and a sense of social cohesion which is unusual in peasant villages. 'Handzlówka is a collective farm,' said a peasant's son, a proof of the feeling of social solidarity which prevails.

The conditions described are those of the best villages in Galicia, where there is no actual bread shortage before the harvest. But the standard of living may be judged by the fact that only half of the families can afford to eat their own pig. In the districts farther from the main lines of communication the price of milk is lower and crop yields are poorer.

---

[1] A study of the history of twenty Galician villages in the period 1787 to 1931 shows a continuous decline in the average size of peasant farms; Styś, *Rozdrabnianie gruntów chłopskich w byłym zaborze austrjackim od roku 1787 do 1931*, Lwów, 1934.

GALICIA, Albigowa
Team on larger peasant farm. Dwarf peasant cottage. The field 'chess board'

In Broniszów, in Rzeszów district, a special study (made in 1928) calculated that the amount of food in flour, fat, meat, cabbage, and milk, i.e. a bare minimum, necessary to maintain a family (with no bought food) could not be obtained by the existing methods on less than 3 hectares. As 50 per cent. of the owners have less than this, and only a small percentage of these can earn on the estates, one-half or one-third of the population cannot feed itself.[1]

The villages on the foot-hills of the Carpathians make an impression of unrelieved misery. The low wooden houses are falling into ruin: the family has one room lit by a small pane of glass, and sleep in wooden beds covered with rags. Children go barefoot even in winter. The horses are old and starved, the cows tiny, pigs and geese are few. The infant mortality rate is high.

In Galicia over-population assumes extraordinary dimensions; the problem is specially acute because it is of long standing. The economic conditions of the province are probably the worst in Europe, if we consider the extent of destitution, which seems to affect the peasantry as a whole and not merely the poorest class. The biological effects of over-population are now being felt by the second or third generations. Almost every family has a cripple; rickets and tuberculosis are prevalent.

Farther to the east in the Ruthene territories conditions are still worse.

A belt of Ruthene populated country runs across the boundaries of several States; outside Russia, where the bulk of the Ruthenians are, they inhabit the eastern provinces of Poland, East Galicia, a part of East Slovakia, and the province of Sub-Carpathian Ruthenia, and spread over into Hungary. In Hungary, we have mentioned, is a very bad patch in the Nyírség, a poor rye and potato region on the borders of the Great Plain. Everywhere they have the worst land and the highest birth-rate.

Their fertility rate in the nineteenth century was abnormally high and is still something like 15 births per 100 women of child-bearing age. All this Ruthene territory is extremely remote from industrial and commercial centres and covers regions of poor sandy soil with long severe winters, and in consequence the standard of living is extremely low. Conditions in the

[1] J. Fierich, *Broniszów*, 1933.

Ruthenian province of Czechoslovakia and in East Galicia are not so bad as in the eastern provinces of Poland; but they are always the poorest of the poor.

3. RUMANIA: TRANSYLVANIA[1]

Transylvania, as its name implies, is a forest country: only half its area is farm land. Of the farm land, arable takes up only half; the rest is meadow, poor pasture, or mountain grazing. Economically it has the same character as Central and Eastern Slovakia—poor soil, little land per head, and sheep the main live-stock product. Except for the area in the borders of the Hungarian Plain, the soil is poor podsol, with a high acid content and poor in humus, so that actually the output per head is lower than in the Rumanian Plain, though there the farm system is more primitive. Yields are variable; in good years wheat is 10 quintals per hectare, maize 12 quintals, but every third year or so the harvest is a failure. The density of population is high, 80 to the 100 hectares. In consequence, the food-supply is barely sufficient; in the pre-war period there was much migration to the States—and now there is some migration to Bukarest.

Though the methods of cultivation are better than in Old Rumania, it is only quite recently that the three-field system with fallow has been abandoned; and oats have been introduced in place of the fallow in some villages. Now the rotation is wheat (or rye on poorer land), followed by a hoed crop, maize or potatoes, followed by oats. Animal manure is not properly utilized, but it is used, and rather surprisingly artificial manure is used by most of the peasants: this use of manure is very profitable because the soil is poor in calcium.

Ploughs are made of wood, with an iron share. There is very little machinery in the villages, though some have jointly owned threshing machines. For the most part, threshing is done with the flail.

The live stock is very poor: the working animals are the water buffaloes which in Europe are found only in Transyl-

[1] The conditions described do not refer to the Banat districts which are now included in Transylvania. These are the counties of Arad and Timis, and their farming system has been already described in the previous chapter.

RUMANIA
Dragus in Transylvania
Mountain pasture and poor soil. Water buffalo team on 5 hectares farm

vania and the Balkans, slow-moving, archaic beasts, which need nothing but a daily swim and a little straw, and give very small quantities of very rich milk.

In spite of the somewhat higher level of cultivation due in the main to better technical advisory service, the standard of comfort is lower than in the Old Kingdom. Although forests are so plentiful, houses are small and low, with rooms not more than 10 feet high, and earth floors. Wells are few and shared by several houses.

The nutritional standard seems a little better than in the Old Kingdom, owing to the milk given by the cow buffaloes, of which every family keeps one or two; pig fat is eaten, and wheat bread is fairly generally eaten instead of the injurious *mamaliga* (maize porridge).[1] But the diet is poor; in the words of a returned emigrant, 'They half eat.'

4. JUGOSLAVIA: REGIONS SOUTH OF THE SAVA

Jugoslavia has four main agricultural regions: (1) Croatia north of the Sava (like Transdanubian Hungary), (2) the Voivodina (like the Hungarian Plain), (3) Croatia south of the Sava, and Bosnia, both characterized by Karst formations, and (4) Serbia, with sub-tropical climate and valleys of good soil among poor mountain regions.

In Jugoslavia most of the passive area, i.e. the corn-importing region, should probably be regarded as over-populated. But it is extremely difficult to find any sort of measure for indicating over-population, as the peasants find subsidiary employment in forest work and as shepherds. The whole of the big region south of the Sava, Bosnia, and Herzegovina, where agriculture can only be carried on in the valleys, might be described as over-populated, taking the standard of 1 hectare of arable land as the minimum.

There are also more purely agricultural regions formerly included in Croatia (in the kingdom of Hungary) which show similar overcrowding, and where farm over-population exists on the same scale as in Poland. These districts are Zagorje, a hill region north of Zagreb, and Lika, a high-lying, wide valley

---

[1] Investigations of the diet of the village have been made; see Chapter IV and the League of Nations Nutrition Report.

behind the Velebit range on the coast. Both were emigrant regions in the pre-war time.

The Lika valley has an agricultural problem which is acute in many districts of Jugoslavia—water shortage, in spite of torrential rainfalls. The area is a wide plain, with red earth soil, which under better conditions can be a fertile soil, but its fertility is destroyed by torrential spring rains of sub-tropical character, which wash out the humus content of the soil and drive it down to the valleys, leaving the limestone bare. (In Cirkvice the rainfall reaches its European maximum of 5,000 mm. Rainfall in Gospic is 203 mm., which falls almost entirely in March.) Though the Mediterranean coast, with its mild climate, is only 20 km. distant, the Lika valley suffers extremes of temperature owing to the mountain range between.

In this region arable land is less than half a hectare per head; immediately behind the huts of every village rises the bare limestone rock (the Karst). Yields are poor; the corn output is so small that there are no barns, and the corn is threshed immediately after harvest; live stock are equally poor, with very small Buza cows and a few sheep. Even pigs cannot be kept; there is only one to every two houses. Goats are gradually destroying the shrubs which grow on the Karst, and though the government takes action to prevent destruction of the forest, it proves ineffectual against the plunder of the population. In some districts the peasants even tear out the shrubs to eat. In most over-populated regions forests provide an outlet or a subsidiary income; but here there are no forests.

Technique is most primitive. Wooden ploughs (which prevail all over Serbia, Bosnia, and Bulgaria) are very common. Threshing is done by oxen treading out the corn.

The population lives in extreme poverty on the verge of starvation. Since 1930 the health administration has undertaken to provide a daily meal—beans and bread—to all school-children. Houses are of wood and owing to the timber shortage are built very small, with no chimneys. The usual type is the hut with a hearth-place, a small room opening on one side and a cow stall on the other.

In this district there is really no prospect of improving the condition of the farmers in any way but by abandoning the land

JUGOSLAVIA
Smoke house, typical of Bosnia

Threshing with oxen treading
out the corn

to grazing, when it could support a few families. To overcome the water shortage the government is building cisterns, which are the only means of storage: and the cost of these—£500 or £600 each—is out of all proportion to the return they can bring in from supplying a few houses.

In the vast Bosnian forests, more remote and more primitive than these regions, the peasants endure great poverty. The Moslem peasants live the most primitive life imaginable; each peasant has his family and his cows in three or four huts in a little enclosure, inside a fence, against bears and wolves. The house is a low hut, smoke-blackened and empty, where the family sleep on the floor round the blazing open fire. The soil is turned with a *ralo* (as in Bulgaria and Serbia), a long wooden spike. The peasants walk twenty to thirty miles to market to sell a few pounds of butter or a goat.

As contrasted with the civilized regions of Galicia or Croatia, the peasants in genuinely isolated communities like these suffer hardships rather than deprivation.

Summary

The question is if the intensification of production in Eastern Europe, even given wider markets, would be sufficient to employ the *present* population on the land in all these countries.

The answer to this must be quite certainly 'Yes' in Hungary. The good soil, the low density of farm population, would make it possible to employ the whole farm population at higher standards of living if cultivation were intensified. Probably 'Yes' in the Old Kingdom of Rumania: the possibilities of re-organization are still greater, though the farm density is higher.

But to bring about this improvement would need major changes in economic organization, a degree of State intervention approaching near to collectivization. First, irrigation would be necessary, with electrical power supply, and this would involve large-scale investment. Secondly, the dates of farming operations must be controlled by the State and the seed standardized. If Rumanian maize is not planted immediately after the frosts cease, it cannot avoid the drought which occurs in July and August—hence early planting is absolutely necessary. Mechanization in general is unnecessary, though tractors might be introduced as auxiliary horse-power. With these changes, yields of maize per hectare could be raised to the same level as those of the Argentine, and wheat yields could also be raised. It should be possible for the farm population in Rumania to eat wheat bread instead of the maize so deleterious to health, and sell in place of wheat maize-fed pigs and poultry. With irrigation, vegetables could be cultivated for home consumption and for canning factories. Fruit production could be developed further in the hill regions of Rumania.

Thus with better organization, of a sort which is technically and politically feasible, an increase in output per head of 50 per cent. should be attained.

The difficulty is that this improvement requires a certain amount of capital investment by the State, and up to the present the limited funds available have been used to support wheat prices, not to change the method of production.

Further advances might be made in Serbia and Bulgaria in the very intensive cultivation of special crops, sunflowers, hemp, rice, roses, tobacco, and vines. But with the present population density the peasant cannot much reduce the cultivation of wheat and maize.

All these special crops must be exported. The expansion of internal demand under present conditions must be too slow; with the present high density these crops are only worth cultivating if the peasant can get a high price per acre—he cannot produce big quantities if he needs most of the land to grow corn for his family. Thus the whole outlook of these regions depends on the tariff position.

To summarize then: if Hungary and the Rumanian Plain could export their goods freely to Germany, Austria, Czechoslovakia, and this country, and could standardize and develop their marketing as Bulgaria already has done, they could raise their standard of living enough for over-population to cease to be a problem. But Rumania would still have a serious problem of over-population in Transylvania.

Poland and Jugoslavia (and Bulgaria to a much smaller extent) have a different problem—something like 12 millions (5 in Jugoslavia, 7 in Poland, and 1 million in Bulgaria) who are surplus and on the starvation line. For them there is no remedy

MOUNTAIN PASTURE FARMING
Czechslovakia.   *The poloniny in Ruthenia*
Transylvania.   *Sheep farm in Hateg mountains*

in intensifying farming. Poland's position could be improved if exports of live stock, particularly pigs, could be increased; but this would mean a minor improvement only.

A survey of the districts shows that over-population in Eastern Europe appears in three kinds of farming conditions:

(1) Over-population in the mountain districts, where natural conditions are really only suited to grazing. This state exists in the mountain districts of Eastern Slovakia, Sub-Carpathian Ruthenia (Czechoslovakia), in Bukovina and Transylvania (in Rumania), in Slovenia, much of Croatia, and in the whole of Jugoslavia south of the Sava.

(2) Over-population in the Polish Plain and Galicia. Here the system of land utilization is probably the best for the natural conditions. But the population is too large to be employed on any system. In Galicia this problem is seen in its most acute form, and here it is quite certain that the pressure of population itself is exhausting the soil.

Further intensification and a change in the farming system —by use of increased labour—is impossible owing to the drawbacks of the climate, the character of the soil, and the absence of internal markets.

(3) Over-population in Bulgaria and Serbia. Here there seem to be some possibilities of intensification, and in Bulgaria at least this direction is being followed, but the area of land per head is so small that little remains to be done.

Thus the scope of farm reorganization affects only about one-sixth of the farm population in these five countries, $4\frac{1}{2}$ millions in Hungary, 6 millions in the Rumanian Plain, out of the 60 millions farm population in the agrarian countries of Eastern Europe.

We must now consider the economic and social changes which farm reorganization would necessitate.

CHAPTER VIII

THE ADVANTAGES AND DISADVANTAGES OF PEASANT FARMING

A. ADVANTAGES

THERE are great economic advantages—apart from the political—in the peasant type of farm organization. The peasant system tends to promote better utilization of the existing labour force, to increase output per head, and to increase the volume of savings; it is also able to maintain a more equal distribution of income; and these tendencies, provided that they are not counteracted by investment in non-productive assets, are of course strong arguments in favour of maintaining it.

In the following chapter the influence of these factors will be discussed: first, the general results of peasant farming, as it affects employment and income, and the influence of the land reform; second, the technical defects and their remedies; and third, the effects of small ownership on investment and saving.

1. *The Effect of Peasant Farming on the Distribution of Income*

At present the greater part of the cultivated land in all these countries is worked by small units. It is only in Hungary and in Western Poland that the big estates still take up a big share of the farm area; in all the other regions something like 70 to 80 per cent. is under small farms, worked by the peasant family. Of course 'peasant' is not a very exact term and need not necessarily mean a very small farm. Bohemia, for instance, is a province farmed mainly (40 per cent.) by farms of the 25 to 75 acres class. These would be comparable in area to largish small-holdings in England. But still, such farms as these are hardly typical: the average size in Eastern Europe is about 5 hectares, or 12 acres, and this is a size of farm which in England does not exist at all as a corn-producing unit, though there are many small-holdings of a highly specialized kind producing poultry, eggs, or market-garden produce of the same size.

In classifying farm sizes it is usual to describe farms over 50 hectares (120 acres) as large farms. The division corresponds roughly to a social distinction, for in Poland and Hungary, where this classification is made, farms over 50 acres are, with rare

Division of the Agricultural Land between Large and Small Farms

	Poland, *1931*		Hungary, *1930*		Rumania, *1930*	
	Mill. ha.	%	Mill. ha.	%	Mill. ha.	%
Under 50 hectares (123 acres) . . .	19·50	76·3	4·49	59·2	10·44	81·3
Over 50 hectares* . .	4·60	18·0	3·09	40·8	2·41	18·7
Public Property . .	1·40	5·7	..	..	..	..
Total Agricultural Area .	25·50	100	7·58	100	12·85	100

	Czechoslovakia		Bulgaria†	
	Mill. ha.	% of total	Mill. ha.	% of total
Under 50 hectares . .	6·813	81	3·79	94·1
Over 50 hectares . .	1·663	19	0·24	5·9
Total . . .	8·476	100	4·03	100

* For Hungary the division must be made at 58 hectares. There are no figures for Jugoslavia.

† Under and over 30 hectares (74 acres).

exceptions, the property of the gentry or aristocracy, and employ wage-paid labour. There are some larger peasant farms under 50 hectares which also employ labour, but such farms are unimportant as a class.

In the above table the distribution of farms above and below 50 hectares (123 acres) is compared in the different countries after the land reform.[1]

From the table it appears that the large farms are not important, except in Hungary, where they cover nearly half the total area. In Poland as a whole large farms are not more

[1] These figures relate to agricultural land only, that is, arable land, meadow and pasture without forest land. To give distribution of farm sizes for the whole area including forests would give greater preponderance to the big properties. In all these countries most of the forest land is owned by the big estate owners or by the State.

important than in Rumania, but in the western and eastern districts they predominate.

Both in Poland and in Hungary the contrast between large and small farms is very marked, for the majority of the small farms are dwarf holdings, not large enough to feed a family without the additional earnings of the owner as a labourer. Between the rich man in his castle and the poor man at his gate there is no intervening class of medium-sized peasants. Poland, it has been said, is built of stones and sand with no mortar to hold it together, and hence its eternal indecision and tragic dissensions.[1] It is true that it was the land question which proved fatal to Polish democracy; and the class division, which causes the opposition between a class-conscious democratic peasantry and the reactionary landowners behind the dictatorship, has almost disrupted the new State.

In other countries, where the reform has reduced the share of the big farms to a small percentage of the total, it is more important to characterize the agrarian structure by classifying the peasant farms into large, medium, small, and dwarf holdings. The term 'dwarf holdings' designates a holding which is not large enough to support a family; usually these holdings are classified as under 2 hectares, but in some regions 3 hectares may be the limit below which a family cannot feed itself.

For convenience farms of 2–5 hectares may be described as small holdings, farms of 5 to 20 or 30 hectares medium-sized holdings; and farms from 30 to 100 hectares as large peasant farms as distinct from estate farms.

The following table shows farm sizes on this basis.

From the tables we can see a broad contrast between Czechoslovakia, where small- and large-sized farms each take up about one-quarter of the farm area and medium-sized farms about half; and Rumania and Bulgaria, where the small- and medium-sized peasant holdings predominate. Both in Bulgaria and Rumania one-third of the land is farmed by units less than 5 hectares (12 acres), and about 70 per cent. of the farms average 2 hectares. Bulgaria has no large properties and a low proportion of dwarf holdings.

[1] This is true of the west, east, and south: in Congress Poland (the Central provinces) there is a fair proportion of medium-sized farms.

SIZE OF FARMS: FARM LAND ONLY
Czechoslovakia, 1930

Size Group	Number (000's)	%	Area in '000 hectares	%	Average area in hectares
Dwarf holdings:					
Under 2 hectares or 5 acres .	730	44	572	7	0·8
Small holdings:					
2–5 hectares or 5–12 acres .	438	27	1,393	16	3·2
Medium holdings:					
5–10 hectares or 12–25 acres	258	16	1,686	20	6·5
10–30 hectares or 25–75 acres	188	11	2,638	31	14·0
Large Peasant Farms					
30–100 hectares or 75–247 acres	25	1·5	877	10	34·5
Large Farms:					
Over 100 hectares or 247 acres	9	0·5	1,308	16	148·1
Total	1,648	100	8,474	100	5·14

[Source: Czechoslovak Census of Agriculture, *Czechoslovak Statistics,* vol. xcii.]

Bulgaria, 1934

Size Group	Number (000's)	%	Area in '000 hectares	%	Average area in hectares
Dwarf holdings:					
Under 2 hectares or 5 acres.	175	23	195	5	1·2
Small holdings:					
2–5 hectares or 5–12 acres .	292	39	993	24	3·4
Medium holdings:					
5–10 hectares or 12–25 acres	186	25	1,285	32	6·9
10–30 hectares or 25–75 acres	90	12	1,323	33	14·8
Large Peasant Farms:					
Over 30 hectares or 75 acres	5	1	236	6	48·0
Total	748	100	4,032	100	5·4

[Source: Molloff, *Struktur der bulgarischen Landwirtschaft.*]

The dwarf holdings are, of course, the weak point in a peasant economy, and their large number (in countries with an egalitarian land system) shows the effect of population pressure. In industrial countries a large number of dwarf holdings is not

Rumania, 1930

Size Group	Number (000's)	%	Area in '000 hectares	%	Average area in hectares
Dwarf and small holdings:					
Under 5 hectares or 12 acres	2,460	75	4,600	36	1·9
Medium holdings:					
5–10 hectares or 12–25 acres	560	17	3,110	24	5·5
10–20 hectares or 25–50 acres	180	5·6	1,715	13	9·5
Large Peasant Farms:					
20–100 hectares or 50–247 acres	69	2	1,555	12	22·5
Large Farms:					
Over 100 hectares or 247 acres	12	0·4	1,870	15	154·1
Total	3,281	100	12,850	100	3·9

Hungary: Total Land Area, 1934

Size Group	Number (000's)	%	Area in '000 hectares	%	Average area in hectares
Dwarf, Small, and Medium holdings:					
Under 29 hectares or 72 acres	1,262·1	97·96	4,341	46·65	3·4
Large Peasants:					
29–115 hectares or 72–254 acres	19·8	1·54	962	10·34	48·7
Large Farms:					
115–288 hectares or 254–711 acres	3·9	0·30	684	7·35	176·6
288–575 hectares or 711–1,412 acres . . .	1·4	0·11	574	6·17	400·0
575–1,151 hectares or 1,412–2,740 acres . . .	0·6	0·05	517	5·56	799·0
1,151–5,755 hectares or 2,740–14,100 acres .	0·5	0·04	1,144	12·29	2,297·2
Over 5,755 hectares or 14,100 acres . . .	0·08	0·01	1,084	11·65	13,060·2
Total	1,288·4	100·0	9,306	100·0	7·2

[Source: J. de Konkholy Thege, 'Estate and Operating Relations in Hungarian Agriculture,' *Journal de la Société Hongroise de Statistique*, 1936.]

necessarily a bad sign, since they are not the owner's only source of income, but represent part time or subsidiary holdings. In Czechoslovakia, for instance, the Census of Agriculture shows that 60 per cent. of the owners of these holdings have an occupation other than farming; and of the 40 per cent. who have to live off their holdings most live in the agricultural provinces of Slovakia and Ruthenia. But in Poland and the Balkans these dwarf farms are the sole source of the peasant's income. In Bulgaria, for instance, the Agricultural Survey shows a large number of farms under 2 hectares, which employ three, four, or five persons permanently.

For Poland the size-group figures unfortunately do not serve to show the position of the dwarf holders: indeed, the official statistics are designed to conceal the main features of the land system. For 1921, however, there are figures which show that in Galicia half the holdings were less than 2 hectares in size—a larger proportion than any region where the dwarf holdings are full-time farms.

The Hungarian figures show the inequality of the land system in broad outline only, as they do not classify the smaller size groups. The very large scale of farming operation appears clearly; 35 per cent. of the land is owned and farmed in units over 700 acres in size, 24 per cent. in units over 2,740 acres. (About a quarter of this land is forest, which is always owned by large estates.) The low average size of farms in the under 29 hectares class shows the prevalence of dwarf holdings.

Thus, apart from Hungary and in part also Poland, the type of farm organization does suggest a dispersion of capital into many small separate units, and in labour operations a lack of control or uniformity or specialization—which runs contrary to the tendencies of economic development which are observable in industry, and even (though to a much less degree) in agriculture also.

To a large extent the present system is the outcome of deliberate choice, and a choice made in quite recent times, in the post-war period. Under the agrarian reforms which were carried through in the years immediately after the war, on a wave of revolutionary and nationalistic enthusiasm, much of the land under big estates was transferred—violently or with some compensation—to the peasants. The present land-tenure system has been shaped by political changes, and it is, of course, precisely on these grounds that the reform has been criticized: that it put certain ends—the more equal distribution of property, or the liberation of the peasants from dependence on an employer—above the end of securing the productive efficiency of the farming system, and attained one at the cost of the other. It is therefore from this standpoint that the reform should be examined: to what extent were the political ends achieved, and did they conflict with the efficiency of the farming system?

The political aims were to liberate the peasantry from their dependence on a landowner class, and to create a more equal distribution of income. How necessary this redistribution of property was can be seen by the distribution of land in present-day Hungary. There the land system gives rise to a more unequal distribution of income even than in England. Forty per cent. of the farm area is owned by 0·1 per cent. of the total number of landowners. Of the total farm population 50 per cent. have no land; of those who have, about 35 per cent. are dwarf peasants who cannot produce enough to support a family. Before the reform, similar conditions existed in Czechoslovakia: 10 proprietors owned 838,000 hectares (2 million acres) and the Schwarzenberg estates alone covered 200,000 hectares (500,000 acres). It was these large properties which the land reform legislation attacked. Obviously a small State, mainly agrarian, could not tolerate such big concentrations, and the property had to be redistributed.

From this standpoint land reform did achieve a positive result. It has created communities with a much higher degree of equality of income distribution than had existed previously.[1]

---

[1] To some extent the reform acted as a property tax. The small estates (over 250 hectares in Czechoslovakia) were exempt from the expropriation. Larger ones were expropriated, and some graduation was applied by fixing lower rates of compensation for large estates.

In Poland the method of arranging the transfer appears to have favoured the very large estates. The reform legislation provided for a gradual transfer of property to the peasants, by fixing each year a certain minimum area to be divided up and sold in each province. Which estates were to come 'on the list' seems to have depended on the discretion of the administration. Much of this discrimination seems to have been due to national divisions: many of the estates in Central Poland and Galicia are owned by the Polish aristocracy

Most of the largest estates in Czechoslovakia were broken up (though landowners were allowed to retain a certain proportion), and the land redistributed among the small and medium-sized peasant farms. Nor is there any sign of new concentration of property occurring.

Of course, in agrarian Europe there is not so much equality of income as those who idealize the peasant state would like to think. Nowhere has the reform completely abolished the proletariat on the land. Take, for example, Slovakia, where, although about a quarter of the land was redistributed, there is still a large section of the farm population without land—about 20 per cent. of the total, and even of the owners of land a large number (something like 30 per cent.) have only dwarf holdings. Still, the fact remains that the distribution of land is much more equal than it used to be, and far more equal than in present-day Hungary.

2. *Employment and Labour Conditions*

On the side of production and employment the results of the reform are more complex. As a general principle it can be said that there was nothing fundamentally unwise in trying to create peasant farms in place of the big estates, and it was reasonable to expect that an increase in output per head and in employment would result from this policy.

The main argument for peasant farming is, of course, its success in Western Europe—success in the sense that the peasant farm does give a standard of living good in the national conditions and reaches a good standard of technique. It increases employment, in the sense that it maximizes the volume of employment for a given labour supply on the land. This is a point which perhaps needs emphasizing in any discussion about the relative efficiency of different farm sizes.

The economic significance of peasant farming, as contrasted with estate farming, is that it carries more cattle to the acre than

and some of these seem to have been fairly successful in keeping 'off the list'; at any rate they still retain large properties. The German landowners in the western provinces have also got off lightly: until quite recently they have been almost entirely exempted from the reform legislation. The reform has been most vigorously applied to the eastern provinces where the Russian aristocracy owned the land.

the large farm, that is to say, more capital. This contrast between peasant farms and large farms is observable everywhere, but is particularly striking in Germany, Hungary, and Poland. In so far as it promotes more intensive production through investing in farm live stock, peasant farming tends to increase the volume of employment.

But, it may be asked, is not this intensification of production necessarily at the cost of lower earnings? It is very often argued that the peasant only produces more to the acre by reducing his standard of living. If intensification is profitable, why should not the big farm undertake it?

This argument overlooks the seasonal factor. Big estates of the Hungarian sort depend entirely on having large supplies of casual labour at critical periods in the year. For instance, a Hungarian farm with 7,500 acres (3,000 hectares) will employ 360 workers permanently throughout the year, and 1,200 seasonal labourers for a month or two months in the harvest. Such a farm carries no excess labour capacity, and can only produce at low costs because this supply of very cheap casual labour is available. The wages of casual labour are paid entirely in corn, the whole gang of casual labour taking a share of the crop—usually one-thirteenth of the harvest.

The peasant farmer, on the other hand, must regard his family labour as a fixed factor—something which must be maintained whether working or not—and he will try therefore to fill in spare time by keeping live stock which will add to his output, and will utilize this fixed factor more fully. His earnings per hour may be less than on the big farm, but his total earnings will certainly be bigger. Consequently peasant farming means a better utilization of the labour force.

By intensifying live-stock production, the family farm also tends to maintain the fertility of the soil. It has even been claimed by Dr. O. E. Baker[1] that only the family farm can be relied upon to maintain soil fertility, and though this may be an exaggeration, yet obviously the family farm is likely to be more efficient in this respect than the capitalist farm, since the farmer's cost calculations relate to a longer period of time.

These important aspects, the unutilized labour supply and

[1] In an article in Harmsen und Lohse, *Bevölkerungsfragen*, 1936.

the maintenance of soil fertility, are too often neglected in a discussion of the relative efficiency of capitalistic and family farms. Usually the question is stated as if the relative efficiency of farm sizes could be judged by calculating the costs which the individual entrepreneur would have to incur to produce a certain crop.[1]

But in agriculture the difficulty of calculating the value of long period investment, and the importance of seasonal labour, make it misleading to calculate costs in this way. The nature of agricultural production makes it inevitable that returns on investment should be very slow, and that in the slack intervals work is done which might not be undertaken if paid for at regular wage rates. In consequence, the costs which are to be attributed to a particular crop and which the farmer has to incur to produce that crop may vary with the nature of the land system itself. If there is a landless proletariat on the land, the large employer can get cheap labour for short periods, without having to bear the cost of maintaining the labour supply when unemployed, and obviously the costs of production will be low. But the community must bear the cost of unemployment in some other form, either through the provision of relief, or through the degeneration of the labour supply. Under a system of family farms the cost will be borne by the farm population, which will seek to employ itself by increasing live-stock production.

As to the maintenance of soil fertility, the large-scale capitalistic farm is not likely to take a long view since it aims at a quick return, which may be obtained by letting the value of the land decline. This tendency may not be universal; the big

---

[1] For instance by A. W. Ashby, 'The Family Farm,' *Proceedings of the International Conference of Agricultural Economists*, 1934. 'If a social engineer or statesman were considering how he could obtain a given supply of foodstuffs from the agricultural area of Great Britain, with the least necessary expenditure of human energy, and the least necessary contribution of raw materials; and at the same time afford the persons concerned with production the highest standard of living and the greatest amount of leisure consistent with the maintenance of low prices to consumers; providing also for progressive technical development and for stability of the general industry in relation to market requirements; it is practically certain that he would not seek these ends by the strengthening or extending of the family farm system.' No evidence is given in support of this view, even on this narrow cost basis.

estates in Hungary, however, are certainly capital consumers. As the experience of the United States shows, the loss through declining fertility must be borne by the community, and the longer the decline continues the more severe the loss is likely to be.

Under a family farming system, therefore, it seems likely that the costs of maintaining the farm labour supply and the cost of maintaining soil fertility may be lower to the community in the long period, than they would be under a system of large-scale farming. A very advanced type of society might succeed in meeting these costs through social insurance and State control of investment, but to do so would need a degree of development which no modern State has reached.

Peasant farming also means a great improvement in the conditions of labour, which on the big estates are extremely wretched. Farm labour in an agrarian country can never be effectively organized: the labourer has to suffer both the disadvantages of feudalism, in that he is not free to move, and of capitalism, in that he is subject to unemployment. Enough has been said about conditions in Hungary to make it clear that the farm workers are unable to resist exploitation; no minimum wage contracts can be enforced (though these exist) when the supply of labour enormously exceeds the demand. All the provisions in wage agreements to secure better housing or better labour conditions can be evaded.

The real significance of peasant farming can be seen only by comparing villages of peasants with villages of farm labourers working in closely similar economic conditions. For instance, in North Hungary, where they often lie side by side, housing conditions in the peasant villages are strikingly better, their food is more varied, employment is more regular, and the whole manner of life is different. The life of the country-side seems undermined by the misery of the farm labourers and their severance from the soil. It cannot be doubted that, in these conditions, if the ownership and management of land is widely distributed, the farm population is better off.

But it is essential to remember that there are special conditions in Western Europe which favour the peasant type of farming, which, as we have argued in Chapter V, do not exist in the

east. Consequently, the hope that peasant farmers of the same
type could be created was doomed to disappointment.

For another reason, peasant farms were likely to be less
successful; the post-war period has seen the development of
machine methods, and, still more important, methods of dry
farming—treatment of the surface of the soil, which are essentially methods for large-scale farming, and might give good
results in Eastern Europe. By choosing the peasant type these
States were rather precluded from taking advantage of the new
methods.

Thus as a general result it can be said that the reform was
successful where the natural conditions resembled those of
Western Europe, and where they were very dissimilar it was a
failure, because it did not introduce any collective organization.

In the regions where conditions are more like those of Western
Europe (Austria-Hungary and Poland) farming was already
rather intensive. In these countries, where big estates were big
farms, the reform has been quite limited in scope. In Bohemia
about 17 per cent. of the farm area was transferred to the peasant
farms which already covered a large part of the area. In Central
Poland only 10 per cent. was transferred. Peasant farms existed
side by side with the big farms and farmed on much the
same methods, though with higher intensity of live-stock production. The reform meant a transfer of land to the peasantry,
and the result was an increase in live-stock output. On
peasant farms in Poland, as compared with the big estates,
there has been a marked increase in live-stock production even
since the depression. Wherever intensification by increasing
live-stock production was possible, we can conclude that the
extension of peasant farming meant an improvement in the welfare of the peasant community, since it implies more employment.

So far as the utilization of capital is concerned it does not
seem likely that the reform has caused any decline in efficiency.
The big estates did not as a rule work with large-scale indivisible capital equipment; for the most part they used large
numbers of ploughing teams, and such machinery as they
employed could be used equally efficiently on smaller areas.
Generally the big units were extensively farmed and could

be divided without impairing their economic efficiency. Sometimes, however, they were integrated units with large-scale industrial plant (distilleries or sugar-beet factories), and these estates were generally exempted from division.

In the regions where the density of farm population was already high, the frontier regions of the old Hungary (Slovakia, Transylvania, and Croatia), the reform transferred a rather greater proportion of the farm land (20 to 25 per cent.), leaving 15 to 20 per cent. still under large farms. In these regions the reform has increased the numbers of very small peasant holdings—a course which was inevitable in view of the large land-hungry population, but which could not, of course, lead to much permanent improvement. In these remote and poor regions the reform has not been followed by much intensification. In such conditions the land reform has only assisted a process of subdivision which was already occurring, by enabling the peasants to buy land on more favourable terms. In Galicia, where land hunger is most acute, the post-war legislation was quite ineffective; only 6 per cent. of the farm land was transferred in the years 1921–31, a slower rate of subdivision than that of the pre-war period.

In these regions there has long been a tendency for farms to split up, apart from the land reform. Big estates have been broken up by a gradual process of attrition, as the peasants bought land off the gentry at high prices, out of all relation to income yield; and, at the same time, peasant farms have been split up into smaller and smaller units with each generation. This is, of course, a result which prohibits full employment of the labour force, and indeed makes its rational utilization impossible. But this is not an argument against the peasant farm. Where there is a high density on the land there will be rural unemployment in any case, whether the system is one of big estates or peasant farms: but even in this case the peasant farms can offer more employment, and distribute work more evenly.

In the over-populated regions, therefore, the land reform, though it has not been followed by much intensification, did benefit the peasants in that it meant a temporary alleviation of rural poverty. But as there was little intensification, there could not be much permanent improvement. Even when intensification is possible, of course, subdivision cannot go on indefinitely, dividing the land further and further. Once the change to live-stock farming has been made there can be no further change in the same direction (except in the tropical regions). Consequently the reform, even though it did improve the conditions of the peasantry for a limited period, could only be successful within a very limited scope.

In the Balkans, large estates were simply large properties. Landlords did not farm themselves, but let the land to peasants under a share-cropping arrangement, sometimes taking as much as half the crop, though the peasant supplied the labour and the working capital.

In Rumania, where the scope of the reform has been much wider (affecting 50 per cent. of the farm land), it has been a failure from the standpoint of increasing productivity, and has led undoubtedly to a degeneration of farming technique. One reason for this is that the landlord system did provide a control of farming operations in two ways which were quite essential in Rumanian conditions—the selection of seed, and the regulation of the date at which sowing should begin. Since the reform the wheat has degenerated in quality, and crops have been reduced by failure to get sowing done in time—both defects which with government intervention could be avoided. Neglect of these practices has been responsible for the decline in yields. Further, there has been no intensification of live-stock farming: one-third of the farmers have no cow and no draught animals, and most farmers have no pig.

In Jugoslavia the effect of the reform has been on the whole good. In the southern part of the country, mainly Bosnia, the system resembled that of Rumania. The peasant paid a share-rent for his land, which varied from one-third to one-half of all produce of the land. In these regions the old system had the peculiar feature that the rent was taken from the corn only and not from live stock: consequently the peasants kept as much live stock as possible and reduced the corn area to as much as would cover their needs, leaving about half the land fallow. In consequence the main effect of the land reform in these provinces has been to cause a large extension of the cultivated area, and an increase in corn production.

To summarize, then, the effect of the reform: it led to some increase in employment and output, which relieved the pressure of population to some slight extent in the worst provinces. In the regions where the peasants are now well-to-do, mainly Bohemia and Moravia, it has been a success, and carried through a necessary redistribution of property. In the agrarian countries the real mistake of the reform was not that it destroyed highly efficient farming enterprises, but that it perpetuated all the defects of individualistic farming.

In general the peasant farm, simply because it maintains and increases the capital invested in farming, must necessarily increase the amount of employment for the existing farm population. But it need not necessarily increase the volume of employment in the future, and indeed it appears likely that precisely because it increases employment at the moment, it may check the shift to other occupations, and so diminish future employment. Peasant farms aim chiefly at maintaining the capital already invested in the farm, or strive to add to it, and to some extent this probably shortens the supplies of capital available for investment in industry or in large-scale farming equipment. In so far as the farm system has this effect, the increase of demand for labour in new branches of production will be restricted and employment will not expand. Consequently, although the peasant farm system does give the best conditions of labour possible in a poor community, if it fails to accumulate sufficiently for the future it will not be able to maintain employment as population grows. How far the failure to keep up output is to be attributed to the over-investment tendency we shall see in the next section. For the moment it is only necessary to point out that maximizing the employment of the existing labour supply is not the same thing as increasing the demand for labour in the future, and may even be incompatible with it.

Could more be done by further measures of land reform? Only in Hungary is there a great opportunity for raising the rural standard in this way. There is much rural unemployment among the underpaid casual labourers, who constitute a quarter of the total farm population. The methods of production are too extensive for the natural conditions, and could be intensified, given better organization. In Hungary the prospects of settlement are exceptionally good, because the farm density is low and the rate of increase very slow. Under the threat of Nazi aggression, large measures of reform are now (1938) being promised, which should be successful, if sufficiently radical in scope.

Elsewhere the density of farm population is too high, and the area under large estates is now too small.

In Poland the subdivision of estates is still continuing. Unlike the other States, where the area to be divided was transferred immediately, the Polish legislation arranged for 'parcellization' of land in gradual stages. A certain area is put 'in the list' for division each year. Up to 1930 the law was fulfilled, about 200,000 hectares being divided each year; since then, under the influence of the landowners who support the dictatorship, it was abandoned. Since 1936 it has been resumed, under the pressure of growing distress, on the initiative of the Minister of Agriculture, Poniatowski, whose policy is very radical, aiming at complete expropriation of the big estates, though it seems unlikely that he can carry out this policy in the present government.

In Poland the future scope of the land reform is now very limited. An inquiry has been recently carried out into the minimum sizes of farm which can employ a family in certain districts, and this minimum has been compared with the actual size of holdings which have been created by the sale of private estates and by the holdings created under the reform. These show that in Central Poland the average is slightly above the minimum (6–7 hectares), well above it in the east, but generally below the minimum in the south. In the later period, 1931–5, the average amount is smaller, a sign that the land supply is getting exhausted.

Though the big estates still take about 20 per cent. of the farm land, the amount of land still available for division is not large enough to relieve the pressure of population considerably. The most radical reform possible would barely equip the peasant families with enough land to be fully occupied. Poland cannot create enough new farms for her population to subsist on even at a very low level. This is not an excuse for discontinuing the reform, but the extreme poverty of the peasants in Galicia cannot be relieved by a more active settlement policy in the east.

In Rumania continuance of the land reform now means local redistribution of the population. This promises well, as there are areas in Bessarabia and Dobrogea with good soil which are not very densely settled. Since the land reform about 40,000 settlers have been moved to these districts and 314,396 hectares settled.

B. DISADVANTAGES

Although, as we have seen, farming methods vary from one region to another, there are certain obvious weaknesses which appear almost everywhere.

These are of two kinds, those which can be called the technical defects, and the other, the defects of organization, due to mis-investment. The first group covers the defects due to low intensity of live-stock production to the acre, coupled with an excessive number of working live-stock and lack of large-scale machinery. Another bad defect is the field system. The second, the defects of organization, are due to the tendency to over-invest in the farm.

All these arise from small-scale ownership, and it might be argued that the only way of eliminating them would be col-lectivization or some kind of State farming. But collectivization inevitably means a social upheaval likely to cause severe econo-mic losses which may even outweigh the benefits of large-scale operations, and it is necessary to decide how serious an obstacle to better farming individual ownership really is.

1. Technical Defects

The main defect, of course, is that the farm system in Eastern Europe is much too extensive. This is not a result of family farming. In itself there seems no reason to regard the family farm as an inefficient unit; it can exist under all kinds of economic conditions, as a large mechanized unit, or as a small labour intensive unit. There is no great contrast in social structure between farming in the United States and in Europe; the proportion between hired labour and the labour of the farmer and his family is almost the same in the United States and in Germany. Family farms exist in widely different conditions; they prevail in the United States where land is cheap and labour dear and where big changes of production can be quickly carried through; in countries with highly specialized agricultural export industries such as Denmark and Switzerland; and in the over-populated parts of Europe, where methods of production are static.

There are, however, as we have already said, quite definite and fixed conditions under which the family farm can succeed on a small acreage in European conditions, in the sense of giving full employment to its members at rates of earnings which are sufficient to guarantee a standard of living adequate in the national conditions. For the type of animal husbandry in connexion with arable farming which is prevalent in Western Europe and Great Britain needs a lucky combination of economic factors, technical methods, and market conditions. First, market conditions favour pork and veal, which a peasant farm can well produce. Second, technical conditions in Western and Central Europe favour farming in family units, owing to the regular labour requirements of meat and milk production, and the possibility of investing extra crop production in additional live stock. Labour can be expended on maintenance of farm buildings, or cultivation of the soil, at rates much below the market rate for free labour; but much of the labour can be regarded as investment for the future. In these special conditions the family farm has the merit of conserving the fertility of the soil.

Third, the natural conditions are favourable: this type of farming is limited to the areas where rainfall is sufficient to produce good crops of roots or green crops. In dry districts, with rainfall less than 24 inches, intensive feeding is impossible and few live stock can be kept: the peasant is not a farmer but merely a cultivator of the soil. The merits of conserving the fertility of the soil cannot be claimed for the family farm in conditions where animal husbandry plays no part. Over large areas of the world's surface the amount of rainfall is insufficient to allow the type of mixed farming characteristic of Western Europe. In Southern Russia, in the Hungarian Plain, and in

Australia the soil can maintain its fertility without the use of organic or artificial fertilizers: it needs water rather than these chemical constituents.

Such areas are not suited to the family farm type of settlement because, in the first place, production is too uniform and labour too seasonal. In such districts the right date of sowing, the selection of crops for early maturity, the uniformity and rapidity of cultivation, are more important in increasing the yield of the soil and maintaining its fertility than manure. Irrigation works need large-scale investment. To keep enough horses to do the work of cultivation puts too heavy a burden on the peasant farm. When such areas are settled by peasant farms, as in the Hungarian Plain and the Danube basin, the weakness of the family farm is very apparent: the fertility of the soil declines, the labour force and the horse power is not fully utilized.

These conditions were of course the main reason for the weakness of the peasant farm in Russia, where intensive cultivation of the steppe by peasants would always have been impossible, owing to lack of water. In fact the main reason why the family farm is best for Germany, and the collective farm for Russia, is not that the one accords with Hitler's ideology and the other with Stalin's, but that in Germany the annual rainfall is over 30 inches, and in South Russia less than 15.

In dry regions the great weakness of the peasant farm is the excessive number of live stock which have to be maintained to work the soil which bring in no return as meat or milk.

In typical peasant regions of Eastern Europe the number of working animals per hectare is as high, and sometimes even higher, than in the regions of intensive peasant farming of Western Europe. Both the peasants and the big farmers in Poland kept fantastic numbers of horses in relation to the crop yields.[1] Rumanian and Hungarian peasants keep a pair of oxen on small farms of 5 hectares. In the densely populated and remote districts the number of working animals increases more than the yield of the land. Though the climate does place limits

---

[1] Naturally social considerations play a part. A horse-peasant ranks much higher in the social scale than a cow-peasant, and a couple of good horses is an end in itself for Pole, Slovak, or Magyar.

to the live stock which can be kept, more cattle could be kept for meat production if the working animals could be reduced, and their work done by machinery. An excessive number of working animals is a result of the peasant system of land tenure.

The only way of increasing meat and fat production would be to increase the output of pigs and poultry fed on maize in the Plain regions. (In Poland an increase might be achieved by feeding on potatoes.) Feeding on roots or green crops is out of the question. But live-stock production could not be increased unless more maize were produced to the acre, and this requires the use of lucerne in the rotation. In Hungary and in Bulgaria this change to better rotations is already beginning. Rumania seems backward in this direction, and where the population density is high the urgent needs of the poorest peasant for bread crops stands in the way.

Machine cultivation would help to overcome this difficulty; the use of tractors would enable the peasants to reduce their live stock and increase their yields at the same time. In regions with surplus working live stock the advantages of mechanization would be very great, and collective cultivation would be simple. In Bessarabia and Dobrogea, where peasant farms are larger, the population relatively sparse, and the land good, a small number of villages have formed tractor co-operatives entirely on their own initiative, with good results.

In the wetter regions the economies to be gained by machine cultivation might not be very large, because live stock are used for milk and meat production as well as for field work, and the more intensive cultivation and use of manure necessitates many journeys in the fields.

An experiment in collectivization which began in Germany in 1932 suggests that in these conditions the cost reduction may be too small in relation to the capital cost. A German village, Haüsern, in Württemberg, composed of large peasant farms, undertook an experiment in mechanization with financial help from a rationalization committee; the farmers began to cultivate the land with jointly owned large-scale machinery—a tractor with complete equipment—each farmer keeping the crop of his area of land but cultivating it in common. Technically it was a success, but commercially a failure because, though the tractor work increased the yields per acre, the number of horses in the village could only be reduced by three: thus there was no cost saving.[1]

Of course, the low cost of labour, as well as the land system, tells against the use of machinery. Many big Hungarian estates use ploughing machinery, either tractors or steam ploughs. But there is great diversity of practice in this respect, and some big estates continue to plough with oxen and wooden ploughs. Many estate owners assert that steam ploughing is very much more costly than horse ploughing, at least three times as dear. Tractor ploughing is also said to be dearer, and this is confirmed by the fact that many farms had tractors bought in 1926–30 now lying idle. So long as a large supply of landless labourers exists the ox or horse team must be cheaper: if the supply of labour were reduced, by industrialization or by land reform, the use of the tractor would become economic.

In the dry areas there can be no doubt that the use of tractor machinery as supplementary to horses could be introduced with benefit, assuming that wheat and maize cultivation are to be the main products.

Even apart from mechanization, there are certain possibilities of raising output per head by abolishing the present field chaos. The outstanding defect of the farm system is the splitting up of each holding into small strips. This defect is by no means peculiar to Eastern Europe: it is very general in Southern Germany, Switzerland, and parts of France. (Northern France, Northern Germany, and Denmark are countries of enclosed farms.) It is universal in Central and Eastern Europe (the only large area where single homesteads are general is the Hungarian Plain). In all these regions the land of the peasant owners lies distributed in strips and squares in different parts of the village fields—sometimes 4 or 5 acres in 20 to 30 pieces—sometimes two miles distant; there are no fences, and no boundaries between them. Live stock grazes in summer on a communal pasture and in the fields after harvest.

[1] Cf. A. Münzinger, 'An Experiment in Co-operative Machinery Employment by Peasant Farmers,' in *Proceedings of the International Conference of Agricultural Economists*, 1934.

In Poland some progress has been made in commassation (i.e. combining the strips) under the administration of the land reform: the more progressive villages in Congress Poland have carried it through, and can show an improvement in corn yields of about 20 per cent. in the east; when it goes hand in hand with land reclamation it is proceeding quite rapidly. But in general the work of commassation is slow, and in Galicia the very smallness of the holdings and the poverty of the peasants make the cost of commassation insuperably high.

Whether the creation of separate farms is really worth paying for in such conditions depends on the kind of farming which is to be undertaken; for arable farming only it is not worth while. Under mechanized conditions it is just as easy to plough right across the strips as to plough land in small farms, indeed easier.

In the Hungarian Plain, where the farms are settled already in single homesteads, it would be much easier to introduce more intensive feeding of pigs and poultry, cultivation of vegetables and fruit, than large-scale machinery. In Rumania, on the other hand, where the strip system is general, it would be easy for the government to run some Machine Tractor Stations, as supplementary to the peasants' own cultivation, which is always delayed.

It cannot be concluded that large-scale farming should be introduced over Eastern Europe as a whole. In view of the present market position for wheat it would be unwise to invest in machinery with the object of selling more corn in the export markets; for sale in the home market the return would not be great enough. Intensification simply on the basis of the present system, maize-fed pigs, poultry, fruit, and vegetables, could be undertaken within the framework of the present system, and in the richer districts at least this sort of change could occur easily, given the development of irrigation, without a fundamental change in farm organization.

2. Capital Investment

The effects of small ownership on capital investment.

In examining the effects of the land reform it appeared that the division of big estates did serve as a temporary alleviation of rural poverty, though the standard of living of the farm population was not greatly improved. From the technical standpoint there is no real reason to regard the family farm as an unsuitable unit except in the dry districts, where its defects could be corrected by enforcement of standardization and of seed and farming operations, through the State administration.

But whereas the peasant system certainly cannot be criticized for making inefficient utilization of the existing labour force, it may exert a more serious influence of a long-run character, in that it may cause the size of the population actually on the land to be larger than can be fully employed; and this might be the result either of fostering a rapid rate of population growth, or of keeping too large a share of the population on the land.

Is there any causal connexion between the existence of big estates and the growth of industry? Or between peasant farming and the growth of rural population? In view of the great diversity in agrarian conditions in Eastern Europe as a whole, it is difficult to find any obvious connexion. The fact that the beginning of industrialization in its modern form has often coincided with agricultural distress—in England in the eighteenth century, in Germany in the nineteenth, and in present-day Japan—does lend colour to the theory (put forward by Schulze Gaevernitz and other German historians) that agricultural distress and peasant expropriation may contribute to, or even cause, the development of industry. Against this view, it can be pointed out that there are countries where domestic industry developed to large-scale modern industry, Switzerland, Central Germany, and Bohemia, while the surrounding peasantry was free and prosperous. Clearly it would seem wise to seek the determinants of the rate of industrialization in the conditions of capital accumulation, the development of trade, rather than in rural unemployment. It is true, of course, that rural poverty drives the population to find other occupations—but in itself it can only cause the growth of non-capitalistic industry (such as can be seen in Slovenia, where there are old-established hand industries, like straw hats and sieves, with an international market).

Nor, on the other hand, does it seem possible to hold that the prevalence of small ownership causes a very rapid growth of population, or causes the size of the population on the land to be larger than it would be otherwise. It is, of course, true that the areas under big estates are less densely populated than the peasant regions; this can be proved for Hungary.[1] But it is the families of the poorest farm labourers which increase most rapidly. There are peasant regions, such as the German villages in Hungary, the Magyar villages in the Ormansag district, and the Banat in Rumania, where very rigid family limitation is in force: others—above all, the Ruthenian regions in Czechoslovakia and Poland—where the rate of increase is abnormally fast.

But it is true that a peasant system with very widely dispersed ownership shows marked tendencies to over-invest in land, and thus prevents capital accumulation for investment in industry, on the scale which its rate of savings would permit; in so far as it does this, of course, it must necessarily reduce the rate of economic progress.

Is this tendency inherent in the peasant system as such?

The effect of peasant ownership of land on investment is, naturally, to promote investment of the peasant's savings in his own farm, in the purchase of live stock, and in the purchase of land, and the possibility of doing this increases the volume of savings.

The total volume of savings in a peasant economy is certainly greater than it would be under a system of large estates: peasants in all regions where a money economy is established tend to save a very high proportion of their income, even when the income is much smaller than that of a wage-earner. But these savings are invested in land purchase. In countries with widely dispersed peasant property the price of land tends to rise higher than its income-yielding capacity, if this were estimated by the rate of interest (although of course in these countries it is difficult to speak of a current rate on savings in general). In the densely populated districts the price of land is higher in proportion to the prospective yield than in the less densely

[1] Cf. Matolcsy, *Az új földreform munkaterve*, Budapest, 1936.

populated districts,[1] and has fallen only slightly since the commodity price fall of 1929. In the western districts of Poland since the crisis the price of land has fallen roughly by one-half, that is, by as much as the fall in crop prices: but in Galicia the price of land, measured in quintals of corn, has risen.[2] Land prices rise in these regions because the possibility of intensifying production is very small. The efficiency of capital in other investments on the farm is very low, and consequently all peasants who can save, hoard, to buy more land. The result is that savings are invested which cannot bring in an increase in productivity.

The existence of many small farms therefore drives savings into many small channels; and in consequence there are no reserves available for investment in large-scale capital construction which would cause an increase in productivity. The same volume of savings, if mobilized and invested in irrigation or electrical supply, might permit a great increase in agricultural productivity: but it cannot be mobilized. Under existing conditions, small investments here and there will not lead to an increase in the productivity of labour: for an increase in output of any magnitude it may be necessary to reframe the whole system,

[1]	Price of land in Rumania			
	Price of arable land in 100 lei 1929, per hectare	Arable land per head	Average yield 1923–27	
			Wheat	Maize
Danube Plain . .	20·1	1·22	11·4	9·0
Dobrogea . .	10·8	1·87	9·2	8·3
Bukovina . .	44·0	0·52	14·4	11·2
Plain of Transylvania.	30·0	0·61	12·8	10·2
Banat . . .	33·9	0·96	11·3	9·2

[2] Price of land in Poland (measured in quintals of wheat per hectare) in the district of Rzeszów, Galicia:

	Wheat	Rye
1927 . .	42·6	51·0
1928 . .	62·8	70·1
1929 . .	78·8	118·7
1930 . .	121·6	221·9
1931 . .	124·2	150·3
1932 . .	105·9	135·1
1933 . .	97·0	164·2
1934 . .	124·5	167·2

and to get control of bigger areas of land than under the present system is possible. But no amount of small-scale investment will bring about this change.

To give an instance of this kind of investment: in Slovakia there are many villages where the aggregate savings of the emigrants who have returned in the past ten years would have been enough to invest in co-operatively owned tractors and machinery; but because the savings are individually invested, all this money has gone to buying land, or horses, or re-roofing the houses. Another instance can be found in the villages of Northern Hungary. Here in quite poor villages some of the richer peasants with small farms have acquired tractors which would be enough to plough the whole land of the village; but, because the land is divided into strips, they are utilized only for threshing machinery.

All this wastage of savings is due, of course, to the defects of the field system which has already been described.

Owing to this individualism in investment, agricultural communities seem prone to stick at a stage in economic development. Consequently capital shortage exists, although the community may be saving more out of its existing income than richer communities do. Of course, large estates do not promote large-scale investment either; on the contrary, where they predominate, the tendency seems to be towards capital consumption rather than over-investment. Both in Hungary and Poland big estates are driven to sell off bits of land to pay debts.

As regards the supply of capital, a great difference exists between countries which have a well-developed co-operative system and those which have not. The Bulgarian peasants, with their highly developed co-operative system, and a bank in every village, have mobilized their savings: with assistance from foreign capital they have constructed the Vilcza hydro-electric power station for irrigation, and built factories for canning and packing fruit pulp: consequently a much greater degree of intensification is possible. In Poland and Rumania the co-operative system is weak, and no such development has occurred. Although Bulgaria has a much denser population on the land, a lower output per head in agriculture, and a lower proportion in industry, yet savings per head are higher in Bulgaria than in Poland, and output per head is being maintained. The peasants show much greater enterprise in changing over to new branches of production than they do in either Rumania or Poland. Thus the co-operative system may apparently serve to correct the tendency to over-invest.

For the peasant State, the real problem of farm organization is not to find the best size of farm, but to create favourable conditions for capital formation. No political system can increase the national income except in so far as it does this. If peasant ownership tends to lower the rate of capital accumulation, then chronic under-employment must result: and thus the real danger into which a peasant society may fall is that it does not exploit the worker enough to save for investment. All the usual neo-Marxist criticism of the peasant is based on superficial social ideals: he is a producer on a small scale, unmechanized, and not highly articulate, and so does not fit into a planned and disciplined system. But in fact the only real criticism to make of the peasant economy on economic grounds is that it does not apparently provide the means of growth.

If this criticism is true, it implies that a society with income relatively equally distributed, and without a capitalist class, cannot be a progressive economy, because the political institutions will not force investment enough to maintain the standard of living as population grows. In these conditions change can only come through gradual pauperization, or colonization by another economic system.

Can we conclude, then, that there is a general tendency in peasant communities not to save on a scale sufficient to maintain the general standard of living, i.e. that societies with widely dispersed ownership will have too little concentration of capital to industrialize?[1] Will peasants be forced to combine by growing misery? This conclusion cannot be drawn from the East European situation: the difficulties of adjustment to world conditions and tariffs on food would have adversely affected incomes and savings in Eastern Europe whatever system of land tenure had prevailed.

[1] Cf. Mitrany, *Marx and the Peasant*, in *London Essays in Honour of Edwin Cannan*, where this question is answered in the negative. The writer, however, does not give due weight to the influence of population growth.

Certainly one cannot find evidence of any inherent tendency in peasant society to consume too much, but rather to save and to misdirect the saving, though the less the credit organization is developed, the greater the tendency to hoard. Where co-operatives exist, they mobilize the capital and make the savings productive. Bulgaria is an example of what can be done to promote large-scale investment by co-operation and State intervention.

The fact that the co-operatives are now very weak is due to the waning of peasant influence in political life. In most provinces co-operatives and political parties are closely inter-dependent: before the War, in Slovenia, Moravia, Transylvania (to a lesser extent in Bohemia and Slovakia), they were identified with each other. For this reason the dictatorships have destroyed the co-operatives and done great harm to the economic structure.

In Poland, on the other hand, conditions do closely resemble the Russian, and the slow rate of accumulation does give support to the view that pauperization is now occurring. In very insecure political conditions, where hoarding is general, a peasant country may fail to invest sufficiently to maintain the standard of living; and when the peasants' parties have lost control of political affairs the danger of this occurring is still greater.

At present, therefore, it is the political situation of these countries which is the main check to capital investment in large-scale undertakings, and not the peasant structure as such which stands in the way of improvement. Most of the defects described are of minor importance, and if abolished would only cause minor improvements. Farm collectivization as a measure of improving farm efficiency would probably not achieve much, unless accompanied by industrialization and large-scale investment in irrigation.

In fact, of course, collectivization in Russia is a means of stimulating industrialization, rather than a way of increasing the productivity of labour on the farm. To regard it as an experiment in institutions, as the Webbs do, or as a revolution in technique, is to miss its significance. Its real meaning can only be seen in a setting of rural over-population, and it is from this standpoint that we must examine its results, in order to see how far collectivization is a remedy for the farm problem in Eastern Europe.

CHAPTER IX

THE RUSSIAN SOLUTION

1. THE RESULTS OF COLLECTIVIZATION

THE process of collectivization which began in 1929 is now complete. In a period of five years 18 million peasant farms were combined into a quarter of a million big units, using the most modern methods of cultivation—a social and economic transformation of such magnitude that its significance is difficult to grasp. Most of all, it is difficult to appreciate its economic results, for to the official communist mind the social change is all-important: in fact, from the official standpoint the social change must solve the economic problem: the elimination of capitalist peasants, the combination into big mechanized units, must themselves mean greater economic efficiency. But it is possible to conclude that collectivization is an experiment and not the application of a fool-proof system; original plans are thrown over, vital social principles are waived, in the effort to realize the idea of progress. It seems essential to refuse for the moment to be impressed by the vastness of the conception, and to estimate its results in economic terms, to see how far the experience can help to solve the farm problems of Eastern Europe.

Collectivization represents a second stage in socializing economic life and was, in fact, more revolutionary than the revolution itself. By the overthrow of Tsarism the large landowners were expropriated and their land and buildings were taken by the peasants and farmed; and in some cases they have been taken over and worked by 'artels'—groups of town workers who farmed jointly. These organizations vegetated for years; the bulk of the land was held by the peasants.[1]

[1] The rapidity of the change to collective farming is easily seen when one considers that before 1930 the number of collective farms was increasing by less than 30,000 per annum: in 1930 there were 86,000 collective farms. At the end of 1931 this number had jumped to 211,000, and the percentage of farmers' families under the collective system had increased from 23·6 to 52·7. Now 80 or 90 per cent. are included in the collective farms. By 1935 there were 4,364 Machine Tractor Stations as against 158 in 1930.

Collectivization aimed at expanding these artels to include all the peasants, and making of each village a collective farm, cultivating the common land with large machinery collectively owned. Its object was to carry out a revolution on the land, on which 70 to 80 per cent. of the population still existed, and to complete, therefore, the intervention of Socialism in economic life which had hitherto only touched its fringe. All the motive power came from the social theory; the peasant was a capitalist and must go. (Actually, of course, this view is a perversion of the facts, since the capitalist's real job of accumulating capital was never performed by the peasant.) Economic motives, except the naïve workshop of the big machine, were really absent. Yet as an economic policy collectivization of farming in Russia was absolutely justifiable: it was in fact the only way of tackling the two great dangers which were pauperizing Russia—inefficient land utilization and misdirected investment, and if the methods of carrying it through to a large extent defeated its object, it must not be concluded that the principle behind it was not a sound one.

In the territories of the Soviet Union, collectivization is a policy which promises success for two reasons. One, the scale of over-population was much greater in pre-war Russia than it is now in any European country (except perhaps Poland). The density of agricultural population in European Russia was 100 farm population to the 100 hectares of arable land[1]—a degree of density which is usually taken to indicate over-population. But in the Central Black Earth area, Little Russia and the Ukraine, the density was even greater—150 farm population to 100 hectares of arable land. Over Russia as a whole output per head was, and still is, lower than it is in Eastern Europe. At the same time, great areas were left uncultivated, owing to the lack of capital to exploit the soil in the dry regions. Thus, although the density of rural population was low over Russia as a whole, the bulk of the population was balled up in the most fertile provinces of European Russia. The real necessity of economic policy was to spread the population wider, and

---

[1] Arable land is taken rather than 'farm land' because the pastures usually included in this classification are very extensive and yet of little value. See Chapter III.

to check the rapid increase of rural population. Collectivization therefore tackles two quite distinct problems: one, the transformation of the peasant village into a mechanized farm; the other, the colonization by men and machinery of new areas where formerly no villages existed.

Secondly, the problem of land utilization was much simpler than it is in Europe; the main feature of Russian agriculture is the remarkable uniformity of the soil types over vast areas, and the immense contrast between the two main types. Russian soil science has evolved its own method of classifying soil types; classification is based on climatic differences, and is therefore much wider than that used in European countries, because the climatic contrasts are so much greater. Owing to the uniformity of soil conditions, agriculture is much more uniform than in Europe—corn is still the main product of farming. Roughly, European Russia falls into two divisions,[1] the poor podsol of the north (like Eastern Poland), and the rich black earth of the south (like Rumania). In neither of these great areas, apart from certain districts, is there any farming, in the European sense of systematic treatment of the soil to conserve its fertility by rotation and animal manuring: partly because the soil is too rich to need it in the south, and in the north too poor to show much return for it. To get good crops from the podsol type of soil it is necessary almost to make the soil by adding humus in the form of green manure and animal manure. The Czernozem soils by contrast are very rich in humus, and only need moisture.

Live-stock farming is still very extensive: so far as can be seen the same type of farming existed in the north as in the most primitive regions of Poland, and in the south the same system as in Rumania. Ukraine was cultivated fairly intensively, but there were steppe regions of primitive cultivation. Hence, to introduce machinery is much easier in Russia than it would be in Western Europe. The first condition for agricultural progress is to get the seeds sown in good time and to give the surface of the soil the right treatment to retain the moisture. In the new areas it was impossible that the work of cultivation should ever have been done by horses, and the tractor and

[1] The line of division runs roughly from Kiev to Sverdlovsk. See Mikhaylov, *Soviet Geography*, 1936.

combine are indispensable. So far as one can judge by the Russian experience to date, it has been mainly successful in these special conditions, that is to say, Southern Russia, that is, Ukraine, and the steppe area. It appears to have been a failure, whether temporary or permanent it is impossible to judge, so far as live-stock produce is concerned. Other branches of production, fruit, poultry, for which the Danubian basin is well suited, do not appear to have been tackled on new lines.

For these reasons, wholly outside the Marxist doctrine, collectivization was necessary to force an increase in output per man by forcing a high rate of capital accumulation, and treating Russia as a colonial region to be developed.

The first essential was to increase output per man, and from this standpoint the immediate results were disastrous. To prevent collectivization the peasants destroyed their cattle; almost half the live stock was slaughtered. For a poor country with so little capital this was a disaster of the first magnitude. For several years grain production fell short of its previous level and only recovered in 1935. The struggle was evidently terrible: on most of the farms I visited I heard accounts of the burning of crops and slaughtering of live stock in 1931–3. It is quite certain that this disaster could have been avoided if the peasants had been allowed to keep their live stock, as they are now encouraged to do. As proof of this it is only necessary to refer to Louis Fischer's description of the brilliant results of collectivization in the small republic of Kabardo-Balkaria,[1] where the wisdom of Kalmikov allowed peasants to keep their beasts on joining the collective. Had this course been followed in general, the disastrous decapitalization would not have taken place, and production might have been maintained.

Since the years immediately following the collectivization drive, the situation has improved. The food shortage of 1932–3 is over, and no actual starvation now occurs. Output of bread crops has increased since 1933, but meat and dairy products could not recover to the 1928 level until 1938, owing to the enormous decapitalization. Prices of these products are accordingly high. In June 1936 bread was 1 rouble (10d. nominal, 2d. actual, exchange value in sterling) per kilogram (2·2 lb.).

[1] Louis Fischer, *Soviet Journey*, 1935.

Butter was 22 roubles in Moscow and 17 in Rostov per kilogram, margarine 10 roubles. Milk was 1·30 roubles per litre (1¾ pints) (best quality, pasteurized), cheese 22 roubles per kilogram, eggs 4 roubles per 10. Sugar was 3·80 roubles per kilogram. Meat (sausage) was 28 roubles per kilogram, and tinned chicken 7·15 roubles for ½-lb. tin. These prices are those prevailing in State shops. Peasants sell butter and milk in the open market at slightly cheaper rates—butter 15 roubles per kilogram and milk 0·08 roubles per litre.

At the 1936 rate of exchange (25 roubles to £1) this is enormously high: but the actual purchasing power of roubles was then about one-fifth the exchange value. Calculated on this basis bread and eggs are cheap, but butter and meat are extremely dear. The consumption of meat and dairy products must be very low, as the average wage for the U.S.S.R. (their figure) is 200 roubles per month. The food situation certainly is not as good as it was before collectivization; questions which I was frequently asked were: 'What is the price of butter in England?' 'Do the workers eat meat?'

It is evidently too soon to speak of the collectivization as a successful measure so far as concerns its short-run effects on the volume of agricultural production in the already cultivated areas. But as a long-run policy the results are more promising. Mainly as a result of extension of the cultivated area, production has increased fast enough to keep pace with population growth. Grain production in 1936 and 1937 reached a total of 1,000 million quintals, 25 per cent. higher than the production of 1913. Total population in the same period had increased by the same amount, by about 20 to 25 per cent., from 140 to 170 or 175 millions.[1] Since exports (formerly 5 per cent. of the total) have declined to nothing, there must have been—though in the past two years only—a slight increase in consumption. (If, however, the average for the years 1909–13 is taken for comparison when the grain harvest averaged 750 million quintals, the results are more favourable, and show that the increase in grain production has been 33 per cent. up to 1937.)

The main reason for the increase is not higher production

[1] Estimate by author on the basis of rate of increase up to 1933; possibly the rate of increase is now slower.

per acre, but a big extension of the cultivated area. Thirty million hectares of arable land (an area three times as large as the agricultural land of England and Wales) have been taken into cultivation since 1913, and this increase has been more rapid since 1928. Yields in 1935 were only slightly higher than

Corn Production in U.S.S.R.

	1913	1929	1930	1931	1932	1933	1934	1935
Sown area (mill. hectares) .	105·0	118·0	127·2	136·3	134·4	129·7	131·5	132·8
Yields (quintals per hectare)	8·5	7·5	8·5	6·7	7·0	8·8	8·5	8·7
Corn production (mill. quintals) .	801·0	717·4	835·4	694·8	698·7	898·0	894·0	901·0

	1913	1929	1930	1931	1932	1933	1934	1935
Sown area (mill. acres).	259·5	291·6	314·3	336·8	332·1	320·5	324·9	328·2
Yields (cwt. per acre) . .	6·8	6·0	6·8	5·3	5·6	7·0	6·8	7·0
Corn production (million metric tons)	78·8	70·6	82·2	68·4	68·8	88·4	88·0	88·7

in 1913. As compared with the very low yields of the pre-war period, 1909–13 (7·5 quintals to the hectare), yields have now risen by about 10 per cent., and great efforts are now being made to increase them further. During the period immediately following collectivization, yields fell, and in consequence, in spite of the extension of the area, the average total production of cereals for the years 1930–4 was no higher than in 1913. Output per man and consumption must have fallen considerably, as the rural population had increased from 1914 to 1933 by 12 per cent., the total population 18 per cent. By 1933, however, production had exceeded the pre-war level by 12 per cent., and in the years 1934 and 1935 was maintained at this level. In 1936 and 1937 corn production is estimated to have risen to 1,000 and 1,140 million quintals, 25 per cent. above the pre-war level. Yields in 1937 rose to 10·9 quintals per hectare.

To calculate output per man is more difficult, as there are no figures to show the change in farm population in recent years. In 1933, however, the rural population of Russia ceased to increase, for the first time in history, and it can be presumed that the rate of increase of the farm population is slower, and even possibly that its numbers are declining, and that there must have been therefore an increase in output per head, from roughly 8 to 9 quintals per head in 1935, to 10 quintals in 1937.

So far as live-stock production is concerned, output per head

Live-stock Production in U.S.S.R.

million head

	1916	1929	1932	1933	1935	1936
Horses	35·8	34·0	19·6	16·6	15·9	16·6
Cattle	60·6	68·1	40·7	38·4	49·2	56·7
Sheep	121·2	147·2	52·1	50·2	61·1	73·7
Pigs	20·9	20·9	11·6	12·1	22·5	30·4

must have fallen by more than 50 per cent., since about half the cattle were destroyed after 1929, when horses, cattle, pigs, and sheep had more than recovered their pre-war level. Cattle have now recovered their 1913 level, and so have pigs. Sheep and goats in 1936 were still only half of their 1913 level.

Apparently, then, most of the increase in output could have been achieved by extending the State farms in the sparsely settled and uncultivated regions, without collectivizing the peasant villages in the already settled parts; had there been no collectivization, then all the loss of capital through live-stock slaughter would have been avoided, and corn production in 1931 and 1932 could have been maintained.

Was the upheaval due to collectivization in the settled regions therefore really unnecessary? To increase food production was essential owing to the rapid increase in population, but in fact the increase has been made by colonizing new areas, not by transforming the farming system, and it is not the new methods of farming which have made collectivization successful, but the possibility of colonizing new areas by machinery. With the high density on the land, and much unemployment in the settled areas, resettlement was obviously far more likely to improve the position of the farm population than providing them with

machines. In any case, in the settled areas it would never have
been economic to use machinery: labour on the land would have
always been cheaper than labour-saving machinery, as it is in
Hungary to-day, and though it appears to be the case that the
rural population has ceased to grow, yet there cannot be any
shortage of labour on the land.

The main purpose of collectivizing the farming system in
these settled areas was to give the central planning authorities
control over agricultural production during the period of investment in heavy industries and construction goods, which
was the basis of the Five-Year Plan. While the work of construction is in process it is necessary to provide the industrial
workers with adequate food-supplies; in other words, to secure
a certain wage level to them, which would be impossible so
long as the peasants retained control of grain production and
would only sell their produce in return for industrial goods.
To speed up industrialization it was necessary to force the
peasants to make a larger grain delivery than they would have
supplied had they been left free to sell or not. During the period
of construction supplies of manufactured goods must necessarily
be short, and the purchasing power of the money which the
peasant receives must necessarily be low. In other words, the
State artificially widens the gap between the earnings of town
workers and the peasants, in order to force the pace of investment in industry. Eventually, of course, the production of
industrial goods will increase, and if the increase in industrial
production is more rapid than the increase in food production,
then the price of industrial goods will fall in terms of food
products and the peasants will find that the purchasing power
of their output is higher. In fact, there are already signs that
this is happening; for the time being the purchasing power of
food is rising.

In so far as the peasants' income is reduced in this way, and
conditions of life in the towns are improved, there will be a
strong movement to the towns. But, of course, so long as the
rate of population increase is so fast as it now is, it is unlikely
that there will be much reduction in the actual numbers on the
land.

How fast the rural exodus is proceeding cannot be estimated

because the census gives a figure for rural population only, and does not show the number of workers in agriculture. The percentage of rural population declined from 82 to 74 per cent. according to the official figures in the five years 1929 to 1933. The terribly rapid rate of increase of the agricultural population, the great problem of pre-war Russia, has at last been checked,

	Total population, millions	Town population, millions	Rural population, millions	Rural population, % of total
1897 . .	106·4	15·8	90·6	85
1914 . .	139·3	24·6	114·6	82
1926 . .	147·0	26·3	120·7	82
1929 . .	154·2	27·6	126·7	82
1933 . .	165·7	39·7	125·4	74

and the problem of rural over-population has been tackled by reducing the numbers on the land and by resettling them in new areas.

When considering the actual change in technique which has been accomplished, it is important to distinguish the types of farming in the great regions.

In the northern districts only the first problem emerges, that of converting peasant villages into collectives, and, judging by appearances, the policy has not met with much success. In the northern provinces, between the Polish frontier and Moscow, the bad level of cultivation is extremely striking; crops are poor, and light, and uneven, obviously suffering from lack of manure. In places weeds are excessive, occasionally last year's crops are still standing. (This, I was told, was much more frequent three years ago.) In these northern provinces agriculture is very extensive; stretches of poor pasture take up about one-third of the area, uncultivated and probably not worth cultivating; odd cows graze at intervals. The arable is poor rye and potato land (average yield of rye 6½ cwt. per acre). In part, no doubt, this state of affairs is due to destruction of live stock which deprived the soil of its natural manure. To make good the loss by artificial fertilizers is at present impossible as the greater part of the supplies—which are quite inadequate—are sent, under the plan, to the cotton- and flax-growing districts in the south. The northern districts have, therefore, gone short—which is inevitable, if the policy of treating food-supply as secondary to industrial production is consistently followed.

The impression of bad farming is probably not due, however, entirely to the plan or collectivization. In these districts agricultural technique before collectivization was very much more primitive than it is in Eastern Europe to-day (except in the eastern parts of Poland). Three-field rotation still existed, winter crop, spring crop, and fallow—with no root or fodder crop—and consequently yields per acre were very low. This rotation is all but extinct on these soils in Europe; in general, root crops and green fodder crops were introduced everywhere in the latter half of the nineteenth century. To make the transition to modern rotations peasants needed a big increase in live stock, in order to get the winter crops in in the short autumn, and to provide manure for the fallow. The tractor does the one but not the other—the winter sowing can be done much more quickly, but this alone, without an increase in the supply of live stock, will not go far to raise yields per acre. In these regions, to skip a century in technical progress by introducing tractors is impossible if the live stock is simultaneously destroyed. Hence it is not surprising that the level of cultivation is not noticeably higher (and, in the opinion of many observers, lower) than before collectivization. To plough right across the separate strips, to get good quality seed and sow better and uniformly, to speed up the ploughing processes and plough deeper, would mean enormous progress if adequate fertilizer supplies were available. These desolate regions have the same sandy soil as Poland and East Prussia —not worth farming without very intensive use of manures— hence the deficiency of manures is catastrophic, as elsewhere it is not.

In the south the picture is entirely different, which may explain why foreign observers give such diverse accounts of collective farming. In two great corn-producing areas, Ukraine and the North Caucasus, tractor cultivation alone means an enormous advance and the destruction of live stock has been less disastrous.

On the steppe tractor cultivation is indispensable. There are vast areas formerly almost uncultivated, sparsely inhabited by Cossacks, who were violent opponents of collectivization. Their resistance is now crushed, and settlers from Ukraine and White

Farms in North Caucasus

	Total area hectares and acres	Cultivated area (exc. rough grazing)	Families	Workers	Total cattle (collect. and individ.)	Wheat yield, quintals per hectare
Kolkhoz 1 Zaviet Lenina (The Bequest of Lenin)	1,300 (3,212)	1,000 (2,471)	250	500	204	9¼ (7·6 cwt. per acre)
Kolkhoz 2 (The 9th of January)	2,300 (5,684)	1,630 (4,028)	157	300	510	9 (7·2 cwt. per acre)
Kolkhoz 3	2,102 (5,194)	1,498 (3,702)	206	545	..	..
Kolkhoz 4	2,054 (5,076)	1,475 (3,645)	515	1,090	..	..

(Milk yields: Zaviet Lenina, 1,300 litres annual average, i.e. 290 gallons.)

Russia have been put on collective farms. The farms I visited are described in the table below. In view of the quality of the soil and the proximity of Rostov it was bad farming (yield 9 quintals per hectare, or 7½ cwt. per acre), but the state of the fields was better than in the north. The amount of live stock kept was small, the cows poor, the milk yields low, and the dairy equipment primitive (though with only well water it can hardly be otherwise). There were not enough tractors to get round the work.

Artificial manures were used in 1936 for the first time. With better root crops and adequate tractor equipment they ought to double their milk and wheat production easily.

The future possibilities can better be seen on the State farms (Sovkhozy) in this district. These are quite distinct from the kolkhozy; they exist mainly in districts where there was no previous village settlement, and consequently were not hampered by social resistance. The workers are in the same position as industrial workers, and have not the same status as the collective farmer (uncertain though that is). Some, like Zernograd, are experimental stations and training schools for the new generation of tractor engineers as well as farms. These farms own their own tractors and combines.

Zernograd[1] is a town of six thousand people, isolated in the steppe, dry, and mirage-haunted. Its area is 29,000 hectares (71,000 acres); it was originally four times this size, but this proved unmanageable 'even by aeroplane', so it was divided into four farms. This is, of course, prairie farming with little live stock and no roots or green crops. Grain is sown continuously, two years winter wheat, two years spring wheat, with a fifth year fallow (the bare fallow, well cultivated in the State farm, is usual in the province).

The tractorists on the farm (and in the whole Union) are among the highest paid workers (excluding the scientific). The farm is a training station for tractor engineers, and it is interesting to note that these are predominantly drawn from the town proletariat and not from collective farm peasants: of 653 students of the Institute, 509 are workers and only 30 of peasant origin.

The average wage is 400 to 450 roubles per month (£16 to £18 at the 1936 exchange rate, £3 to £4 in purchasing power), and in addition to this workers receive 2,000 to 5,000 kilograms of flour and keep their own cows.

Although the relation of costs and prices gives no true indication of whether this farm is working at a profit (the price of petrol is fantastically low, and also the machinery), there cannot be much doubt that it is. If 17 quintals to a hectare (13½ cwt. to an acre) can be produced with no manure, and with an average area per tractor of 1,000 acres and wages of £3 4s. per month, wheat can be produced below the world market price.

Ukraine is a complete contrast to the steppe; evidently well-farmed for generations; densely settled with enormous villages

[1] Zernograd (The City of Grain), North Caucasus.

Area	Total population	Workers	Management	Institute	Students
29,000 ha.	6,800	200	800	1,000	600

Sales: Total sales to State 12,000 tons of grain, price 130 roubles a ton (equals £60,000 at exchange rate).

and mud cottages scattered over the fields (as a result of the Stolypin reforms). Farming is incomparably better than in the north; there are big areas under vetch, sainfoin, and lucerne, and superb crops of wheat and rye and sugar-beet. The live stock are few but good—Simmenthal cattle, good local pigs

Farms in Ukraine

	Cultivated area, hectares and acres	Families	Workers	Cattle	Wheat yields, quintals per hectare
1. *Kharkov* Nadia (Hope) .	1,247 (3,081)	..	402	207	13 (10 cwt. per acre)
2. *Poltava* Dawn of Victory .	1,911	270	460	15*	29 (1935) (23 cwt. per acre)
	(4,721)			242†	35 (1936) (27 cwt. per acre) (estimate)
3. *Poltava* Red Dawn . .	1,000 (2,470)	..	250	Few, specializing in poultry	

* Collective.   † Individual.

crossed with Large Whites. With its bees and cherry orchards and gardens the country is wholly European in character.

Here agricultural progress is not a matter of breaking up the soil but of seed selection, animal breeding, and scientific feeding. On two farms, one specializing in pigs, the other in live stock, the inequality in machine equipment was striking; one, the 'Dawn of Victory', had 1,911 hectares and only one tractor. and the other, the 'Red Dawn', 1,000 hectares and 4 tractors, The 'Dawn of Victory' was well farmed by Ukrainian peasants, and had magnificent crops (23 cwt. to the acre and over), the 'Red Dawn' (originally a commune, which failed and was then divided into four collective farms) was run by a hard-boiled set of refugees from Bulgaria, Poland, and Macedonia, and seemed extremely chaotic, with machinery lying about the yard unprotected in heavy storms. The large amount of capital in horses and oxen is evidently no disadvantage to the 'Dawn of

Victory' and suggests that for their conditions it is better to supplement tractor work with horses and oxen and use more manure. The Wisconsin silo (newly built) is used on all farms.

On the technical side the really impressive thing is the close connexion between the scientific workers and the farms. In Ukraine this is mainly due to the two Agricultural Institutes at Poltava. One institute works on grass crop cultivation and experiments with vetches to flower at different dates under different light and temperature. The other institute, under Professor Lewitski, researches on pig feeding. All farms in Ukraine and many in other parts of Russia now use his method of fermentation of food. The collective farm mechanism undoubtedly gives the opportunity of introducing better methods. On each farm there is an agronome with some technical training, and many farms have a laboratory where experiments in seed selection, manures, and dates of sowing are conducted. Thus, farmers get a much stronger guidance from scientific workers than they do in any European country, and are acquiring a more experimental attitude.

2. THE SOCIAL ORGANIZATION

As an institution the *kolkhoz* is hard to classify. Usually it is the former peasant village with five hundred or more inhabitants and one or two thousand hectares. It is not in any intelligible sense co-operative, nor is it fully socialistic. It is difficult to understand how the land is owned; and in the minds of my informants it certainly was not clear. Recently, a new law has been passed which gives the land as collective property to the collective farm (i.e. to the former peasant village, minus the intransigents) as a perpetual lease. This appears to mean that the collective cannot forfeit the land to the State nor can the collective sell the land. Thus the village owns jointly what it previously owned as individuals. The bulk of the capital, however, the big machinery such as tractors, combines, and plate harrows, is not owned by the collective farm, but by Machine Tractor Stations (M.T.S.) which exist in every district and serve about thirty collectives each. (At present not all farms are served by the M.T.S., and some are in possession of their own tractors, but this is a temporary phase.) Live stock and smaller machinery (drilling machines, harrows, horse-ploughs) are the property of the collective farm, as are also the buildings, usually the old buildings of the landowner's estate with additions and improvements. But much live stock is individual property; each peasant has the right to keep a cow, a pig or two, poultry, and a garden. On most of the farms visited the individual cows outnumbered the collective cattle.

Thus on the majority of collective farms there is not a complete socialization of property. They distinguish between the 'artel' in which some private property is retained and the 'commune' in which *all* property is socialized.

The communist standpoint is, of course, that the commune is 'a higher form'—meaning that it is absolutely better than individualism—apart from its technical advantages. This form they attempted to introduce without success: the attachment to pig and cow proved too strong even for Stalin, and after many attempts have failed, 'the commune', he reassures them, 'is premature'. Some examples, like the Seattle Commune, near Rostov, remain. It appears that there is within limits a return to individualist ownership, for the purposes of increasing live-stock production. A decree has just been issued to give credits to individual peasants to enable them to buy cows, pigs, and sheep from the collective; and the management of the farm *must* act on this decree.[1]

Thus the system is not complete Socialism. How much control of management do the collective farmers exercise? The degree of management has to be compatible with, first, the requirements of the plan as to crop production; second, the use of the tractors from the Machine Tractor Station.

The plan, it must be understood, does not cover agricultural production as such. Agricultural production is planned to a much less degree than in the U.S.A. or in Germany. From time to time resolutions are made saying 'we must aim at producing so many tons of sugar-beet per hectare', but *total* production is not decreed. Only the output of tractors is included in the Five-Year Plan, and some special crops, like cotton and flax, for industrial raw material. According to two foreign observers,

[1] Credits are to give each individual farmer means to acquire 1 pig, 25 sheep, 1 cow, and 2 young beasts.

the agronomes are the real entrepreneurs, as indeed they must be, since they control the use of the machine capital.

Hence one is sceptical as to whether there is much scope left for independent action by the collective. The disposal of the product is, within limits, a matter for the members to decide. A certain proportion of the crop—about one-third—must be sold to the State, and 600 litres of milk from every cow: and also, on the breeding farms, pedigree pigs. The remainder the members can sell (collectively) to the co-operatives, or can divide among themselves, or invest in the farm. As they are apt to invest too much in the farm—just as peasants do—a provision has been introduced in the Statute of Artels by which not more than 10 to 20 per cent. of the product is to be invested. So the essential decision is the same as that of an ordinary agricultural co-operative, i.e. how much dividend, how much investment. The party members are, of course, the driving force. The peasants who would have been the leaders in co-operative enterprise, the *kulaks*, are not there.

3. INCOMES AND STANDARDS OF LIVING

To discuss the effect of collectivization on the standard of living of the rural population is difficult indeed. In a country where the housing shortage is still so acute, and which has only recently emerged from famine conditions, people cannot possibly think of their income as entitling them to minimum diets or minimum housing space. Though manufactured goods, cotton shirts and dresses, canvas shoes, can now be purchased, their prices are so high that consumers cannot possibly buy them regularly. Thus it seems better to speak solely of earnings per worker, and to distinguish between special classes of skilled workers and the ordinary agricultural workers who were formerly poor peasants. The tractorists get high wages (500 roubles a month, i.e. £20 at exchange rate, £4 at one-fifth exchange rate); they are paid by the Machine Tractor Station and their wages have no relation to the amount or price of farm production: the wages of the 'collective farmer', on the other hand, vary with the amount and price of output of their own farms.

Are they better or worse off than they would be as individual peasants? The only way of answering this question is to

...tion per hectare and population in U.S.S.R. compared with other European countries

	Total farm population, millions	Arable* land, million hectares	Arable land per head, hectares	Average yield of four chief corn crops 1928–32, quintals	Arable land, million acres	Arable land per head, acres	Average yield, cwt. per acre
of rural population)	112·5 (1933)	132†	1·2	8·2	310·9	3·0	6·5
	19·3 (1931)	18·4	0·9	11·3	45·5	2·2	9·0
	4·4 (1931)	5·5	1·2	13·0	13·6	3·0	10·4
	5·1 (1933)	5·8	1·1	16·8	14·3	2·8	13·4
	13·6 (1933)	21·2	1·5	19·0	52·4	3·8	15·1
	4·0 (1931)	3·7	0·9	11·3	10·1	2·2	9·0

compare their earnings with those of peasant farmers in East European countries, and in making such a comparison it is difficult to distinguish the effects of collectivization from the effects of natural conditions. In all agricultural countries which are mainly self-supporting, the condition of the worker on the land is determined by the density of population, quality of the soil, and proximity to the market to a much greater extent than by the size of the producing unit or the nature of economic organization. For instance, a peasant in Ukraine, under whatever system he worked, ought to have a bigger income than a peasant in Galicia, or on the marshes and sands of Polesia; population cannot move about enough to equalize the return in different districts.

The table opposite shows the number of workers engaged in agriculture at the last census and the average production per hectare in Russia, Germany, and Eastern Europe. Calculated from these figures, the average gross corn output per man would be 9·8 quintals in Russia, 11 quintals in Poland, and 28 quintals in Germany. Since 1937 the average gross corn output in Russia may be over 10 quintals.

On this basis, the income of the peasant in Russia before collectivization and during its early years was lower than that of the peasantry in Eastern Europe, because the amount of arable land per head was less and yields were lower; at this time, and even in the good years of 1934 and 1935, Russia would come below the 10 quintals per head standard which has been taken as the minimum indicating adequate feeding. Now, in the last two years, 1936 and 1937, production has increased about 25 per cent. as compared with 1913. This, as we have said, means that it has kept pace with the growth of total population. Output per head must now be over 10 quintals per head of farm population, if it can be assumed that since 1933, the last date of the census, the farm population has not increased (or has increased only slightly). On this assumption output per head is now slightly higher than it is in the poorest regions of Eastern Europe, though not as high as it is in Rumania, or Poland, as a whole, mainly because yields remain low.

This, however, does not take into account the purchasing

power of the produce. In the peasant countries of Eastern Europe the proportion of production sold varies from 20 to 80 per cent., and is determined by the market price, on the basis of some sort of utility calculation.

In the Soviet Union there is no calculation of this kind. Farmers are forced to sell a large part of their produce on very unfavourable terms. This, as we have said, is necessary to the Five-Year Plan. If the pace of industrialization is to be forced, the level of agricultural earnings must be depressed in relation to industrial prices: some degree of exploitation of the peasant is essential to its fulfilment. In Eastern Europe industrialization is forced in essentially the same way, by imposing tariffs on manufactured goods, so that the peasant exchanges his product on worse terms, but with the difference that he is free to retain his produce if industrial prices rise too high: in Russia he is not.

The method of fixing the grain delivery is as follows: each farm must deliver a certain quantity of grain, a fixed amount per hectare, and in return it receives a low price. As a political measure this is wisely calculated, since it is not a tax on production: if more is produced, the farm retains it and a price is given. Thus the proportion delivered varies from farm to farm: in general it is about one-third of the total. The 1936 price was 11–12 roubles per quintal. What remains after the compulsory grain delivery may be purchased by the State, sold in the market, or retained for consumption. If sold, it is marketed to co-operatives, also at a controlled price, but this price reflects more or less the state of the market and may be ten times as high as the price paid for the State grain delivery. The prices paid (120–180 roubles per quintal) are fairly high, but farmers do not sell much in this way, presumably because the State grain delivery takes most of their surplus.

The following table shows how the proportion sold has increased.

The town proletariat until now has taken a bigger share of food from the agricultural population than it would have been able to do under a price system. Obviously, the standard of the farmers has not risen, except in so far as production has increased. In the last two years grain production has increased rapidly from the low level of 1930, but as agricultural production

Disposal of Grain Crops*

	1932	1933†	1934	1935	1932	1933†	1934	1935
	million quintals				*million cwt.*			
Harvest in ear	699	898	894	920	1334	1714	1706	1756
Grain losses	179	258	214	170	341	492	408	324
Granary harvest	520	640	680	750	992	1221	1298	1431
Grain sold and delivered	197	252	282	315	376	481	538	601
Grain supplies	323	388	398	435	616	740	760	830
Compulsory grain deliveries	188	227	226	255	359	433	431	487
Sales	9	11	43	50	17	21	82	95
Other deliveries	..	14	13	10	..	27	25	19
Total sale and delivery	197	252	282	315	376	481	538	601
Per cent. of statistical harvest.	28	28	32	34	53	53	61	65
Per cent. of granary harvest .	38	40	42	42	73	76	80	80

in general has only just recovered its pre-collectivization level, it is clear that so far collectivization cannot have much improved the position of the workers on the land.

As we have said, as the volume of industrial production increases, the ratio must change in the farmer's favour or there will be no market for the industrial products. This stage has now been reached; the State is trying to pump back purchasing power for industrial products on to the land, and the State price for wheat has been raised recently. As things are at present, on the basis of purchasing power, the Russian farmer is certainly not so well off as the peasants in Poland

Thus the physical output per man in corn is slightly higher in Russia than in the very poorest regions of Eastern Europe, and the value in terms of industrial products certainly lower. Is the output per man sufficiently high to compensate for the low purchasing power of wheat? To make an estimate it is necessary to calculate the earnings of a peasant farmer or of an estate worker in Poland in the same way as those of a Russian worker, i.e. to take the gross product and assume that one-third is sold. The only figures for earnings obtainable for Russia relate to farms in the neighbourhood of industrial towns, and all (except near Moscow) on extremely good soil; thus they are much above the average.[1]

The figures for comparative gross incomes per worker are as follows: in wheat and rye, on Ukrainian collective farms near towns, 900 kilograms; on three Polish farms—peasant with 5

---

[1] The method of calculating income on collective farms needs explanation, as it is a complicated method of piecework and profit-sharing. Earnings are calculated 'per labour day'. This is an abstract term, referring not to a real day but to an amount of work. On each farm certain pieces of work—ploughing a certain area, cleaning stables, milking cows—are described as labour days, so a tractorist can do three labour days in 10 hours, an old man who watches the orchards takes several days to count one. At the end of the year each worker has a total of 250–450 'days' to his credit. This determines the ratio in which total production is divided among producers: if the total production is 900,000 kilograms (9 quintals per hectare × 1,000 hectares), and there are 300 workers each with 300 days to his credit, the total is divided by 9,000: which gives 10 kilograms per worker per day. About half is sold to the State as grain delivery or in the market which gives the income in money—2·4 roubles—and the remainder, 5 kilograms, is consumed. Each worker gets 2·4 roubles and 5 kilograms multiplied by the number of labour days to his credit.

acres in a remote village (Broniszów), peasant with 5 acres in a village close to a town (Albigowa), and workmen on an estate in Central Poland, respectively 750, 850, and 1,400 kilograms. In money, the respective earnings were 600 roubles (120 zloty), 135, 171, and 120 zloty.

Thus, in good conditions in Poland where yields are high, and the number of cows kept per worker is higher, the income is higher also. In the poor Galician village it is lower. This is on account of the better prices obtained; on the good peasant farms the physical production per worker would be lower than on the Russian.

In the Russian farms and less remote Polish villages there is no starvation if this rate of income is obtained by all. However, the food-supply is not adequate from a nutritional standpoint. On the Russian farms meat consumption must be much lower than in Poland, and milk consumption must be lower also.

Over the country in general, apart from the State farms where a new generation is learning new jobs, there cannot possibly have been much improvement in earnings as compared with the pre-collectivization period. Grain output per head is not higher by more than a small amount.

Looking at the achievement to date, it seems surprising that food prices should be higher, and incomes of agricultural workers lower, in a country which has gone over to big units and mechanized production, than in countries which carry on the old methods under all the drawbacks of the strip system. The reason is that the method of carrying through the change was violent and sudden; destruction of live stock inevitably means a decline in production for a long time; and the industrialization drive necessitates a low level of incomes on the land. Under any system, it would be impossible to increase the volume of production in agriculture and raise the income of workers, if at the same time decapitalization in agriculture and forced invest-ment in industry were occurring on a large scale. For the present, like the Russian country-side, the policy is 'too vast to admit of excellence', but there is no doubt that in the future there must be an increase in food-supplies and a rise in the standard of living. From the standpoint of a country with a rapidly increasing population and a policy of self-sufficiency, it has been the only course to take.

It is clear that the present state is not Socialism; collective farms in some sense own their land, and peasants get higher incomes where the land is better, because the grain delivery does not vary with the yield. The ultimate ideal is to urbanize agriculture completely, to assimilate *kolkhoz* to *sovkhoz*, and make agro-cities with a town proletariat. In the south, where stone for building materials is cheap, such cities are already under construction. But this ideal is still very far from the mud-huts and thatch of the Ukraine.

In spite of the tendency to return to individual ownership of live stock, it does not seem likely that there will be a return to individual farming. The increase in productivity in the Caucasus and Ukraine may be so great that they will suffice to feed the Union, so that the poor soils of the north can abandon rye and wheat. In pre-war Russia such a possibility of plenty could not even be contemplated. The critics of communism can easily point to instances of uneconomic use of the factors of production; such wastage indubitably occurs. It cannot be doubted that the tractors, for example, are less economically utilized than they would be under a price system; but it cannot be doubted either that under a price system the tractors would not be there at all. Only through collectivization is it possible to develop the agricultural resources of the Soviet Union in such a way that the problem of their economic use arises.

4. COLLECTIVIZATION AS A REMEDY FOR EASTERN EUROPE

As a means of increasing productive efficiency in the immediate future, collectivization looks rather like a failure. The chief object of revolutionizing farm organization should be, in the peculiar conditions of Russia and of Eastern Europe, to make better use of the existing capital and increase the output per man: and collectivization certainly had the contrary effect, as a short-run measure; it caused the destruction of about half the live-stock capital, and production declined. From the social standpoint much modification has been necessary. The ideal of making peasants a proletariat has not been reached: private ownership of cattle has been allowed; the peasants have been given some sort of property in land and security of tenure, and a promise of democratic activity. If one simply takes into account the effect of farming methods it is difficult to urge collectivization as a remedy for the farm problem of Eastern Europe. The peasants as a whole are not much better off than before, and not better off than peasants in Eastern Europe, except those in the very poorest regions.

For Russia, on the other hand, it must be a successful policy in the long run, because it must stimulate the accumulation of capital; and as the progress of industrialization leads to a bigger output of manufactured goods, the purchasing power of the peasants' income must rise.

But in its broad lines, as a policy for speeding up capital accumulation, collectivization seems unlikely to succeed in Eastern Europe, both because the economic conditions for its success are not present, and because the social forces which might carry it through do not exist.

The situation in Eastern Europe now resembles to some extent that of pre-war Russia—chronic under-employment, a falling level of agricultural technique, which may eventually lead to destruction of the fertility of the soil. In Russia the state of rural over-population was consistent with the existence of vast agricultural areas which could not be brought into cultivation, and natural resources which could not be exploited, owing to lack of capital: the population was balled up very densely in Ukraine and the Central Black earth region, and could not be spread over the rest of the area because under a system of semi-feudalism the long-period investment could not be undertaken from the country's own resources. Investment, if forced, can yield a big return, because the area to be colonized and the resources to be utilized are already in existence. But Eastern Europe has little or no uncultivated land and few mineral resources; the policy of a forced industrialization would therefore lack its foundations. The essential condition for the success of forced industrialization is that there should be a reserve of natural resources, which new development will make available, and without these resources to draw upon industrialization and the extension of the cultivated area alike would be impracticable.

The main reason which promises success to the Russian plan is because it is a colonization programme, not merely a reorganization of farming methods, and Eastern Europe has no hope of dealing with surplus population in this way.

How far, then, is collectivization likely to be successful, considered simply as a means of reorganizing farming? As we have said, its chief merit is that it does permit a more general application of the results of scientific research over large areas. Scientific farming, of course, may be merely a phrase: ten years ago in the United States the kind of farming which has been responsible for soil erosion was acclaimed as scientific. Another danger is that scientific farming may mean the introduction of standards of technical methods which are only successful in other conditions, for instance, the introduction of Simmenthal cattle in Rumania, which was undertaken with State assistance. But in spite of these dangers, there is great scope for the application of results of scientific research, mainly in the sense of study of the conditions of cultivation in dry climates. The work of Manninger in Hungary[1] is a striking proof of the need for scientific farming in a genuine sense, and of the ease with which results can be applied when the scale of operation is large.

The problem, however, is to find a way of reconciling control of operations over large areas with the responsibility of the workers on the land, which is always a valuable asset, apart from its social significance. In farming, complete State control is as impossible as complete individualism. But a peasant society like that of Bulgaria can go a long way towards enforcing good standards, and stimulating corporate investment, without sacrificing the independence of the producers, and the fact that it does not enforce collective cultivation is not such a great disadvantage, if farming can turn over to new crops.

Can collectivization do more than this? At present the Russian system seems to have centralized control too far, destroying the independence of the producers, without having achieved results on the technical side which would outweigh the losses of the early years. The critical question, of course, is whether it really has created a new mentality among the serf-peasants, or whether they still regard the government as their enemy.

[1] See Chapter V, p. 107.

On this question it is hard to form an opinion: something has undoubtedly been done to create a new spirit among the leaders of the younger generation. But after all, the collectivization was undertaken as a campaign against the peasants, and resulted in a partial victory only; the winning side lost through the food shortage, the peasants won the right to keep cows. Its material success is not great enough to have obliterated the psychological effects of the struggle. The Webbs argue that these methods were necessary because the Russian peasant was so extraordinarily primitive that he could not see the advantage of collectivization, but this is not, of course, the Marxist argument. The true Communist view was that the peasants would be eliminated as capitalists, and that to subordinate them to the ends of another class is to remove a social injustice. The ruthless enforcement of this doctrine must inevitably have left a legacy of bitterness.

Planning in the Five-Year Plan sense might help the agrarian countries up to a point; if they could evolve State schemes for raising the rate of capital accumulation, for investment in large-scale undertakings, irrigation, industrialization, and (to some extent, in some areas) in mechanized farming, they could certainly make some advance. A survey of peasant farming has shown that individual ownership of land and individual investment, without control by co-operatives or by the State, will not lead to the best utilization of the land. Peasant farms give better conditions of labour to the farm population than estate farms; but unless there are ways of mobilizing savings and controlling investment, there tends to be a surplus supply of labour.

Of course this is a defect of individualism rather than of peasant farming. Even in countries with much higher standards of farming technique, and much greater supplies of capital, the same problem arises. Planning is necessary in agriculture in the sense of planned investment and production control, because the great factors of soil fertility and animal breeding and disease do not fit into the cost and profit schemes of the individual farmer. If to these factors is added a rapid rate of population growth, then it is clear that the best utilization of the soil is a matter of vital concern. Where there is land shortage, the decline of fertility will be far more serious and difficult to arrest than it is in the United States. For this reason it is countries like Africa and Eastern Europe which can learn most from the Russian example.

But it would be unwise to suppose that a more scientific attitude towards soil fertility and some State intervention can do for Eastern Europe what Communism can do for Russia. The real value of Communism is that it is doing for Russia what free trade and capitalism did in the nineteenth century for England: it speeds up the rate of capital accumulation, spreads population over new regions, and so can counter the effects of rapid population increase. But it is a plan which depends for its success on having great undeveloped resources of iron, coal, oil, and electrical power. Since these resources do not exist in Eastern Europe on a large scale, there is not much scope for planning, in the sense of speeding up capital accumulation, although in Rumania the peasant problem might be solved, given the better methods to be attained through State control.

In the sense of a scheme simply aiming at reorganizing village farming, without an industrialization policy, collective villages could realize some degree of technical progress if the lessons of the Soviet collectivization were studied. These lessons are two-fold. One is that the live stock should not be collectivized. The other is that if the peasant gives up the land he must retain some security of a share in the harvest. If the peasant holds on to the land it is not because he is a capitalist; it is not a means of production which he can hire out, but his only security in a world of uncertainty. Given such a guarantee, it ought to be easy to introduce communal cultivation and machinery. But without wider markets, and the possibility of migration, this reorganization could not do much to raise the standard of living.

CONCLUSION

WHAT, then, is the future of the peasant States? Their economic position—the population surplus—and their geographical location seem to expose them to a choice between two State systems, in political and economic methods rather similar, but fundamentally different in their economic purpose: Nazism aiming at increasing Germany's economic power, Communism aiming at raising the standard of living by industrialization.

As we have seen, the Russian transformation of peasant agriculture into large-scale farms is not a solution, unless reserves of land are available. With the present farm density, Eastern Europe cannot evolve a type of farm organization which can raise its standard of living appreciably, on its own resources; no country in Europe which has an adequate rural standard has a density of this level, nor ever has had.

Without access to markets in which the supply of capital is more plentiful, and where food products command higher prices, it is impossible for Eastern Europe to obtain the means of accumulating capital. The extension of German economic control over these areas does appear to hold out the prospect of immediate gain. But planning, in the Nazi sense, offers limited possibilities of expansion.

Nazism is a system of State control which aims simply at making Germany self-sufficient, and in such a plan Eastern Europe must play an essential part. But Nazism could only include Eastern Europe in the German economic system on a footing of dependence: agriculture would turn over to cultivation of industrial raw materials, which can be produced cheaper elsewhere. In Germany itself planning in the sense of control of food-production and prices has not been successful in causing much increase in production, and it is not this kind of regulation that the peasant States need. The Nazi economic system has introduced no new principles of economic organization: the special institution for agriculture, the Farm Inheritance Law, which ties the farm to the farm family, has no significance whatsoever in over-populated regions. What the peasant States need is not price-regulation but rising prices: they need integration with the economic life of industrial Europe, in the sense of access to markets with rising standards of living and cheap capital.

How far closer connexions with Germany can offer these advantages is a matter for controversy. The German market could certainly absorb the whole of the export surpluses from the Danubian regions, though only on unfavourable terms. But so long as wages remain low, it seems unlikely that there can be much further increase in consumption of meat and fat. So far as capital is concerned, Germany has little capital available for investment in agriculture or in consumption goods industries, as long as it pursues its present investment policy.

Since the extension of German control is likely to follow only as a result of successful power politics, it is desirable in the political interests of these countries to find a European solution, in which the agrarian states will find a market for their produce while maintaining their independence.

How far would a European custom union go towards solving the problem of the agrarian states, assuming that it took the form of free trade between European countries, and worked out as an exchange of products between the agrarian East and the industrial West, excluding imports of food from overseas countries?

Such a union would cause a very far-reaching adjustment in the economic structure of the industrial regions of Europe. At present the relatively sparsely settled farm population in each of the industrial countries has secured a monopoly of its home market, in which wages are relatively high and in which consumption is extremely stable. Prices are maintained at roughly twice the level of prices in Eastern Europe, and imports from the agrarian states would therefore bring down wheat prices considerably, meat and milk prices also. This fall in prices would cause a fall in farmers' incomes in the industrial countries, and much unemployment among the farm population. No doubt the fall in bread prices would lead to some increase in meat and milk consumption, but the scope of the increase cannot be very large. A contraction in wheat production must inevitably mean a contraction in labour requirements on the land. As wheat production in the West declines, the higher price in the East would stimulate more intensive cultivation, yields would rise and production shift to the Danube region.

In Western Europe the industrial population would gain through cheaper food, but would find the adjustment in the labour market through the influx of labour from the land a very serious one. How serious the adjustment would be can be judged by comparison of the farm populations in Eastern and

	Western Europe		Eastern Europe		Europe, except U.S.S.R.
	Millions	Per cent. of Europe	Millions	Per cent. of Europe	
Occupied agricultural population .	38·6	50·3	38·1	49·7	76·7
	Million quintals				
Cereal production .	789·2	58·3	565·2	41·7	1354·7

Western Europe. At present about half Europe's farm population lives in Eastern Europe, about half in the West, and the East produces about 35 per cent. of the wheat harvest. Free trade inside Europe would inevitably mean a big displacement of labour in the West.

To make the necessary adjustment the farm population of Europe as a whole would have to be reduced considerably. To get an adequate income, it is necessary in European conditions that a farm family should produce enough food to feed at least three families, including itself. At present, of Europe's total population of 350 millions, about 45 per cent. are now dependent on agriculture; thus to raise the level in agriculture in Europe as a whole the proportion of farm population would have to fall to 30 per cent., even if Europe were self-sufficient.

Undoubtedly this shift in production would improve the position of the Eastern regions. But it would not cause a big all-round improvement. The increase in the demand for food in Western Europe would not be very large, since wheat produced in European conditions will tend to be dear in relation to wheat produced overseas, owing to land shortage and transport costs in Europe. In the future the divergence in rates of population growth, the decline in the West, and the increase in the East, will mean that food consumption in the high standard regions tends to decline, while in the East food producers still increase. Even, therefore, if agrarian Europe does become the granary of Germany, or of Western Europe as a whole, the growth of population on the land will not be absorbed in agriculture. Europe would still have an excessive number of farmers. Either the agrarian countries must industrialize, or their population must migrate.

From the general economic standpoint, migration is the most desirable solution. When regard is had to the soils available for cultivation in overseas countries, and even in Europe itself, it is absurd that the Polesian sand should be cultivated at all. Even where there is no sign of declining yields, much of the soil now used for arable farming is not really suitable for corn-growing, and only a starvation standard forces this kind of land utilization. If the world as a whole was over-populated, the problem would be a different one. But there is no reason for thinking that it is.[1]

The following table shows the contrast between the land resources of Eastern Europe and those of the overseas producers, so far as arable land only is concerned.

	Arable land million hectares (1930)	Farm population* millions (1930)	Arable land per head of farm population (hectares)
U.S.A. . . .	137	21·0	6·5
Australia . .	12	1·1	11·0
Canada . . .	23	2·2	10·0
Argentina . .	25	5·0†	5·0
Poland, Rumania, Bulgaria, Jugoslavia	42	48·0	0·86

     * Estimated as twice the active agricultural population.
     † Estimated.

Further, the dynamic aspect must be borne in mind. Europe's subsistence basis is shrinking as its population grows, while the decline in population in overseas countries will mean that they

[1] According to an estimate by Bowman the amount of cultivable land per head in the world in general amounts to 3 acres, i.e. is above the European subsistence level of 1 hectare (2·4 acres). See *The Limits of Land Settlement*, 1937.

cannot rely on the natural increase of their population to develop their resources.

Apart altogether from the instability which arises from the disparities of standards in Europe, there is a case for redistribution of farm population, from the point of view of the overseas countries now producing surpluses for export. Unless these countries can find a market for their products through an increase in consumption the benefits of technical progress will be hindered by price fluctuations of great violence.

So long as the difference persists between standards of living in countries with dense populations and countries with large reserves of land, a slight rise in the world prices of agricultural products will cause a large increase in food-production in overseas countries; but this cannot be followed by an expansion of consumption because the overpopulated regions cannot buy. Clearly it would be possible to secure a greater measure of stability through international migration, if food-consumption could be increased in the overseas exporting countries and in Eastern Europe itself.

As the effect of the difference in rates of population growth and capital accumulation begins to be felt, therefore, overseas countries may see the wisdom of taking more immigrants to mitigate the difficulties of adjustment. For the staple industries also will be to some extent in the same position as agriculture, and will benefit if the countries on the lowest standards of living are enabled to increase their consumption of industrial products.

At present the demand for redistribution of the world's productive resources has been made in terms of political prestige; the demand is made by countries which are not over-populated in the same sense as Eastern Europe is; in consequence, the demand loses its force. But that there is a case for such a redistribution so far as agricultural production is concerned is undeniable, if the world is to take advantage of the new resources and new methods. Without a redistribution of farm population to regions outside Europe, Europe's farm problem cannot be solved in a way which can be reconciled with economic progress and political stability.

INDEX

Population (cont.):
production, 43–51, 61–3, 84, 85, (table) 197; growth of farm, in E. Europe, 44–5, (table) 47; surplus level of density, 67–72; standard of rural density, 67; density of farm, 1931 (table), 69, 76; amount of land per head of farm, in Europe, 1930-1 (table), 70; arable land per head of farm (table), 72; causes of high density of farm, 72–8; production per head of farm (table), 84. See also Agriculture.
Potocki, Polish landowning family, 39.
Prices, fall in food, 4, 5, 34; rise in food, 32; fall in agricultural, 49, 53; fall in corn, 56, 75; Germany and high food, 59.
Proceedings of the International Conference of Agricultural Economists, 1934, 18 n., 149 n., 160 n.
Property, distribution of, 10–13, 44, 146.
Protection for agriculture, 1, 2, 27, 31–4, 37, 51, 72. See also Tariffs.
Prussia, extension of properties, 10; the feudal landlord, 12; peasant emancipation, 15.

Radić, peasant leader, 39; theories of, 39 n., 40 n.
Radziwill, Polish landowning family, 39.
Regions, classification of, 97–102; intensive, 102–10.
Rome, International Institute of Agriculture, 80.
Rotation, three-field system, 9, 10, 177; scientific, 10; as practised in Europe, 104, 110, 116–17, 122, 125, 129, 134.
Rumania, a peasant state, 13; standard of living, 21, 88–9, 89 n., 91–2, 92 n. 2, 116, 118–19; character of peasantry, 24; creation of peasant community, 25; peasants' political independence, 36; peasants' loss of power, 40–1; land shortage, 43, 65; farm population, 44, 46, 46 n., 102, 156, 163; grain and corn output, 46, 48; cereal consumption, 48; wheat and other exports, 52–3; oil exports, 53 n.; opposition to Hungary, 59; rural density, 67; surplus population, 69, 70; census of occupations, 69 n. 2; increase in population,

76–7, 119; distribution of income, 86; decrease in yields, 86; adequate diet, 88–9; infant mortality, 89; industrial goods purchased, 95–6; Bata factory, 96; live-stock production and crop yields, 98, 100, 116–19, 153; regions classified, 101, 112, 115; arable land per head, 116; description of Goicea Mica, 117–18; primitive system, 117–19; lack of machinery, 117–19, 161; output per head, 138; size of farms, 142; degeneration of technique, 153; price of land, 164 n. 1; co-operative system, 165–6. See also Transylvania.
Rural density, see Population.
Russia, peasant emancipation, 15; collective farming, 28, 35, 158, 167; method of density analysis, 66; development of railways, 75; comparison with Europe, 72, 177, 184–6, 188–9; increase in population, 76, 76 n., 77, 77 n., 172–5, (table) 176, 185; wheat yields, 97; Five-Year Plan, 168, 175, 182, 186, 193; machine tractor stations, 168 n., 181–3; results of collectivization, 168–81; mechanization, 169, 170, 174–5, 177–8, 180–2, 189, 193; output per head, 169, 171, 173–4, 185, 188–9 ; population density, 169; classification of soils, 170; live-stock production, 170–1, (table) 174, 177–8, 182, 190; manures and fertilizers, 170, 176–8; cost of food, 171–2; grain and corn production, 171–2, (table) 173, 174, 178, 186; meat production, 171; extension of cultivation, 172–4; industrialization, 175, 186, 189, 191, 193; regions classified, 176; rotation, 177; tractor cultivation, 177–81, 190; the *kolkhozy*, 178, 181, 190; milk production, 178, 183; the *sovkhozy*, 178–9, 190; description of Zernograd, 179; social organization, 181–3; incomes and standard of living, 183–90; the statute of Artels, 183; production and population compared with Europe, (table) 184, 185; arable land per head, 185; state grain delivery, 186, 190; disposal of grain crops (table), 187; 'labour day' as basis of income, 188 n.; collectivization as remedy for E. Europe, 190–4.
Ruthenia, birth-rate, 33; increase in

For Product Safety Concerns and Information please contact our EU
representative GPSR@taylorandfrancis.com Taylor & Francis Verlag GmbH,
Kaufingerstraße 24, 80331 München, Germany

Printed and bound by CPI Group (UK) Ltd, Croydon, CR0 4YY
11/04/2025
01844009-0004